Gita
for
Everyday Living

A *Vedanta Kesari* Presentation

Sri Ramakrishna Math
Mylapore, Chennai - 600 004

Published by
Adhyaksha
Sri Ramakrishna Math
Mylapore, Chennai-4

Total number of copies
printed before: 11,500

VI-2M 3C-9-2013
ISBN 978-81-7823-520-2

Printed in India at
Sri Ramakrishna Math Printing Press
Mylapore, Chennai-4

Publisher's Note

Bhagavad Gita is a perennial source of inspiration and strength for millions of people all over the world. For centuries, it has been the guiding light for anyone interested in living a spiritual life and having a wiser and matured outlook towards life. No wonder, the Gita has a universal appeal and all-inclusive readership.

An eternal scripture like Gita too, however, needs to be restated and reiterated with the change in circumstances. Its eternal teachings need to be rephrased and rearticulated in order to meet the contemporary needs. In the process of doing this, it becomes more accessible and new insights are brought into focus.

Keeping this in mind, *The Vedanta Kesari*, the English monthly published by this Math, brought out a special issue in December 2008 entirely dedicated to this theme. It received an overwhelming response and an additional 2000 copies had to be reprinted to meet the demand.

We are pleased to present the same in the present form and hope it will be received with the same enthusiasm and interest and reach even larger number of spiritual seekers.

Swami Ramakrishnananda Jayanti
20 July 2009

CONTENTS

Chapter One

Gita Today: An Introduction

SWAMI ATMASHRADDHANANDA

Gita's Timeless Significance

How important and relevant is the message of the Bhagavad Gita today? We might as well ask the question: 'How important and relevant is the sun today! Or the air? Or the water? Or all the elements of nature?' In other words, the term 'relevance today' in the context of the *Gita* is redundant and rather bemusing.

Having said this, we should also confess that like the importance of air-water-earth-and-all-else, the message of Gita also needs to be restated again—and again, until we are able to live our lives according to it. The message by itself has never been irrelevant and out of place. It cannot. Based as it is on the solid rock of the eternal principles underlying the human personality, life and its ultimate purpose, the Gita is becoming ever more relevant in today's context. In today's world of growing consumerism and rising violence—leading to restlessness, anxiety and confusion in life—Gita's teachings are becoming even more significant than before. They are an eternal spring of wisdom required for developing right judgement, emotional balance, strength and for discovering the ultimate destination of human life.

1

Such is the appeal of Gita's message that there is hardly anyone who has known something of Hinduism and India and has not read the Gita. Beginning with its first English translation appearing some 200 years ago, the Gita continues to be translated again and again. One keeps coming across a 'new translation', a new interpretation, a fresh elucidation of its essential teachings published every year. All the great *acharyas* that India has produced as well as numerous men and women from diverse fields of life have commented on the Gita. One compelling truth about Gita is its pan-Hindu universality. It is accepted by all Hindu sects as authoritative. Gita's glories, like the truth it preaches, are eternal and unending.

Though well-known, the Gita is rather little known among today's large populace of youth and modernized (read materialistic) people. This reminds one of a verse in the Gita about the varieties of responses to the idea of the Self. 'Some look upon the Self as marvellous. Others speak of It as wonderful. Others again hear of It as a wonder. And still others, though hearing, do not understand It at all.'[1] A similar response can be observed with regard to the Gita. Some *look* upon the book as marvellous, a scripture of extraordinary (or mysterious) value; some others *speak* of the book as wonderful and some *hear* of it as wonderful. And still others, though hearing its teachings, do not *understand* its wonderful significance! No wonder, once a teacher wanting to educate a child about the Gita, asked him: Do you know Gita? 'Of course, I do,' replied the child, 'that is the name of my next-door aunt!' Aunt! He had only heard of Gita—and had *his* own meaning of it in his mind.

An Everyday Appeal

What does Gita contain? It contains everything that a person wanting to live a life of meaning and fulfilment would like to know. A popular verse on Gita compares its message to milk of the cow called the Upanishads. Milk is the best part of a cow. It has a rich supply of all essential vitamins and other nutrients that a staple food should contain. Again, milk can also be consumed directly or by converting it to other forms such as butter, curds and buttermilk.

The Gita-milk too has all the ingredients necessary to make it a perfect drink for moral and spiritual nourishment without which no healthy living is possible. The Gita-milk enriches the malnourished human mind by frequently reminding it of the undying Self that lies at the core of human personality. A mere idea of the eternity of the Self itself brings a great solace to the despairing heart. Yes, we might face troubles in life, commit mistakes and fall into crises but there is Something in us which is never affected by all this. What gets affected is mind and this mind can be trained and disciplined to overcome these influences. It can be purified and strengthened. A spiritually educated mind is always fixed on the Self and that state of steadiness is the source of unending joy, strength and peace. Using a clear and exact language, Gita helps us to reach that state and quietly tells that reaching that state is the goal of life.

This ultimate ideal of life is stated in various ways—Self-realization, knowing the Brahman, becoming a Yogi, getting established in God-consciousness, going beyond the *gunas*, gaining perfect control over senses and the mind, perfecting one's devotion and so on. In Gita one finds an amazing wealth of expressions to denote spiritual perfection and a mere reading about it can be a rewarding experience. Rightly did Gandhiji call it his 'spiritual dictionary'. All spiritual concepts and shades of meaning can be found in the Gita.

The Gita-milk also nourishes one with the knowledge of various paths to reach that state (called Yoga-s). It discusses in depth the subtleties of human needs and frailties and how to gradually overcome them. Like a mother, it holds our hands gently but firmly and teaches us to walk the path of inner peace and fulfilment. One might stumble and slip here and there, but the Gita, the Mother, is always present to help us stand up and walk the path of perfection again.

Gita's teachings, again, cover the entire spectrum of paths to spiritual perfection that human beings follow. An interesting anecdote of Sri Ramakrishna aptly describes this all-inclusiveness of the Gita thus:

A certain man had a tub. People would come to him to have their clothes dyed. The tub contained a solution of dye. Whatever colour a man wanted for his cloth, he would get by dipping the cloth in the tub. One man was amazed to see this and said to the dyer, 'Please give me the dye you have in your tub.'[2]

The multi-faceted quality of the dye, which has several colours in it, is similar to that of the Gita. This, however, has to be properly employed in colouring or re-colouring our life and personality with spiritual orientation and conviction. As someone said, 'It is not the question of memorizing the Gita but *internalising* the truths it contains.'

Gita, hence, contains teachings for people at various stages of growth, in different stations of life and having diverse temperaments. Gita has much philosophy to teach but also many practical hints for solving issues that we confront in our daily lives. As Aldous Huxley says:

> The Bhagavad Gita occupies an intermediate position between scripture and theology; for it combines the poetical qualities of the first with the clear-cut methodicalness of the second.[3]

Gita not only accommodates but also harmonises all paths. A Bhakta has as much to learn from the Gita as a Jnani or a Yogi or a man of action. In Gita one finds a grand harmony of all Yogas and a possibility for discovering new ways to reach the highest state of being. What about those who seem least interested in any path? Whose minds are not clear if they should take a path or not? 'It is My path that men tread in all ways,'[4] says Sri Krishna. Even the pathless ones? Yes, because even the pathless ones, too, seek happiness, peace and security in life. There is no one who seeks unhappiness, turmoil and insecurity. Hence, all men, even those who are not spiritual seekers in the conventional sense, are seeking God alone though their definition and concept of God may not be as explicitly stated as a spiritually educated man would do. Gita has enough to teach even them.

Gita's teachings are accessible, acceptable and applicable to all seekers of Truth. Since they were delivered just before the beginning of the Mahabharata War—which is symbolic of the inner war between our good and bad tendencies—the Gita easily becomes related to the harsh realities of everyday life. The advice that Sri Krishna gives to Arjuna sounds so reasonable and applicable that one never feels the aloofness and other-worldliness that is often associated with many other scriptures. As Gita deals with certain everlasting issues of life—the true purpose of life, solving moral dilemmas, taming the restless mind, learning the art of doing actions without getting attached, understanding love, compassion, charity and so on—it occupies a central position among the scriptural traditions of the world.

The Ideal of Gita

The Gita not only speaks of the goal of life's journey but also of various stages of the journey. It teaches one how to counter problems and challenges of life and also how to be preventive with regard to various crises and emergencies of life. This, of course, it does not do by asking us to take an insurance cover but by asking us to develop right orientation to life and by equipping ourselves with strength and faith. The real happiness, says the Gita, is not in acquiring the objects of sense pleasure but in training our senses. If we do not train our senses, we become slaves to them. And what can a slave expect from a master—from a ruthless master?

When one develops self-control through proper training and patience, one develops a peaceful mind—this, and not meaningless acquisition and reckless pampering of senses and ego, is the real source of happiness. It is not just temporary 'peace of mind' that Gita speaks of but getting established in Peace with a capital P. It teaches us how to seek it and become free from all sorrow forever. 'In the tranquillity of mind, all sorrow is destroyed. For the intellect of him, who is tranquil-minded, is soon established in firmness.'[5]

Contrary to what popular consumerist culture advocates, Gita's way to peace and joy is to search for it *within*. Sri Krishna describes a man who has found this inner source thus:

> Whose happiness is within, whose relaxation is within, whose light is within, that Yogi alone, becoming Brahman, gains absolute freedom.[6]

In another place, the Gita describes three types of joys—originating from three gunas namely, *sattva*, *rajas* and *tamas*:

> That which is like poison at first, but like nectar at the end; that happiness is declared to be *sattvika*, born of translucence of intellect due to Self-realisation.

> That which arises from the contact of objects of senses, at first like nectar, but at the end like poison, that happiness is declared to be *rajasika*.

That happiness which begins and results in self-delusion arising from sleep, indolence, and miscomprehension, that is declared to be *tamasika*.[7]

In his evolutionary march towards greater wisdom and maturity, man learns and progresses from tamasika to rajasika happiness and to sattvika happiness and even beyond. This happiness is not inviting at the beginning but seeking which it finally leads one to a joy which is free from all remorse, guilt and anxiety. It is the pure joy of our being.

In Gita is found the message not only of personal development but a plan for collective good and development. Sri Krishna cautions all men, especially leaders and elders, to be careful in whatever they do. Freedom entails responsibility. It is not mere freedom to act but the freedom to *be* that is vital and necessary for growth and true well-being. Says Gita:

Whatever the superior person does, that is followed by others. What he demonstrates by action that people follow.[8]

Through its ideal of following one's *svadharma* [duty based on one's station in life] and *svabhava* [temperament or sum total of inclinations a person has], the Gita has provided an irrefutable solution for harmonising social and individual aspirations.

In one of the verses in praise of Gita that appears in an auxiliary work, Sri Krishna says. 'Gita is My heart'. The word *Gita* itself means a song and when it comes from the heart of God, it should be taken to mean the *best* advice Sri Krishna, the Godhead personified, has to give to anyone. Of course, whatever God gives is best and good for others but we should not forget that when a man is joyful, he bursts into a humming melody and a song emerges from his heart. It may be the song that he has heard and admired earlier or a song which he composes impromptu. Singing a song is thus a spontaneous outburst of a joyful heart. In the same way, Gita, Sri Krishna's outpouring in the form of his song, the Song of God, is born of joyfulness and goodwill. And it comes from God's *heart*. In other words, the Gita is born of His deep concern and love for humanity.

Finally, Swami Premananda, a direct disciple of Sri Ramakrishna, said to a novice once, 'My boy, say I am reading [the Gita]. Never say I have read the Gita. One can never finish reading the Gita.' It is a statutory warning for all complacent students of the Gita and a call for being devoted to its study with humbleness and openness. What comes in the following pages is an attempt to explore and state the message in a contemporary perspective.

The Vedanta Kesari brought out a Spotlight Issue on Bhagavad Gita in 1983. It examined the continued relevance of the Gita from various angles. Obviously, being the fountainhead of spiritual and cultural legacy of entire mankind, Gita lends itself to ever newer perspectives. With changed socio-cultural contexts, and the challenges they have thrown up, a keen need was felt to re-examine the message of the Gita for newer and contemporary meanings and applications. Hence, after

25 years, this year's Spotlight Issue focuses on the Gita again. It is not just an attempt to paraphrase the teachings of the Gita but to examine them from new perspectives. After all, as in *Varaha Purana*, Sri Krishna says, 'Standing on the wisdom of the Gita, I maintain the worlds,' we all need the wisdom of the Gita for living fuller lives in this world!

References

1. *Gita*, 2:29
2. *The Gospel* , p.305
3. *The Song of God,*
   Tr. Sw. Prabhavananda and
   Christopher Isherwood, p.2
4. *Gita*, 3.23
5. *Gita*, 2:65
6. *Gita*, 5.24
7. *Gita*, 18.37-38-39
8. *Gita*, 3.21

Chapter Two

Gita—'The Essence of All Scriptures'

From the Gospel of Sri Ramakrishna

You see, there is no need to read too much of the scriptures. If you read too much you will be inclined to reason and argue. Nangta used to teach me thus: What you get by repeating the word 'Gita' ten times is the essence of the book. In other words, if you repeat 'Gita' ten times it is reversed into 'tagi', which indicates renunciation.[1]

The essence of the Gita is: 'O man, renounce everything and practise spiritual discipline for the realization of God.'[2]

An aspirant entitled to the Knowledge of God is very rare. It is said in the Gita that one in thousands desires to know

God, and again, that among thousands who have such a desire, only one is able to know Him.[3]

It is said in the Gita that if a man is respected and honoured by many, whether it be for his scholarship or his music or his oratory or anything else, then you may know for certain that he is endowed with a special divine power.[4]

It is said in the Gita that whatever one thinks in the hour of death, one becomes in the after-life. King Bharata gave up his body exclaiming, 'Deer! Deer!' and was born as a deer in his next life. But if a man dies thinking of God, then he attains God, and he does not have to come back to the life of this world.[5]

One must surrender the result to God. . . That is the view of the Gita.[6]

How long should a man perform his duties? As long as he identifies himself with the body, in other words, as long as he thinks he is the body. That is what the Gita says. To think of the body as the Atman is *ajnana*, ignorance.[7]

You no doubt need money for your worldly life; but don't worry too much about it. The wise course is to accept what comes of its own accord. Don't take too much trouble to save money. Those who surrender their hearts and souls to God, those who are devoted to Him and have taken refuge in Him, do not worry much about money. As they earn, so they spend. The money comes in one way and goes out the other. This is what the Gita describes as 'accepting what comes of its own accord'.[8]

[Referring to a Bengali play, M said] 'Quoting from the Gita, Bhavani said: "He who sees Me in all things and all things in Me, never becomes separated from Me, nor do I become separated from him. That yogi who, established in unity, worships Me dwelling in all beings, abides in Me, whatever his mode of life. O Arjuna, that yogi is regarded as the highest who judges the pleasure and pain of all beings by the same standard that he applies to himself."' Sri Ramakrishna responded by saying, 'These are the characteristics of the highest bhakta.'[9]

The Gita speaks of temperance in eating. Sattvic food, rajasic food, tamasic food; sattvic kindness, sattvic ego, and so on—all these are described in the Gita. It contains the essence of all the scriptures. . . . Do you know the meaning of karma yoga? It is to surrender to God the fruit of all action.[10]

No food can harm a jnani. According to the Gita, the jnani himself does not eat; his eating is an offering to the Kundalini. But that does not apply to a bhakta.[11]

A sannyasi may or may not keep with him another book, but he always carries a pocket Gita.[12]

As is the disease, so must the remedy be. The Lord says in the Gita: 'O Arjuna, take refuge in Me. I shall deliver you from all sins.' Take shelter at His feet: He will give you right understanding. He will take entire responsibility for you. Then you will get rid of the typhoid. Can one ever know God with such a mind as this? Can one pour four seers of milk into a one-seer pot? Can we ever know God unless He lets us know Him? Therefore

I say, take shelter in God. Let Him do whatever He likes. He is self-willed. What power is there in a man?[13]

Chaitanyadeva set out on a pilgrimage to southern India. One day he saw a man reading the Gita. Another man, seated at a distance, was listening and weeping. His eyes were swimming in tears. Chaitanyadeva asked him, 'Do you understand all this?' The man said, 'No, revered sir, I don't understand a word of the text.' 'Then why are you crying?' asked Chaitanya. The devotee said: 'I see Arjuna's chariot before me. I see Lord Krishna and Arjuna seated in front of it, talking. I see this and I weep.'[14]

Haven't you read the Gita? One truly realizes God if one performs one's worldly duties in a detached spirit, if one lives in the world after realizing that everything is illusory.[15]

References

1. *The Gospel of Ramakrishna*, Sri Ramakrishna Math, Chennai, p.484

2. *ibid.*, p. 255   3. *ibid.*, p.502   4. *ibid.*, p.625

5. *ibid.*, p.631   6. *ibid.*, p.592   7. *ibid.*, p.582

8. *ibid.*, p.506   9. *ibid.*, p.686   10. *ibid.*, p.849

11. *ibid.*, p.564   12. *ibid.*, p.772   13. *ibid.*, p.329

14. *ibid.*, p.105   15. *ibid.*, p.956

Chapter Three

Bhagavad Gita: 'The Best Authority on Vedanta'

SWAMI VIVEKANANDA

The Background

The Gita requires a little preliminary introduction. The scene is laid on the battle-field of Kurukshetra. There were two branches of the same race fighting for the empire of India about five thousand years ago. The Pandavas had the right, but the Kauravas had the might. The Pandavas were five brothers, and they were living in a forest. Krishna was the friend of the Pandavas. The Kauravas would not grant them as much land as would cover the point of a needle.

The opening scene is the battlefield, and both sides see their relatives and friends—one brother on one side and another on the other side; a grandfather on one side, grandson on the other side. . . .When Arjuna sees his own friends and relatives on the other side and knows that he may have to kill them, his heart gives way and he says that he will not fight. Thus begins the Gita.

For all of us in this world life is a continuous fight. . . .Many a time comes when we want to interpret our weakness and cowardice as forgiveness and renunciation. There is no merit in the renunciation of a beggar. If a person who can [give a blow] forbears, there is merit in that. If a person who has, gives up, there is merit in that. We know how often in our lives through laziness and cowardice we give up the battle and try to hypnotise our minds into the belief that we are brave.

The Gita opens with this very significant verse: 'Arise, O Prince! Give up this faint-heartedness, this weakness! Stand up and fight!' Then Arjuna, trying to argue the matter [with Krishna], brings higher moral ideas, how non-resistance is better than resistance, and so on. He is trying to justify himself, but he cannot fool Krishna. Krishna is the higher Self, or God. He sees through the argument at once. In this case [the motive] is weakness. . .

There is a conflict in Arjuna's heart between his emotionalism and his duty. The nearer we are to [beasts and] birds, the more we are in the hells of emotion. We call it love. It is self-hypnotisation. We are under the control of our [emotions] like animals. . . .[To reach] the eternal consciousness, that is the goal of man! There emotion has no place, nor sentimentalism, nor anything that belongs to the senses—only the light of pure reason. [There] man stands as spirit.

Face the Life!

Now, Arjuna is under the control of this emotionalism. He is not what he should be—a great self-controlled, enlightened sage working through the eternal light of reason. He has become like an animal, like a baby, just letting his heart carry away his brain, making a fool of himself and trying to cover his weakness with the flowery names of 'love' and so on. Krishna sees through that. Arjuna talks like a man of little learning and brings out many reasons, but at the same time he talks the language of a fool.

'The sage is not sorry for those that are living nor for those that die.' [Krishna says:] 'You cannot die nor can I. There was never a time when we did not exist. There will never be a time when we shall not exist. As in this life a man begins with childhood, and [passes through youth and old age, so at death he merely passes into another kind of body]. Why should a wise man be sorry?' And where is the beginning of this emotionalism that has got hold of you? It is in the senses. 'It is the touch of the senses that brings all this quality of existence: heat and cold, pleasure and pain. They come and go.' Man is miserable this moment, happy the next. As such he cannot experience the nature of the soul. . . .

There is nothing in the universe that can change [the Changeless]. Though this body has its beginning and end, the dweller in the body is infinite and without end.

Knowing this, stand up and fight! Not one step back, that is the idea. . . .Fight it out, whatever comes. Let the stars move from the sphere! Let the whole world stand against us! Death means only a change of garment. What of it? Thus fight! You gain nothing by becoming cowards. . . .Taking a step backward, you do not avoid any misfortune. You have cried to all the gods in the world. Has misery ceased? . . . You are infinite, deathless, birthless. Because you are infinite spirit, it does not befit you to be a slave. . . .Arise! Awake! Stand up and fight! Die if you must. There is none to help you. You are all the world. Who can help you?

The Mystery of Living the Life

But if you say that killing all these people is sinful, then consider this from the standpoint of your own caste-duty. . . . 'Making pleasure and misery the same, making success and defeat the same, do thou stand up and fight.'

This is the beginning of another peculiar doctrine of the Gita—the doctrine of non-attachment. That is to say, we have to bear the result of our own actions because we attach ourselves to them. . . .'Only what is done as duty for duty's sake. . .can scatter the bondage of Karma.' There is no danger that you can overdo it. . . .'If you do even a little of it, [this Yoga will save you from the terrible round of birth and death].'

'Know, Arjuna, the mind that succeeds is the mind that is concentrated. The minds that are taken up with two thousand subjects (have) their energies dispersed. Some can talk flowery language and think there is nothing beyond the Vedas. They want to go to heaven. They want good things through the power of the Vedas, and so they make sacrifices.' Such will never attain any success [in spiritual life] unless they give up all these materialistic ideas.

That is another great lesson. Spirituality can never be attained unless all material ideas are given up....What is in the senses? The senses are all delusion. People wish to retain them [in heaven] even after they are dead—a pair of eyes, a nose. Some imagine they will have more organs than they have now. They want to see God sitting on a throne through all eternity—the material body of God. ...Such men's desires are for the body, for food and drink and enjoyment. It is the materialistic life prolonged. . .'

We have identified ourselves with our bodies. We are only body, or rather, possessed of a body. If I am pinched, I cry. All this is nonsense, since I am the soul. All this chain of misery, imagination, animals, gods, and demons, everything, the whole world—all this comes from the identification of ourselves with the body. I am spirit. Why do I jump if you pinch me? . . .Look at the slavery of it. . . . What are we? Living hells, that is what we are.

Who can work without any attachment? That is the real question. Such a man is the same whether his work succeeds or fails. His heart does not give one false beat even if his whole life-work is burnt to ashes in a moment. 'This is the sage who always works for work's sake without caring for the results. Thus he goes beyond the pain of birth and death. Thus he becomes free.' Then he sees that this attachment is all delusion. The Self can never be attached. . . .Then he goes beyond all the scriptures and philosophies. If the mind is deluded and pulled into a whirlpool by books and scriptures, what is the good of all these scriptures? One says this, another says that. What book shall you take? Stand alone! See the glory of your own soul, and see that you will have to work. Then you will become a man of firm will.

The Secret of Non-attachment

Arjuna asks: 'Who is a person of established will?'

[Krishna answers:] 'The man who has given up all desires, who desires nothing, not even this life, nor freedom, nor gods, nor work, nor anything. When he has become perfectly satisfied, he has no more cravings.' He has seen the glory of the Self and has found that the world, and the gods, and heaven are. . . within his own Self. Then the gods become no gods; death becomes no death; life becomes no life. Everything has changed. 'A man is said to be [illumined] if his will has become firm, if his mind is not disturbed by misery, if he does not desire any happiness, if he is free of all [attachment], of all fear, of all anger. . . .'

'As the tortoise can draw in his legs, and if you strike him, not one foot comes out, even so the sage can draw all his sense-organs inside,' and nothing can force them out. Nothing can shake him, no temptation or anything. Let the universe tumble about him, it does not make one single ripple in his mind.

Then comes a very important question. Sometimes people fast for days. . . .When the worst man has fasted for twenty days, he becomes quite gentle. Fasting and torturing themselves have been practised by people all over the world. Krishna's idea is that this is all nonsense. He says that the senses will for the moment recede from the man who tortures himself, but will emerge again with twenty times more [power]. . . .What should you do? The idea is to be natural—no asceticism. Go on, work, only mind that you are not attached. The will can never be fixed strongly in the man who has not learnt and practised the secret of non-attachment.

How to Worship God

We will understand more clearly if we once get rid of the idea that religion consists in doctrines. One idea of religion has been that the whole world was born because Adam ate the apple, and there is no way of escape. Believe in Jesus Christ—in a certain man's death!

But in India there is quite a different idea. [There] religion means realisation, nothing else. It does not matter whether one approaches the destination in a carriage with four horses, in an electric car, or rolling on the ground. The goal is the same. For the [Christians], the problem is how to escape the wrath of the terrible God. For the Indians it is how to become what they really are, to regain their lost Selfhood. . . .

Have you realised that you are spirit? When you say, 'I do,' what is meant by that—this lump of flesh called the body or the spirit, the infinite, ever blessed, effulgent, immortal? You may be the greatest philosopher, but as long as you have the idea that you are the body, you are no better than the little worm crawling under your foot! No excuse for you! So much the worse for you that you know all the philosophies and at the same time think you are the body! Body-gods, that is what you are! Is that religion?

Religion is the realisation of spirit as spirit. What are we doing now? Just the opposite, realising spirit as matter. Out of the immortal God we manufacture death and matter, and out of dead dull matter we manufacture spirit. . . .

If you [can realise Brahman] by standing on your head, or on one foot, or by worshipping five thousand gods with three heads each—welcome to it! . . .Do it any way you can! Nobody has any right to say anything. Therefore, Krishna says, if your method is better and higher, you have no business to say that another man's method is bad, however wicked you may think it.

Again, we must consider, religion is a [matter of] growth, not a mass of foolish words. . . All these people fighting about what God's nature is—whether He has three heads in one body or five heads in six bodies. Have you seen God? No. . . .And they do not believe they can ever see Him. What fools we mortals be! Sure, lunatics!

Each one thinks his method is best. Very good! But remember, it may be good for you. One food which is very indigestible to one is very digestible to another. Because it is good for you, do not jump to the conclusion that your method is everybody's method, that Jack's coat fits John and Mary. All the uneducated, uncultured, unthinking men and women have been put into that sort of strait jacket! Think for yourselves. Become atheists! Become materialists! That would be better. Exercise the mind! ...What right have you to say that this man's method is wrong? It may be wrong for you. That is to say, if you undertake the method, you will be degraded; but that does not mean that he will be degraded. Therefore, says Krishna, if you have knowledge and see a man weak, do not condemn him. Go to his level and help him if you can. . . .

Understand the Workings of *Prakriti*

Whence comes all this bondage of action? Because we chain the soul with action. According to our Indian system, there are two existences: nature on the one side and the Self, the Atman, on the other. By the word nature is meant not only all this external world, but also our bodies, the mind, the will, even down to what says 'I'. Beyond all that is the infinite life and light of the soul— the Self, the Atman. . .

We always act under some compulsion. When hunger compels me, I eat. And suffering is still worse— slavery. That real 'I' is eternally free. What can compel it to do anything? The sufferer is in nature. It is only when we identify ourselves with the body that we say, 'I am suffering; I am Mr. So-and-so'—all such non-sense. But he who has known the truth, holds himself aloof. Whatever his body does, whatever his mind does, he does not care. But mind you, the vast majority of mankind are under this delusion; and whenever they do any good, they feel that they are [the doers]. They are not yet able to understand higher philosophy. Do not disturb their faith! They are shunning evil and doing good. Great idea! Let them have it!. . .They are workers for good. By degrees they will think that there is greater glory than that of doing good. They will only witness, and things are done. . . .Gradually they will understand. When they have shunned all evil and done all good, then they will begin to realise that they are beyond all nature. They are not the doers. They stand [apart]. They are the . . .witness. They simply stand and look.'

'Even those who know the path act impelled by their own nature. Everyone acts according to his nature. He cannot transcend it.' The atom cannot disobey the law. Whether it is the mental or the physical atom, it must obey the law. 'What is the use of [external] restraint?'

What makes the value of anything in life? Not enjoyment, not possessions. Analyse everything. You will find there is no value except in experience, to teach us something. And in many cases it is our hardships that give us better experience than enjoyment. Many times blows give us better experience than the caresses of nature. . . . Even famine has its place and value . . . .

According to Krishna, we are not new beings just come into existence. Our minds are not new minds. . . . In modern times we all know that every child brings [with him] all the past, not only of humanity, but of the plant life. There are all the past chapters, and this present chapter, and there are a whole lot of future chapters before him. Everyone has his path mapped and sketched and planned out for him. And in spite of all this darkness, there cannot be anything uncaused—no event, no circumstance. . . .It is simply our ignorance. . .

Now Sri Krishna says: 'Better die in your own path than attempt the path of another.' This is my path, and I am down here. And you are way up there, and I am always tempted to give up my path thinking I will go there and be with you. And if I go up, I am neither there nor here. We must not lose sight of this doctrine. It is all [a matter of] growth. Wait and grow, and you attain everything; otherwise there will be [spiritual] danger. Here is the fundamental secret of teaching religion.

Instead, we start a religion and make a set of dogmas and betray the goal of mankind and treat everyone [as having] the same nature. No two persons have the same mind or the same body. . . .

. . .If you and I organise, we begin to hate every person. It is better not to love, if loving only means hating others. That is no love. That is hell! If loving your own people means hating everybody else, it is the quintessence of selfishness and brutality, and the effect is that it will make you brutes. Therefore, better die working out your own natural religion than following another's natural religion, however great it may appear to you.

'Beware, Arjuna, lust and anger are the great enemies. These are to be controlled. These cover the knowledge even of those [who are wise]. This fire of lust is unquenchable. Its location is in the sense-organs and in the mind. The Self desires nothing.'

There is a man stealing there. Why does he steal? You punish him. Why can you not make room for him and put his energy to work? . . .You say, 'You are a sinner,' and many will say he has broken the law. All this herd of mankind is forced [into uniformity] and hence all trouble, sin, and weakness. . . .The world is not as bad as you think. It is we fools who have made it evil. We manufacture our own ghosts and demons, and then. . .we cannot get rid of them. We put our hands before our eyes and cry: 'Somebody give us light.' Fools! Take your hands from your eyes! That is all there is to it. . . .We call upon the gods to save us and nobody blames himself. That is the pity of it. Why is there so much evil in society? What is it they say? Flesh and the devil and the woman. Why make these things [up]? Nobody asks you to make them [up]. 'None, O Arjuna, can swerve from my path.' We are fools, and our paths are foolish. We have to go through all this Maya. God made the heaven, and man made the hell for himself.

Be Strong In Every Way

It is a tremendous error to feel helpless. Do not seek help from anyone. We are our own help. If we cannot help ourselves, there is none to help us. . . . 'Thou thyself art thy only friend, thou thyself thy only enemy. There is no other enemy but this self of mine, no other friend but myself.' This is the last and greatest lesson, and Oh, what a time it takes to learn it! We seem to get hold of it, and the next moment the old wave comes. The backbone breaks. We weaken and again grasp for that superstition and help. Just think of that huge mass of misery, and all caused by this false idea of going to seek for help!

There is only one sin. That is weakness. When I was a boy I read Milton's *Paradise Lost*. The only good man I had any respect for was Satan. The only saint is that soul that never weakens, faces everything, and determines to die game.

Stand up and die game! . . . Do not add one lunacy to another. Do not add your weakness to the evil that is going to come. That is all I have to say to the world. Be strong! . . . You talk of ghosts and devils. We are the living devils. The sign of life is strength and growth. The sign of death is weakness. Whatever is weak, avoid! It is death. If it is strength, go down into hell and get hold of it! There is salvation only for the brave. 'None but the brave deserves the fair.' None but the bravest deserves salvation. Whose

Die game : to maintain a bold, unyielding spirit to the last ; to die fighting.

hell? Whose torture? Whose sin? Whose weakness? Whose death? Whose disease?

All weakness, all bondage is imagination. Speak one word to it, it must vanish. Do not weaken! There is no other way out. . . .Stand up and be strong! No fear. No superstition. Face the truth as it is! If death comes—that is the worst of our miseries—let it come! We are determined to die game. That is all the religion I know.

Where one sees another, one hears another, so long as there are two, there must be fear, and fear is the mother of all [misery]. Where none sees another, where it is all One, there is none to be miserable, none to be unhappy. [There is only] the One without a second. Therefore be not afraid. Awake, arise, and stop not till the goal is reached!

Chapter Four

Sri Krishna,
the Teacher of the Gita

SWAMI VIVEKANANDA

A few words about the life of Krishna. There is a great deal of similarity between the lives of Jesus and Krishna. A discussion is going on as to which borrowed of the other. There was the tyrannical king in both places. Both were born in a manger. The parents were bound in both cases. Both were saved by angels. In both cases all the boys born that year were killed. The childhood is the same. . . . Again, in the end, both were killed. Krishna was killed by accident; he took the man who killed him to heaven. Christ was killed, and blessed the robber and took him to heaven.

Almost the same circumstances which gave birth to Buddhism in India surrounded the rise of Krishna. Not only this, the events of that day we find happening in our own times.

This Krishna preceded Buddha by some thousand years. . . .A great many people do not believe that he ever existed. Some believe that the worship of Krishna grew out of the old sun worship. There seem to be several Krishnas: one was mentioned in the Upanishads, another was king, another a general. All have been lumped into one Krishna. It does not matter much. The fact is, some individual comes who is unique in spirituality. Then all sorts of legends are invented around him. But, all the Bibles and stories which come to be cast upon this one person have to be recast in [the mould of] his character. . . .

Krishna was a married man. There are thousands of books about him. . . .Since I was a child I have heard about Krishna's life. I take it for granted there must have been a man called Krishna, and his Gita shows he has [left] a wonderful book. I told you, you can understand the character of a man by analysing the fables about him. The fables have the nature [of decorations]. You must find they are all polished and manipulated to fit into the character. For instance, take Buddha. The central idea [is] sacrifice. There are thousands of folklore, but in every case the sacrifice must have been kept up. There are thousands of stories about Lincoln, about some characteristic of that great man. You take all the fables and find the general idea and [know] that that was the central character of the man. You find in Krishna that non-attachment is the central idea. He does not need anything. He does not want anything. He works for work's sake. 'Work for work's sake. Worship for worship's sake. Do good because it is good to do good. Ask no more.' That must have been the character of the man. Otherwise these fables could not be brought down to the one idea of non-attachment.

He is the most rounded man I know of, wonderfully developed equally in brain and heart and hand. Every moment [of his] is alive with activity, either as a gentleman, warrior, minister, or something else. Great as a gentleman, as a scholar, as a poet. This all-rounded and wonderful activity and combination of brain and heart you see in the Gita and other books. Most wonderful heart, exquisite language, and nothing can approach it anywhere. This tremendous activity of the man—the impression is still there. Five thousand years have passed and he has influenced millions and millions. Just think what an influence this man has over the whole world, whether you know it or not. My regard for him is for his perfect sanity. No cobwebs in that brain, no superstition. He knows the use of everything, and when it is necessary to [assign a place to each], he is there. Those that talk, go everywhere, question about the mystery of the Vedas, etc., they do not know the truth. They are no better than frauds. There is a place in the Vedas [even] for superstition, for ignorance. The whole secret is to find out the proper place for everything.

Then that heart! He is the first man, way before Buddha, to open the door of religion to every caste. That wonderful mind! That tremendously active life! Buddha's activity was on one plane, the plane of teaching. He could not keep his wife and child and become a teacher at the same time. Krishna preached in the midst of the battlefield. 'He who in the midst of intense activity finds himself in the greatest calmness, and in the greatest peace finds intense activity, that is the greatest [Yogi as well as the wisest man].' It means nothing to this man—the flying of missiles about him. Calm and sedate he goes on discussing the problems of life and death. Each one of the prophets is the best commentary on his own teaching. . .The great men think, and you and I [also] think. But there is a difference. We think and our bodies do not follow. Our actions do not harmonise with our thoughts. Our words have not the power of the words that become Vedas. . . .Whatever they think must be accomplished. If they say, 'I do this,' the body does it. Perfect obedience. This is the end. You can think yourself God in one minute, but you cannot be [God]. That is the difficulty. They become what they think. We will become [only] by [degrees].

Krishna talks of himself as God, as Christ does. He sees the Deity in himself. And he says, 'None can go a day out of my path. All have to come to me. Whosoever wants to worship in whatsoever form, I give him faith in that form, and through that I meet him. . .' His heart is all for the masses.

Independent, Krishna stands out. The very boldness of it frightens us. We depend upon everything—upon a few good words, upon circumstances. When the soul wants to depend upon nothing, not even upon life, that is the height of philosophy, the height of manhood. Worship leads to the same goal. Krishna lays great stress upon worship. Worship God!

Krishna saw plainly through the vanity of all the mummeries, mockeries, and ceremonials of the old priests; and yet he saw some good in them. So the ceremonials,

worship of gods, and myths, are all right, Krishna says
. . . .Why? Because they all lead to the same goal.
Ceremonies, books, and forms—all these are links in the
chain. Get hold! That is the one thing. If you are sincere
and have really got hold of one link, do not let go; the
rest is bound to come. [But people] do not get hold.
They spend the time quarrelling and determining what
they should get hold of, and do not get hold of anything.
. . .We are always after truth, but never want to get it.
We simply want the pleasure to go about and ask. We
have a lot of energy and spend it that way. That is why
Krishna says: Get hold of any one of these chains that are
stretched out from the common centre. No one step is
greater than another . . . Blame no view of religion so far
as it is sincere. Hold on to one of these links, and it will
pull you to the centre. Your heart itself will teach all the
rest. The teacher within will teach all the creeds, all the
philosophies. . . .

In Krishna we find . . . two ideas [stand] supreme
in his message: The first is the harmony of different ideas;
the second is non-attachment. A man can attain to
perfection, the highest goal, sitting on a throne,
commanding armies, working out big plans for nations.
In fact, Krishna's great sermon was preached on the
battlefield.

How hard it is to arrive at this sort of non-attachment!
Therefore Krishna shows us the lower ways and methods.
The easiest way for everyone is to do [his or her] work
and not take the results. It is our desire that binds us. If

we take the results of actions, whether good or evil, we will have to bear them. But if we work not for ourselves, but all for the glory of the Lord, the results will take care of themselves. 'To work you have the right, but not to the fruits thereof.' The soldier works for no results. He does his duty. If defeat comes, it belongs to the general, not to the soldier. We do our duty for love's sake—love for the general, love for the Lord . . . .

There are a great many similarities in the teaching of the New Testament and the Gita. The human thought goes the same way. ...I will find you the answer in the words of Krishna himself: 'Whenever virtue subsides and irreligion prevails, I come down. Again and again I come. Therefore, whenever thou seest a great soul struggling to uplift mankind, know that I am come, and worship . . . .'

This was the great work of Krishna: to clear our eyes and make us look with broader vision upon humanity in its march upward and onward. His was the first heart that was large enough to see truth in all, his the first lips that uttered beautiful words for each and all.

Glory unto the great souls whose lives we have been studying! They are the living gods of the world. They are the persons whom we ought to worship. If He comes to me, I can only recognise Him if He takes a human form. He is everywhere, but do we see Him? We can only see Him if He takes the limitation of man . . . .If men and.

. . animals are manifestations of God, these teachers of mankind are leaders, are Gurus. Therefore, salutations unto you, whose footstool is worshipped by angels! Salutations unto you leaders of the human race! Salutations unto you great teachers! You leaders have our salutations forever and ever!

Chapter Five

Universal Message of the Bhagavad Gita

SWAMI RANGANATHANANDA

The Gita's Wide Appeal

The *Gītā* was first translated into English by Sir Charles Wilkins and published by the British East India Company with an Introduction by Warren Hastings, the first British Governor-general of India, in which we find the following prophetic sentence:

> The writers of the Indian philosophies will survive when the British Dominion in India shall long have ceased to exist, and when the sources which it yielded of wealth and power are lost to remembrance.

A century later, another beautiful rendering of the *Gītā* in English appeared, namely, *The Song Celestial* by Sir Edwin Arnold (1832-1904). He had learnt the Sanskrit language while he was working in India; in Pune and other places. He developed a great love for Indian culture, and after he went to England, he produced this outstanding book and another equally outstanding book about Buddha, namely, *The Light of Asia*. Both have gone through more than fifty to sixty editions. Both go straight to the heart of the reader.

The *Bhagavad Gītā* deals with human problems in a human way. That is why it has a tremendous appeal. It has inspired the human mind in India for centuries and centuries, and today, it is inspiring millions of people in various parts of the world. It is interesting to see that in all these countries, after reading the *Gītā*, people find their whole outlook changed. Thinkers and writers like Emerson, Walt Whitman, and Thoreau in U.S.A, and Carlyle in England, experienced this broadening and deepening of their outlook after studying the *Gītā*, and their writings also began to convey a new message.

Greatness of the Gītā revealed through Ādi Śaṅkara

In the modern period, the *Gītā* has the whole world as its empire. In the beginning, it was known only in India, not even in the whole of India, but known only to a few Sanskrit scholars. For the first time, in the 8th century AD, this book was taken out of that mighty epic, *The Mahābhārata*, by Śaṅkaracārya, who wrote a great commentary in Sanskrit on it and placed it before the people. Till then it had been lost in the *Bhīṣma Parva* of the mighty epic. Swami Vivekananda expressed great appreciation for this great work of Śaṅkaracārya. To quote his own words from his lecture on 'Vedanta in All Its Phases':[1]

The great glory of Śaṅkaracārya was his preaching of the *Gītā*. It is one of the greatest works that this great man did among the many noble works of his noble life—the preaching of the *Gītā*, and writing the most beautiful commentary upon it. And he has been followed by all founders of the orthodox sects in India, each of whom has written a commentary on the *Gītā*.

Even then, it was still limited to a few scholars and saints. Later, others wrote commentaries and slowly the book entered into our national languages; *Jñāneśvarī* in Marathi, by the saint Jñāneśvar, a few centuries after Śaṅkaracārya. In the modern period, Lokamanya Tilak wrote his great book, *The Gītā Rahasya,* in two volumes. He wrote it when the British Government had imprisoned him for a few years in Mandalay jail in Burma. He had no books to consult with, but wrote from his memory. That is a remarkable book; many other books have come out since then, and the *Gītā* today is very popular all over India and in many parts of the world. Many editions in world languages are also coming out; and, as soon as the books are out, they are sold out. So, we are living in an age that indeed is being shaped gently by this great book. Its message is universal, practical, strengthening, and purifying. The great Upaniṣads, which expound a science of human resources, a great science of human possibilities, have found their practical orientation in the *Gītā*. We have to study this book from that point of view, as a science of human development and fulfilment. The metre of the 700 verses is also very simple, the usual metre of eight letters in one line, called *anuṣṭup,* though occasionally we come across longer metres also.

Generally, before commencing the study of the text, we study what are called *Gītā Dhyāna Ślokas,* 'the nine Meditation Verses on the *Gītā.*' They are current all over

India, and now, in foreign countries also. We don't know who composed them. Some people believe it was Śrīdhara Swami, a commentator on the *Gītā* and on the *Śrīmad Bhāgavatam,* who lived about three or four centuries ago. The *Gītā Dhyāna Ślokas* refer to the *Gītā,* to Vyāsa, the author of the *Mahābhārata,* and to Śri Kṛṣṇa. . . [Now let us take one of these verses.]

Prapanna pārijātāya totra-vetraika-paṇaye;
Jñāna-mudrāya kṛṣṇāya gītāmṛta-duhe namaḥ

Salutation to Kṛṣṇa, with (the right hand held in) *Jñāna mudrā,* the granter of desires of those who take refuge in Him, the milker of the *Gītā* nectar, in whose one hand is the cane for driving the cows.

Significance of Jñāna-Mudrā

The verse describes Śri Kṛṣṇa with his right hand held in *Jñāna mudrā.* This is a remarkable concept in Indian Vedantic philosophy and spirituality. It holds that there is a deep significance for this particular *Jñāna mudrā,* knowledge pose, when the thumb is opposed to the forefinger and all the three fingers are stretched out. Our body postures have psychological counterparts; as the mind is, so is the body. You are lying down in a particular way; that will show a certain state of your mind. You sit in a particular way; you will find your psyche manifesting in that posture in a particular way. Suppose one constantly shakes one's legs while sitting, that shows a scattered mental state. In all these matters, the body shows the effect of the psyche. So, from that point of view, *Jñāna mudrā* is a remarkable sign of some profound psychic expression. The very name shows that, that *mudrā* represents *Jñāna,* knowledge—knowledge of every type; from the ordinary or secular knowledge to the highest spiritual knowledge. We, in India, never made any wide distinction between secular knowledge and sacred knowledge. To us all knowledge is sacred. Remember that there is only one Goddess, Sarasvatī, who represents all knowledge and techniques. Unity of all knowledge is a profound idea in our Indian tradition. We may create different departments of knowledge for purposes of study; but we should not break up the unity of knowledge. That is our teaching in India. So we have this idea that knowledge is the greatest thing to be sought after—*Vidyā dhanam sarvadhana pradhānam,* 'the wealth of knowledge is supreme among all forms of wealth'. There is nothing in this world so purifying as knowledge, says the *Gītā* (4: 38): *Nahi jñānena sadṛśam pavitram iha vidyate.* That is the motto of one of our universities, namely, the Mysore University.

A human being is human because he has the organic capacity to seek knowledge; no animal can seek knowledge. Animals have only an instinctual apparatus within, and are completely controlled by the genetic system. The human being, however, has been put on the road of making research into the world of knowledge. That world of knowledge may be secular or spiritual, but all knowledge is sacred to us in India. We start with the secular, and continue the search to the spiritual.

Now, how to represent this search for knowledge through a particular posture? Our ancient sages discovered this wonderful *mudrā* which can describe the entire gamut of this search for knowledge; that is something extraordinary. I used to wonder about it. Later on, some years ago, when I studied biology, neurology, and allied subjects, I found one wonderful truth and that is, no animal, not even a chimpanzee, can oppose the thumb to the forefinger, but only the human child can do this. While in Holland, I saw in a film on chimpanzee's behaviour; a chimpanzee holding a branch from a tree with his palm enclosing all the fingers, and beating it on the ground to drive an enemy. When you hold a branch like that, the grip has no strength, and one cannot impart energy to the use of that branch until the thumb comes prominently into operation. In all animals, the thumb does not know how to co-operate with the other fingers, particularly with the forefinger.

However, at the human level of evolution, for the first time, the human being learned to oppose the thumb to the forefinger. That is the beginning of humanity's technical efficiency, his or her capacity to handle tools, his capacity to manipulate the world around him, and acquire knowledge. The human being entered into the world of *jñāna* or knowledge, with this initial physical capacity. That is why this opposing of the thumb to the forefinger is highly symbolic of man's search for knowledge from the most ordinary to the most extraordinary levels. I found this perfectly valid from the scientific point of view. Then I also found that the number of brain cells needed to manipulate these two fingers is the largest compared to all other fingers. If the thumb is cut off, the manipulating efficiency of the hand will suffer automatically. In the *Mahābhārata*, we read of Droṇa, the teacher of archery, asking Ekalavya to cut off his thumb and offer it to him as his guru-dakṣiṇa or offering to the guru, so that he does not successfully compete with his favourite student, Arjuna; and Ekalavya obeyed that command of Droṇa whom he respected as his own teacher. The British rulers of India are said to have cut off the thumbs of our Dacca weavers, who wove fine Dacca muslin, so that they may not compete with their own Lancashire weavers.

The importance of the thumb and the capacity to oppose it to the forefinger, is the beginning of man's march to knowledge, secular and spiritual. There is no distinction between secular and spiritual so far as knowledge is concerned; all knowledge is sacred. On the Sarasvatī Pūjā day, you find all instruments of knowledge placed before Sarasvatī. In my childhood, every year, I used to join the worship of Sarasvatī in my home. I saw carpenters' tools, doctors' medical instruments, and all types of holy books being kept before Sarasvatī, also called *Vāṇī*, 'speech'. She represents the unity of all knowledge. She is a wonderful, austere goddess, so inspiring to the human mind. So long as we worshipped Sarasvatī in the true spirit, our land was devoted to knowledge. But when we left Sarasvatī, and ran after Lakṣmī, the goddess of wealth, both Lakṣmī and Sarasvatī, both wealth and knowledge, vanished from India. Today we have to bring both of them back to our country, first Sarasvati, then Lakṣmī. Lakṣmī is the product of Sarasvatī.

The more knowledge you have, the more wealth you can create; except through efficient work inspired by knowledge, there is no other way to gain wealth. You cannot create wealth by magic and mystery. That lesson we have to learn today. Sarasvatī is primary, and Lakṣmī is a by-product of Sarasvatī. This knowledge must come so that poverty will be eliminated in India. Pure science is Sarasvatī, and applied science is Lakṣmī. Knowledge applied to agriculture improves the wealth of the nation; so also industry. Everywhere these two austere goddesses reign, but we in India have to re-learn how to truly worship them. Merely making *ārati,* waving of light, before their picture is not the way to worship them. Go to the university, study various books, think for yourself—that is how you become students of Sarasvatī. And, hard work, teamwork, trying to improve efficiency— that is how we have to worship Lakṣmī. *Ārati* we can do once a year, but everyday we have to worship Lakṣmī only through this kind of hard work. Then alone Lakṣmī *kaṭākṣa* or grace will come to us.

Therefore, in this modern age, the ideal is *jñāna,* and everyone is to be on the road to knowledge. Nature has given human being the capacity to oppose the thumb to the forefinger, and thus manipulate the world around him or her, and acquire knowledge and power. This is the beginning of human evolution. In the description of Śrī Kṛṣṇa, this wonderful expression is there; *jñāna mudrāya kṛṣṇāya*. In all the iconography of India, of great saints, sages, incarnations, and of the Divine Mother, you will find this particular pose of *jñāna mudrā*. It is especially seen in depicting Śiva as Dakṣiṇāmūrti. By this *jñāna mudrā*, he is able to remove the doubts of students around him. This is the tradition coming down to us from very ancient times and we should apply the essence of this tradition to deal with our own present-day problems. The whole land must become dedicated to knowledge and knowledge-seeking.

Reference

1. *The Complete Works of Swami Vivekananda*, vol. Ill, p. 328

Chapter Six

Gita's Way of Right Activity

SWAMI SMARANANANDA

Gita's Unique Contribution

The Bhagavad Gita, one of the greatest scriptures of the world—or rather the greatest, if one may say—has its eternal message given from various angles. Among them the concept of Karma Yoga is its original contribution. For the first time in the history of world literature, this idea of Karma Yoga occurs in the Gita, even though it finds a mention in the Upanishads in a rudimentary form. For example we may quote here the second verse of the *Ishavasya Upanishad*:[1]

By doing Karma, indeed, one should wish to live here for hundred years. For a man such as you there is no other way than this, whereby Karma may not cling to you.

It is also interesting to note that this message of the Gita was delivered in a battlefield where two large armies had been arrayed against each other—in the battleground of Kurukshetra. Indeed, the battlefield is the place to test one's ability to do one's duty, in spite of being provoked to do otherwise.

Though the *Gita* is a *samanvaya-grantha*—a book harmonizing all the four Yogas such as Jnana, Karma,

Bhakti and Rajayoga—its special contribution is the concept of Karma Yoga. During the medieval period in India, there was a general belief that *Karma*—action of all kinds—is an obstacle to spiritual progress. The Mimamsakas [votaries of the ritualistic practices], however, taking their stand on the ritualistic section (*Karma-Kanda*) of the Vedas, believed that non-performance of the Vedic rituals will result in one not reaching the goal of life—the heaven. This was illustrated through such statements or directives as *yavad jivam agnihotram juhuyat*— 'perform *agnihotra* [the customary fire-ritual performed by a householder] as long as you are alive.'

But the question was raised: 'Can work be done without the bondage it brings?' This was answered by Sri Krishna who emphatically said in the Gita that it is possible to do so. He said, 'The art of right activity [Yoga] lies in doing one's duty skilfully' [*yogah karmasu kaushalam*].[2] In other words, one should learn how to work without being shackled by the bonds of Karma.

Sri Krishna denounces people who set heaven as their goal of life and perform Vedic rituals for that purpose only. He says: 'Those people who have fixed heavenly enjoyments as their goal in life can never attain *vyavasay-atmika buddhi*—an intellect determined on breaking of all bonds; for the Vedas [or the Vedic rituals], too, come within the sphere of the three *gunas*. You go beyond them.'[3]

He did not preach inaction. Referring to the necessity of doing work, Sri Krishna said:

Verily none can ever rest for even an instant without performing action, for all are made to act helplessly by the *Gunas* [constituent qualities of the material world], born of *Prakriti*.[4]

So, how should we work without getting entangled in it? Sri Krishna's answer is, *Yogasthah Kuru Karmani*[5]— 'By remaining rooted in Yoga and doing one's work.' How does one do that? By not getting attached to the fruits of one's action (*sangam tyaktva*). This, then, is the secret of Karma Yoga: work without being attached, looking upon success and failure with equanimity (*samatva*). This is called Yoga, and this is the state of perfection in Karma Yoga.

Sri Krishna calls this method of doing work as *Buddhi Yoga*, because non-attachment to results is an attitude of the *buddhi* or our discriminative faculty. Without this attitude, one cannot become detached to the results of one's actions.

Activity without Attachment

Though popularly the word *yajna* brings to mind a fire-ritual, Sri Krishna gave a deeper meaning to it when he said:

Work done for purposes other than *yajna* results in bondage. Therefore, O Kaunteya, work, freeing yourself from all attachment.[6]

Here *yajna* means making a sacrifice in order to maintain the universal order of give-and-take which forms the basis of all life.

It is this participation in the cyclic nature of life which brings true happiness in life. This means that we will have to convert all our actions into *yajna*—that is, transform all our activities into sacrifice, by eschewing all selfishness or tendency to hoard and possess. In order to renounce selfishness, one should make one's life God-oriented. Only when our mind is directed towards higher ideals that it becomes possible for us to get rid of selfishness.

We often ask: 'Why are people selfish?' To it the simple answer is: Because of desires and a wrong understanding that if desires are fulfilled one can be happy forever!

The fact, however, is otherwise. It is not fulfilling our selfish desires but non-attachment to results of actions which really brings true joy in life. We suffer because we become attached to results and run after money, pleasures, fame and other fleeting objects of life. Suffering comes from following the path of *sakama-karma* [work with a selfish motive].

One should remain active all the time—but without attachment. Sri Krishna himself sets this example of constant activity and shows us how to remain free from attachment. He tells Arjuna,

O Partha, I have no duty to be performed in all the three worlds. I have nothing to be attained; still I go on working.[7] The actions or work do not bind me, nor have I any desire for the results of actions. If one understands this in this manner, actions will not bind him.[8]

Lest people misconstrue this statement to mean that one can then be inactive or lazy, Sri Krishna warns:

> If I were not working without sleep, ordinary people will also follow suit. That would set in motion degeneration of higher values of life.[9]

The Practice of Karma Yoga

Generally speaking, the practice of Karma Yoga is quite difficult. In order to be truly successful in the practice of Karma Yoga, one needs the support of Jnana Yoga or Bhakti Yoga. For Karma Yoga involves giving up attachment which, of course, requires cultivating right attitude towards the action itself and this is what Jnana Yoga and Bhakti Yoga help one to do.

The practice of Jnana Yoga requires exercising our power of discrimination—between the real and the unreal, between the ephemeral and the permanent, between the Absolute and the relative or what Sri Rama-krishna called as *nitya* and *anitya*. Attachment is a mental quality, and we have nurtured it through many births. To get rid of it, one needs to continuously struggle and practice *shravana* [hearing about the spiritual ideal], *manana* [deep thinking about it] and *nididhyasana* [meditation on the truth of it].

Similarly, we should practice Bhakti Yoga or the Yoga of love for God and connect all our actions to God. We will have to dedicate the fruits of all our actions at the feet of the Lord. This is possible only when we develop love for God—not merely doing ritualistic worship, but truly developing intense love for God.

Renunciation is a mental act, and it has to have discrimination and detachment at the background. As the Gita says:

> The Knower of Truth thinks that he does nothing, though he may be performing all kinds of actions. He knows that the sense-organs are working upon sense-objects. He deposits all the results of actions in Brahman, and frees himself from all attachments, and lives like the lotus leaf on water.[10]

In order to renounce attachment to something lower, attachment to something higher is necessary. This attachment to something higher is the attachment to God. If we can love God with all our heart and all our soul, we can then renounce attachment to all things worldly. Then we will be able to do all our actions as duty without getting attached to their results. We will then be able to offer the results of all such actions at the feet of God. As goes the well-known Sanskrit saying: *Yad-yad karma karomi tad-tad akhilam shambho tavaradhanam*—'whatever Karma I am doing O Shambhu, I dedicate all these at your feet.'

Therefore, the secret of Karma-Yoga is to develop the right kind of attitude with which one can do one's duties skilfully. This demands freeing oneself from all wrong identifications and remaining detached in the midst of all actions. This is actually an inner process and begins at the mental level—the level of the *buddhi*. Action itself is not at fault; it is our attitude towards it which makes the difference. It again depends upon our identification with what is being done by the senses, which are themselves the transformation of the three *gunas*. But the Jnani or the Knower of Brahman knows that all actions are only the three gunas acting upon the three gunas in various ways (*guna guneshu vartante iti mattva na sajjate*).[11] Being established in the knowledge thus, he no more identifies himself with them.

Conclusion

So what the Gita ultimately teaches is that we should develop the right attitude toward all actions and this is possible if we make Jnana or Bhakti as the basis of all our actions. Above all, as Swami Vivekananda said, 'Duty is seldom sweet. It is only when love greases its wheels that it runs smoothly; it is a continuous friction otherwise.'[12] Leo Tolstoy, the great Russian litterateur, concluded one of his short stories, entitled *What Men Live By*, with the saying:

I have now understood that though it seems to men that they live by care for themselves, in truth it is love alone by which they live. He who has love, is in God, and God is in him, for God is love.

In other words, only when the leavening of love is added to our actions that it becomes pleasant.

Therefore only when activity is channelled through love that it becomes right activity. This is possible only if 'love' forms the basis of Karma. Sri Krishna uses the phrase *sarva-bhuta hiteratah*[13]—'one who is constantly interested in the welfare of all beings.'

Indeed, if this love for others forms the basis of our actions, then only can we be interested in the welfare of all. And the secret of activity lies in nurturing this power of love which acts as the transforming power behind all our actions.

References

1. *Ishavasya Upanishad*, verse 2
2. *Gita*, 2.50
3. *ibid.*, 2.41-45
4. *ibid.*, 3.5
5. *ibid.*, 2.48
6. *ibid.*, 3.9
7. *ibid.*, 3.22
8. *ibid.*, 4.14
9. *ibid.*, 3:23, 24
10. *ibid.*, 5: 8-10
11. *ibid.*, 3: 28
12. *CW*, 1: 67
13. *Gita*, 12:4

৪৩৪৪

Chapter Seven

Getting Introduced to Bhagavad Gita

SWAMI SRIDHARANANDA

The Setting

According to scholars and also saints belonging to various religious movements in India, the whole gamut of Indian or the Hindu scriptures can be categorized into *prasthana trayas*—the three pillars, as it were. Of the three, first is the Upanishads and the second is the Brahma Sutras which is a compilation of the ideas that are scattered over the Vedic literature by Maharshi Vyasa. Finally comes the Bhagavad Gita, the third of the *prasthana-trayas*.

The essence of Gita can be understood only if we know how this came into light. The fact is that the mighty third son of Pandu—Arjuna—was acclaimed and proclaimed to be the best specimen of a human being at that time of society. This measure of the personality was based on worldly acquisitions. An unparalleled warrior and a unique general, Arjuna had all that goes to make a *kshatriya*.

The Pandavas were greatly wronged and were denied the rightful throne. Duryodhana, the head of the Kuru family had claimed the throne of India. Prior to that, when the Pandavas were exiled in the forest (including living incognito for one year), all sorts of trickeries were laid on them by the Kauravas.

Sri Krishna and Yudhishtira, the two elders of the family, were both very mature people. They tried to exhaust all avenues of a negotiated settlement, knowing full well that war does not solve any problem—which we are yet to learn in today's world. Anyway, at that time also the same question of avoiding blood bath was paramount in the minds of Sri Krishna and Yudhishtira. When in a group, they used to discuss all that, the two brothers of the five, the second brother Bhimsen, and the third brother Arjuna used to move off tangentially, used to get into a tearing raid of the two elders, to the extent they used to abuse the elder brother as coward, and not being worthy of being called a kshatriya.

Arjuna felt that as a kshatriya—kshatriyas are supposed to be the maintainers of equity, justice, righteousness, and also to protect the territory of the nation—they should fight a righteous battle. This was their right and responsibility. Ultimately, it was decided to make it absolutely clear that might is right, and they are going to fight it out in a battlefield, and the winner gets all. This is the setting for the battle royal in Kurukshetra.

In this great drama of Bhagavad Gita, there were two main actors—Arjuna at one end, and Sri Krishna, at the other end. They represent two aspects of life. Arjuna represents the humankind with all its plus points and minus points. Sri Krishna represents the collective wisdom of India's spiritual heritage. This is the setting in chapter one of the Gita. Unless we understand this, we cannot grasp the inner meaning of the Bhagavad Gita.

The Beginning

Dhritarashtra was not in a position to leave his kingdom, Hastinapur. But at the same time, he wanted to be kept posted about the happenings in the war without missing any details. So Vyasa wanted to give him the divine insight whereby sitting in Hastinapur he could see what is happening. Dhritarashtra said, 'What shall I do with this insight, dear! I am blind from birth. Therefore, give that special capacity to my friend, my charioteer, Sanjaya. Let him see and let him narrate.' That is how we find in the Gita, the expression *Sanjaya uvacha* ('Sanjaya said').

In the battlefield, both the armies were ready. War sirens had been sounded by the blowing of conchs, as was the practice then. Krishna decided to be Arjuna's charioteer— literally and symbolically, his friend and philosopher. Charioteering was an art in itself. A charioteer has to be an exceedingly skilled horseman, so that he can tactfully manage the chariot to protect the fighter from being unnecessarily exposed to danger.

When the battle was about to begin, Arjuna asked Krishna, 'Take my chariot and park it between the two armies so that I can behold my enemies who want to raise their arms against me.' It was just a simple demand:

wanting to have a look at the faces of people who have assembled there with an intention to fight. But the attitude with which one expresses intent speaks volumes of how one looks at things. Arjuna spoke in a challenging, derisive tone: 'I will look at these people who have the temerity to raise their arms against me? Do they not know who am I?' His statement was full of self-confidence. This self-confidence is most welcome in every person. But none has the right to transgress the fine borderline of self-confidence entering into the domain of arrogance, vanity, and pride. This is the first catch to study the Bhagavad Gita.

Arjuna's mistake was that he crossed that fine line and became self-righteous. Though powerful, self-pity took over him and he was writhing in pain.

The Teacher par-excellence

Arjuna was fortunate because he had an excellent teacher in Sri Krishna. Though he had the authority to snub Arjuna straightaway and tell him to fight for the sake of posterity and humanity at large, Sri Krishna showed us what it is to be a supremely intelligent teacher. A teacher knows how to guide the student by his nose, without wasting the time.

Hence, Sri Krishna politely and honestly drives the chariot in-between the two armies and very innocently tells Arjuna, 'Look at them—whom you wanted to see, on both sides'. In the process of asking him to see and observe, Sri Krishna plays a very subtle role highlighting the blood relationships and the emotional bonds that Arjuna has had on both the sides.

He starts from the most venerable grand-father of the family, Bhishma; next comes Dronacharya, the teacher of the art of warfare; then comes Kripacharya, teacher of all ethics and sciences of war, and one after the other, the most venerable elders, the most beloved related cousins, and nephews and so on.

Sri Krishna, very silently and sensibly, triggered the scene for the Gita to be delivered. Arjuna starts moaning: 'O Dear! Bhishma! Dronacharya! Kripacharya! All my elders, maternal uncles and nephews.' Though Arjuna was facing his enemies, he forgot that they have to be killed in order to get back his throne. For years, Arjuna was a victim of his own anger and when reality dawned on him, what did he see? He breaks down totally saying, 'I am not prepared to fight.'

What a somersault! How come this enlightened, intelligent, accomplished human being, who had made up his mind as to what he will do, and what he will not do, turns around totally? What has happened to him? Arjuna could not swallow his pride. Here we can see how the funny human ego works. One should have the courage to admit plainly his inadequacy. The human ego and the influence of Maya are such that man is simply caught in the most unavoidable circumstances making him commit more mistakes.

Sri Krishna was waiting for this. He did not stop Arjuna; he allowed him to come out with his vainglory.

Why? Although a highly qualified human being, Arjuna did feel that he is unworthy, unable, unsuited, to face the demands and challenges. He wanted to run away, under the noble garb of renouncing the throne and spend his life as a mendicant monk in the hills and dales of Himalayas, as if that is an answer to life's challenges.

Unable to cope with the situation, and at the same time, unable to admit our short-comings, because of our pride and ego, we create some noble mask, to cover up our weaknesses and shortcomings. That is what the concept of Maya or *ajnana* or *avidya* is. It is a fact of life. I know, my conscience does not spare me. I know I am on the wrong side. But I do not have the moral courage to admit openly, 'Pardon me, I am mistaken. Would anybody correct me?'—we don't have that humility because of the ego which always sticks out like a sore thumb.

Arjuna keeps on creating a wonderful aura, a halo, around him, 'Sir, I have now understood. To enjoy this throne which is bathed by the blood of the near and dear ones, is not worth it. I should not be greedy for the throne. Let them enjoy the throne and let me renounce the world and be a mendicant monk.' It was as if, monkhood would resolve all his defeatism and escapism. And this is what most of us also think.

There are two types of knowledge—*apara vidya* [secular or mundane type] and *para vidya* [dealing with eternal issues of life]. Arjuna was excellent in *apara vidya*. But until now, no occasion had arisen in his life when he could be exposed to *para vidya*, the knowledge of the Reality behind the appearance. He might have learnt the Upanishads or recited the Vedas, but he did not know the art of translating those actions in such a demanding period of his life.

Hence we find, Sri Krishna giving him this freedom to come out with his problem. After Arjuna had finished his arguments, Sri Krishna just put an innocent question, 'Arjuna, you want to leave this battlefield and want to go away? But your intentions and your noble philosophy are known only to me, not to the whole world. When you leave this battlefield, what would others who have gathered here think? They have pawned away their life, as it were, to this war. They may die; they don't care. They are brave people. Now, under this lofty ideology of renunciation and self-sacrifice, you want to leave the battlefield?'

Krishna reminds that if he tries to run away from the battlefield, people will tell, 'We now see Arjuna in his true colour. All along he was growling and howling like a tiger. Now at the crunch in his life, he runs away with the tail in-between his legs.' 'So, Arjuna, are you prepared to suffer this humiliation? This shame? This loss of reputation that is worse than death?' Sri Krishna doesn't say what to do, what not to do. He plays the same card which Arjuna had used—the ego.

Arjuna thus gets a whack on his head. An intelligent teacher does not contradict the egoistic approach of a student. The art is to sow reasonable, rational doubt in his heart, which would slowly and surely erode the imposed self-confidence—the confidence did not actually arise within; it was imposed to cover up his inadequacy. Thus we find in the whole of the first chapter and part of the second chapter, Sri Krishna, actually pricking the bubble of Arjuna's ego, as it were. Finally when Sri Krishna has neutralized the element of *ajnana*, by these probing sentences, Arjuna becomes receptive to new ideas. He says (2.7):

Karpanyadosho-apahata svabhavah pricchami tvam dharma-sammoodha chetah
yacchreyah syannishchitam bruhi tanme shishyas-teham shadhi mam tvam-prapannam

'I know what I am worth—my talents, and my faculties. But I am in such a jam; I don't know how to use it. Therefore, please accept me as your disciple. I surrender myself totally at your command. Please help me to come out of this situation.'

We should not be carried away by the dramatics of it and instead try to understand the catch here. As humans we are liable to go wrong, and that going wrong is because of the mistaken sense of our ego, vanity and pride. Let us humble ourselves, and expose ourselves to nobler thoughts of life which will make us competent enough to cope with the various challenges of life, of which we have no previous warning. It might happen anytime, anywhere. This life—we are in this world, and this life has been compared to a battleground where good, evil, bad, worse, best, keeps churning us all the time.

Sri Krishna, in order to pull Arjuna out of dire straits says (2.1):

kutastva-kashmalam idam vishame samupasthitam
anarya-jushtam asvargyam akirtikaram arjuna

'Wherefrom O Arjuna! Have you imported this darkness of indecisiveness? I have not seen this before. Who is this Arjuna? I don't know. Wherefrom has he imported all this darkness of understanding, unable to take a decision for himself.'

klaibyam masma gamah partha na'etat tvai upapadyate
kshudram hridayadaurbalyam tyaktvottishtha parantapa

'This is not pardonable and acceptable. Arise, awake, and face your life with the full dedication to your duty and learn the art of performing the duties.' (2.3)

Arjuna is back to square one again. Now Sri Krishna's first advice is,

ashochyan-anvashochastvam prjna-vadamscha bhashase
gatasuna-gatasunscha-nanushochanti panditah

'Well, Arjuna, this is something very funny. The objects about which you should not repent or lament, you are repenting and lamenting, and at the same time, you are talking tall. How do I harmonize this Arjuna? Your acts and deeds are not up to your stature. What you are trying to preach to me has nothing to do with this because you have totally, miserably failed. So, listen to me now.' This is the Gita way of administering psychotherapy.

In order to introduce oneself to the study of the Bhagavad Gita, one should place oneself in the position of Arjuna and try to feel how many times, because of our arrogant attitude, we create problems for ourselves. And if one can develop an attitude which has the fullest support of the voice of conscience or God within us, then one will be able to sort out those self-created problems caused by one's egoistic attitude towards situations. This is the crux of the first chapter and part of the second chapter.

Three Parts of the Gita

We read in the Upanishad, Shvetaketu, the young aspirant, asking the question: 'Who am I?' His teacher tells him: *Tat Tvam Asi* ('Thou Art That')

Here are three different words. *Tvam*—you; *Tat*—Atman or Brahman or the Absolute goal; *Asi*— the process of being and becoming, the process of manifesting yourself from what we are today. The Gita exhorts us to get rid of our limitedness, extend the boundaries of our awareness, and gradually become absolutely our true Self, without any limitations. In these words—'Thou Art That'—a human being is described. These words also describe the concept of divinity in various approaches and the processes to reach that goal.

The eighteen chapters of the Gita too have been divided accordingly. The first part, (first to the sixth chapters) deals with various stages of a normal human being—from the depth of depression and non-under-standing, to the end of the sixth chapter, when we are taught how to reach *nirvikalpa samadhi*, the highest experience of union with the Absolute; the *jivatman* merging into *paramatman*. In this section an elaboration of the word *Tvam* ('You') from its bottommost level of awareness and suffering, to the ultimate level where one can potentially reach is done through the elucidation of the concept of Atman, the immutable and indestructible and also such other concepts as Karma Yoga, Dhyana Yoga, Sannyasa Yoga and so on.

The second part, consisting of next six chapters (seven to twelfth chapters) mentions the various concepts of the Divine ('Tat'). These six chapters have one purpose in view—to instill in us the understanding that God is everywhere, every moment of life, looked at from different points of view. These are not to be looked down upon as a distraction, but as a source of spiritual light. They make spiritual life more enjoyable and flavoured.

Once Sri Ramakrishna wanted to listen to veena, the musical instrument quite popular in India. It is said that the purest form of sound, which borders the *anahata dhvani* [the 'unstruck sound', the primordial sound at the root of creation], can be brought out only from Veena. This is the reason that Devi Saraswati, the goddess of learning, has veena in her hands. When Sri Ramakrishna visited Benaras, he expressed his desire to listen to Mahesh Veenakar, a veena maestro, who was in Benaras then. Mathur Babu immediately made arrangements, and Mahesh Veenakar was invited and Sri Ramakrishna was present there. As soon as the first note was played in the veena, the sound was so elevating and unadulterated, that Sri Ramakrishna at once went into *nirvikalpa samadhi*. With great effort and labour he later returned to the normal plane. This is how the Divine can be enjoyed or can be experienced, in thousand and one ways, through infinite attitudes.

This approach of Sri Ramakrishna is to be found in this second set of six chapters of the Bhagavad Gita. It also includes the chapter on *viswa-rupa-darshan*, when Sri Krishna assumed the form of *mahakala*, which destroys everything. Arjuna was scared to see that form and said, *tenaiva rupena chaturbhujena sahasra-bahu*—'O dear Lord, this is good enough for me. I know who you are. But I love to see you in that soft, sweet, pleasant manner of *chatur-bhuja narayana* (the four armed form of Lord Narayana).'

The last set of six chapters—from chapter thirteen to eighteen—deal with the process of becoming one with that ultimate reality. Here Sri Krishna mentions innumerable ways, approaches, perspectives, attitudes, with which one can build up one's spiritual life, and what is the sum and substance of spiritual life? To be one with God at all times, through all avenues of our awareness. The Gita mentions various methodologies, of signs and symptoms through which one can chalk out one's path to reach the goal with a safe yardstick in one's hand. This set of chapters hence deal with *asi*, the process of realizing our true nature.

The Beauty That is Bhagavad Gita

The Bhagavad Gita is an excellent masterpiece of spirituality. It helps us understand what spiritual life is and also instructs us how to live it. The Gita gives us a measuring rod, so that during our journey we do not fall into a false notion that we have reached the goal and become swollen headed. At the same time, the signs and symptoms mentioned of a realized soul, call it by any name, help us gauge ourselves honestly. It also protects us from the charlatans who claim that they have realized God.

Every chapter of the Gita is a yoga—a method of developing an uninterrupted communion with the divine. As to what types of divine attributes one wishes to meditate is left to one's choice. Here is an open invitation for us to pick up. Hence various signs (*lakshanas*) of inner perfection are given: signs of a man of wisdom (*sthitaprajna-lakshana*), signs of a perfected Karma Yogi or Jnana Yogi, man of complete renunciation and so on.

When we study the Gita, we imbibe excellence in all its aspects. It instructs and educates us about what to do and what not to do, how to and when to do it and so on. Everything is precisely kept in its proper place. It is for us to learn and benefit from its study.

The Crowning Glory

The last chapter is a summary of the whole Gita. By this time Arjuna was exposed to the idea who Sri Krishna was: not his friend, not his philosopher, not his guide, not his cousin brother, but an incarnation of the Divine. Arjuna was absolutely convinced of it. Having explained in an extremely exhaustive manner, Sri Krishna concludes by saying, 'I have told you, Arjuna, whatever I had to tell you. I have placed before you, all the options that are available to you. Through your body mind infrastructure, with all the faculties that you have, manifest the potential divinity already present in you. Do whatever you wish (*yatha icchasi tatha kuru*).'

Ah! What a freedom! God telling you; He doesn't command you; He says, 'Here is the table full of your choices. I have played my role. Choose whatever you want. But for heaven's sake, choose that well.'

Finally comes the most assuring statement (18.66):

sarvadharman parityajya mamekam sharanam vraja
aham tvam sarvapapebhyo mokshaishyami ma shuchah

Who can say that but God?! So full of love! 'Do you want to reach the divine? Here are the choices. Has these abundant choices blinded you? Come, I will tell you what to do. Get rid of all these "isms"; get rid of all these intellectual bondages of your achievements.'

Then where do I go? Do I live in vacuum? No! Then?

Answers Sri Krishna: *maam ekam sharanam vraja*— 'Let your life have only one goal. And what is that goal? Follow the ideal that you have chosen.' With no conditions! *Aham tvam sarva papebhyo mokshaishyami*—'I will see it through and through, I take you by your hand, and I will take you across the ocean of life and death and rebirth and I will take you to that promised land. It is my promise.'

Earlier too he affirmed: *kaunteya pratijanihi na me bhaktah pranashyati*—'I swear to you, my dear *Kunti-putra*, Arjuna, a person who has dedicated himself or herself to me, I will see him through.'

And when this assurance came to Arjuna, after all this world of exposure, his response was: *nashta moha smritir labdhva*—'my confusion to fight or not to fight has been totally removed. I have got back my wisdom, my poise, my capacity to remember what to do, what not to do.'

Tvat prasadat mayachyutah sthitosmi—by your unending grace, O Lord, I am now rehabilitated in the concept of converting my duties of life into an endless interaction with the divine. I am now well placed in my conviction, *gata sandeha*—I am no more a victim assailed by doubts and hesitation. I have established myself in my lost glory, the memory of how to convert the duties of my life into an endless interaction with you.

Then he comes to the final statement: *karishye vachanam tava*—'I will follow your instructions.' And he starts his battle of life—no more that Arjuna who with arrogance asked. 'Let me see the soldiers with whom I have to fight (*kair maya saha yoddhavyam asmin rana samudhyame*).' No more of that attitude but as an instrument in the hands of God. Now his attitude is 'I know now what am I to do. I transfer all my resolutions;

I just get rid of my ego and surrender it under your command. Please guide me. Use me as your instrument.'

Conclusion

The Bhagavad Gita is a treasure that the human society can ill afford to lose or forget. If we do so, it will be at our own peril and destruction. As humans we are psycho-physiological beings with such tremendous faculties that we can break open all its boundaries and limitations through proper training and guidance by the guru, and ultimately through the compassion of the Divine, we can manifest the divinity which is already within us. This is the true meaning of getting introduced to the Gita.

Chapter Eight

Gita's Message for Self-Transformation

SWAMI PRABUDDHANANDA

Search for the Self

The self, as we ordinarily understand it, is fluctuating every moment. In spite of its changing nature, however, it is through the self alone we perceive and experience ourselves and the world. The self is the sense of 'I-consciousness' or individuality that we all have, though initially our identity is unclear. It is only after a long, sustained effort that we will be able to realize the true nature of this 'I.' The process of arriving at this knowledge is what we call self-transformation. What gets transformed is really the concept of ourselves; the apparently divided self becomes whole. This is in essence the teaching of the Gita. Truly speaking, self-discovery is the only quest in spiritual life—nay, in life itself. Sometimes this quest is direct; sometimes it is indirect. But ultimately the purpose of life centres around this search for self-knowledge, the true 'I,' whether one is leading a secular or a spiritual life.

It is interesting to note how psychologist Carl Rogers insightfully refers to this self-inquiry in the book, *The Self* :

A frequently raised question is, 'What problems do people bring to you?' . . . I always feel baffled by this question. One reply is that they bring every kind of problem one can imagine. . . . I feel baffled as to how to answer this simple question. I have however come to believe that, in spite of this bewildering horizontal multiplicity, there is a simple answer. . . . Below the level of the problem situation about which the individual is complaining— behind the trouble with studies, or wife, or employer, or with his own uncontrollable or bizarre behaviour, or with his frightening feelings, lies one central search. It seems to me that at the bottom each person is asking: 'Who am I, *really*? How can I get in touch with this real self, underlying all my surface behaviour? How can I become myself?'

Another modern psychologist, Dr. Nathaniel Branden, refers to this search in this way in *Honoring the Self*:

To evolve into selfhood is the primary human task. It is also the primary human challenge, because success is not guaranteed. At any step of the way, the process can be interrupted, frustrated, blocked, or sidetracked, so that the human individual is fragmented, split, alienated, stuck at one level or another of mental or emotional immaturity. To a tragic extent, most people are stranded along this path of development. Nonetheless, the central goal of the maturational process is *evolution toward autonomy*.

How to evolve toward this autonomy?

The Bhagavad Gita, as is well-known, deals with all aspects of life: physical, mental, moral, and spiritual. In this comprehensive scheme, the first step in our evolution is to develop a well-defined personality. An average person's identity or personality is an unstable, bewildering jumble of the external world, body, and mind. As a result of this inner disharmony, many people end up living aimless, thoughtless lives. So in this process of self-discovery, it's imperative that one develops a strong character, a distinct unwavering sense of self-identity and purpose. In the language of the Gita, become manly. 'Do not yield to unmanliness, O Partha, it is not worthy of you.'[1] Have faith in yourself, stand up and fight the battle of life with firmness of mind, clarity and inner strength. This step toward becoming autonomous is what Swami Vivekananda calls manliness, or man-making. That's why Sri Krishna exhorts Arjuna to be a man in the true sense of the word. Become a strong person with self-respect, one who is able to defend his reputation by living up to one's ideals and thereby maintain his position in life with assurance and courage.

Following the Law of Our Being

In this cauldron of man-making, firming up who we really are, the important instruction Sri Krishna gives to Arjuna is that he should do his duty, his *svadharma*. Dharma, in general, is a function of the universal moral order, *ṛta*; it is that which protects and holds us together, nourishing our inner being. *Sva* means that which is one's own. It connotes a feeling of identity, or 'myness.'

Svadharma is the law of one's being, which is determined by an individual's inner tendencies, inclinations, or mental impressions. These tendencies greatly influence our present actions. Therefore we should live according to our psychological makeup—our bent of mind, our aptitudes. In short, be yourself; don't imitate others. Stand on your own feet. 'Better is one's own duty, though imperfect, than the duty of another, well performed.'[2] In the words of Emerson, 'Imitation is suicide.' On the basis of your svadharma, do your duty; what has fallen to your lot. Don't be attracted or misled by the duties of others. As someone said, 'For better or for worse, you must play your own little instrument in the orchestra of life.'

Ascertainment of what our svadharma is, what we should do, requires the use of our intrinsic determining and discerning faculty, or buddhi, which lifts us from a mere mechanical existence. (In Vedanta philosophy, the concept of mind is comprehensive having four divisions defined by function: weighing pros and cons, determination, the sense of 'I-ness,' and memory. Sometimes the terms mind and buddhi are used interchangeably.) Our lives should be governed and determined by a well-trained buddhi. We have the innate capacity to distinguish between right and wrong, true and false, good and bad, etc., and on this basis we are relatively free to make intelligent choices. 'Far inferior is work (prompted by desire) to work done through buddhi yoga, O Dhananjaya. Take refuge in the buddhi,' *buddhau saranamanviccha*.[3] Again Sri Krishna says,

On those who are ever devoted to Me and worship Me with love, I bestow the yoga of understanding [buddhi yoga], by which they come to Me.[4] Solely out of compassion for them, I, dwelling in their hearts, dispel with the shining lamp of wisdom the darkness born of ignorance.[5]

It is through the purification, development and assiduous exercise of the buddhi that self-transformation moves forward.

The Gita describes this process of self-purification or transformation in terms of different conditions of the mind: tamas, rajas, and sattva. These three gunas are the constituents of nature, or *prakriti*, in general and of the mind in particular. Our understanding and judgment are coloured by the gunas which are characterized by certain qualities: Tamas is marked by darkness, laziness, dullness; rajas by attachment, pain, passion, restlessness; and sattva by clarity, luminosity, and healthy-mindedness, *prakasakam anamayam*. When sattva becomes predominant, a person feels mentally expansive and psychologically healthy in spite of the ups and downs in life. As the sattva quality increases within oneself, the mind by degrees becomes integrated and well-balanced. The Gita beautifully describes this mental condition as one that leads to the comprehension of unity in diversity, to non-attached action, and to freedom from selfishness and passion.

The unillumined, unrefined mind, which is dominated by tamas and rajas, however, is our greatest enemy. But the same mind can be educated to be our most reliable friend as well. It is through this friend alone, and through no other, that we can progress in either secular or spiritual life. We have to befriend our mind; be a friend to ourselves, not be inimical to or fight with our self. Sri Krishna instructed Arjuna, 'One should raise oneself through the self . . . for the self alone is one's friend and the self alone is one's enemy.'[6] Self-transformation means attenuating tamas and rajas and increasing the proportion of sattva. When sattva prevails, the mind becomes more transparent and one experiences an enhanced sense of well-being, vitality, and strength. Swami Vivekananda spoke frequently about the necessity of strength. 'The sign of vigour, the sign of life, the sign of hope, the sign of health, the sign of everything that is good is strength.'[7]

There is a striking parallel between the Bhagavad Gita's description of a sattvic mind and positive mental health according to psychologist Marie Jahoda. In her article, *Criteria for Positive Mental Health*, she lists six indicators of a mentally healthy attitude toward self.

❖ *Self-acceptance:* Self-acceptance is a realistic perception of oneself, including awareness of one's pluses and minuses. This assessment of oneself fosters independent thinking and self-confidence.

❖ *Self-actualization:* Self-actualization is the actual process of an individual's growth or becoming based on certain concepts of what one wishes to be and the subsequent striving to unfold one's inner potential. Eric Fromm elaborates this idea further, 'Virtue is the unfolding of the specific potentialities of every organism; for man it is the state in which he is most human.'

❖ *Integration of personality:* 'Integration refers to the relatedness of all processes and attributes in an individual.' But it also implies that the individual is aware of a unifying principle underlying his personality, which broadens his outlook on life.

❖ *Autonomy:* Autonomy or self-determination connotes an individual's ability to deal independently with a variety of environmental factors.

❖ *Perception of Reality:* Perception is considered healthy when it corresponds to what is actually there.

❖ *Environmental Mastery:* Environmental mastery indicates that an individual can readily adapt and adjust to circumstances appropriate to the need or occasion.

Thus sattva is healthy-mindedness which is needed not only in ordinary life, but is a *sine qua non* for the unfoldment of self. A healthy mind is a friendly mind.

Dimensions of Self

A healthy mind is a great gain, no doubt. Becoming a well-developed psychological self, however, is but a phase in our evolution. Being a separate unique individual, though necessary for our growth, is not an end in itself. After all, an individual is a part of nature, which comprises the spectrum of the pairs of opposites. It is an egocentric state of existence and is extremely fragile. At any time our world can fall apart. As one matures, one's awareness of oneself and the outside world expands. Then we will recognize that we are not isolated, separate beings, but in truth are related to one another. In addition to this, gradually we become aware, though indistinctly at first, of a higher power that is guiding and coordinating our lives. We may call it our higher Self or God. Whatever it is, we become conscious of two entities, as it were, within ourselves—the lower self and the higher Self, the apparent and the real man. As our insight deepens, we will feel progressively an inseparable connection between these two. Thereafter, self-transformation is gauged by the strengthening of this relationship between the two aspects of self; ultimately it is the realization of the one Self.

This union occurs in two ways: by expansion of consciousness; that is, including others in our lives more and more by leading an unselfish life and by establishing a connection with the higher Self or God within us. As we practice these two exercises, expanding the self and connecting the individual with the higher Self, the limitations of the empirical self—attachment, ignorance, and their effects such as lust and greed— gradually wear out. Veil after veil drops off and the true 'I' emerges. This process is quickened through spiritual disciplines. In the terminology of the Gita, it is through yoga.

Self-transformation Through Yoga

Yoga as delineated in the Gita is the means of uniting our individualized self with our higher Self by utilising all of our faculties. Yoga has many aspects based on different functions of the mind—thinking, feeling, and willing. Whatever we do is transformed into spiritual practice by following the technique of yoga. According to Sri Krishna, culture of the mind is the bottom line of yoga discipline. In fact, evenmindedness is yoga. He eloquently describes mental balance, or equanimity of mind, starting with the instructions regarding our ordinary daily activities, right up to final realization of becoming a *sthitaprajna*, a person of steady wisdom; one who is unaffected and remains even-minded through all the vicissitudes of life: success or failure, health or illness, profit or loss, happiness or misery, good or bad, and so on.

Established in yoga, O Dhananjaya (Arjuna), perform actions, giving up attachment and remaining even-minded both in success and in failure. This equanimity is called yoga.[8] Regarding alike pleasure and pain, gain and loss, success and defeat, prepare yourself for battle.[9] Even here is the relative existence conquered by them whose mind rests in equality.[10]

As with equanimity of mind, similarly he extols and recommends the practice of same-sightedness, *samadarshana*. Seeing the unity in diversity, by trying to perceive the infinite or God in the heart of all beings and as the centre of the universe, is the essence of *samadarshana*.

The man whose mind is absorbed through yoga and who sees the same (Brahman) everywhere, sees the Self in all beings and all beings in the Self.[11] He who sees Me everywhere and sees all things in Me, does not lose sight of Me, nor do I of him.[12] He who worships Me residing in all beings in a spirit of unity, becomes a yogi and, whatever his mode of life, lives in Me.[13] He who by comparison with himself looks upon the pleasure and pain in all creatures as similar—the yogi, O Arjuna is considered the best.[14]

Another practice of uniting the self is through focusing the mind on the higher Self in meditation. Development of virtues such as self-restraint, truthfulness and noninjury is essential for the practice of meditation and is the bedrock foundation of self-transformation. A true moral sense is an inner awakening in a person that incites him to do what is right and checks him from going astray. Sensitivity to this inner voice of conscience requires life-long discipline. Further as an aid to meditation, Sri Krishna recommends avoiding extremes in daily life.

Yoga is not for him who eats too much nor for him who eats too little. It is not for him, O Arjuna, who sleeps too much nor for him who sleeps too little.[15] For him who is temperate in his food and recreation, temperate in his exertion at work, temperate in sleep and waking, yoga puts an end to all sorrows.[16]

However, in spite of these practices, the main obstacle to successful meditation is the tremendous restlessness of the mind. The antidote for this turbulence is constant practice and dispassion.

The mind is restless and hard to control; yet by practice and dispassion, O son of Kunti, it is controlled.[17] Without these, *abhyasa*, practice and, *vairagya*, dispassion, real meditation is impossible. When the mind, well-controlled, rests in the Self alone, and free from craving for all enjoyments, then is one said to have attained yoga.[18] Restraining all the senses, the self-controlled one should sit meditating on Me. Verily, his wisdom is steady whose senses are under control.[19] Endowed with a pure understanding, restraining the mind with tenacity, turning away from sound and other objects, and abandoning love and hatred.[20] Dwelling in solitude . . . controlled in speech, body and mind, ever engaged in the yoga of contemplation, and cultivating dispassion.[21]

The practice of discrimination or *vichara* is another significant aspect of yoga. Knowledge of the immortal nature of the Self is revealed through discrimination between the real and the unreal. Through vichara one separates fact from fancy; that is, that which is eternal from that which is perishable. The Gita views this issue of the eternal and the non-eternal from a variety of angles. For example, analysis of the nature of the body and the soul reveals that the body is mortal and therefore subject to illness, decay, and death, whereas the soul is undivided, indestructible.

For one who is born, death is certain.[22] The unreal never is. The real never ceases to be. The conclusion about these two is truly perceived by the seers of Truth.[23] That by which all this is pervaded know to be imperishable. None can cause the destruction of that which is immutable.[24] There is indeed nothing so purifying here as knowledge. One perfected in yoga attains that automatically in himself in time.[25] Even as a blazing fire burns the fuel to ashes, O

Arjuna, even so the fire of knowledge burns to ashes the effects of all actions.[26]

Throughout the teachings in the Gita, we find the emphasis on living an active life by following our svadharma, which includes our interactions with other people. 'Yoga is skill in action.'[27] What is this skill? Keeping oneself disentangled while working or dealing with people; that is, avoiding being caught in the intricate maze of activities and relationships. How? By giving up attachment to the results of action, not being satisfied with the immediate, ephemeral fruits, but striving for the highest fruit; that is, Self-realization. Self-realization is really our svadharma, which is living in the Indwelling Self or God, whose dharma or essential nature is purity, freedom, wisdom, love and bliss. Through such action attachment is gradually erased and one's innate freedom manifests.

Men of selfless action, giving up attachment, perform action through the body, mind, intellect, and senses, for the purification of the mind.[28] To work alone you have the right, but never to its fruits. Never let your motive be the fruit of action, nor be attached to inaction.[29] Giving up attachment to the fruit of action, ever content, and dependent on none, though engaged in work, he does no work at all.[30] But even selfless service and other spiritual practices should be performed giving up attachment and fruit—this is My conclusive and final view.[31]

This attitude of non-attachment has to be applied not only to work, but while interacting with others as well. Seeing the Divine in all as the basis of love and service is the means of detaching ourselves from others.

Non-envious, friendly, and compassionate toward all beings, free from ideas of possession and ego-consciousness, sympathetic in pain and pleasure, forgiving, always contented . . . with his mind and intellect dedicated to Me.[32] Alike to foe and friend, unaltered in honour and dishonour[33] They who worship the imperishable . . . all-pervading . . . immovable, and eternal, having controlled their senses, even-minded under all conditions and devoted to the welfare of all beings, attain Me alone.[34]

The Gita concludes, as it were, with yet another salient practice for self-transformation: Offering all activities to the Supreme, which culminates in complete self-dedication, wherein we give ourselves to God. Thus transformed we will become God-centered. The small self loses its smallness and the true Self emerges in all its glory.

Whatever you do, or eat, or sacrifice, or give, whatever austerity you perform, that, O son of Kunti, offer unto Me.[35] By worshiping Him through the performance of duty does a man attain perfection.[36] This divine illusion of Mine, consisting of the gunas, is indeed hard to overcome. But those who take refuge in Me alone, shall cross over this maya.[37] Surrendering, in thought, all actions to Me, regarding Me as the supreme goal, and practising steadiness of mind, fix your heart constantly on Me.[38] He who performs actions dedicating them to the Lord and giving up attachment, is untainted by sin, as a lotus leaf by water.[39] Giving up all duties, take refuge in Me alone. I will liberate you from all sins, do not grieve.[40]

Although a person may be under the spell of bad karma, he will be purified and made holy through worship of the Lord.

Even if the most wicked person worships Me with unswerving devotion, he must be regarded as righteous; for he has formed the right resolution.[41] He soon becomes righteous and attains eternal peace. Proclaim it boldly, O son of Kunti, that My devotee never perishes.[42] Fix your mind on Me alone, rest your thought on Me alone, and in Me alone you will live thereafter. Of this there is no doubt.[43]

The Self Transformed

In the inward journey of self-discovery, we evolve from an indefinite individual to a psychologically well-integrated healthy person, and then ultimately to our true Self which is one without a second. In this process the all-round growth of our personality is harmonious not piecemeal. It is not necessarily a step-by-step progression, but all our faculties work together in unison. Sometimes at a certain stage in our development, emphasis may be given to a particular practice or attitude because of individual need at the time. But on the whole, all of these disciplines are undertaken coordinately for our inner transformation.

The Gita's message for self-transformation is this integrated self-unfoldment. Thus we see self-transformation comes through self-purification. Self-purification leads to self-dedication. The acme of self-dedication is Self-realization.

References

1. *Gita*, 2:3
2. *ibid*. 18:47
3. *ibid*. 2:49
4. *ibid*. 10:10
5. *ibid*. 10:11
6. *ibid*. 6:5
7. *The Complete Works of Swami Vivekananda,* 6: 62
8. *Gita*, 2:48
9. *ibid*. 2:38
10. *ibid*. 5:19
11. *ibid*. 6:29
12. *ibid*. 6:30
13. *ibid*. 6:31
14. *ibid*. 6:32
15. *ibid*. 6:16
16. *ibid*. 6:17
17. *ibid*. 6:35
18. *ibid*. 6:18
19. *ibid*. 2:61
20. *ibid*. 18:51
21. *ibid*. 18:52
22. *ibid*. 2:27
23. *ibid*. 2:16
24. *ibid*. 2:17
25. *ibid*. 4:38
26. *ibid*. 4:37
27. *ibid*. 2:50
28. *ibid*. 5:11
29. *ibid*. 2:47
30. *ibid*. 4:20
31. *ibid*. 18:6
32. *ibid*. 12:13-1412:13-14
33. *ibid*. 12:19
34. *ibid*. 12:3-4
35. *ibid*. 9:27
36. *ibid*. 18:46
37. *ibid*. 7:14
38. *ibid*. 18:57
39. *ibid*. 5:10
40. *ibid*. 18:66
41. *ibid*. 9:30
42. *ibid*. 9:31
43. *ibid*. 12:8

৪৩৫৪

Chapter Nine

Frequently Asked Questions About Gita

SWAMI HARSHANANDA

QUESTION: *What is Gītā?*

ANSWER: The *Bhagavadgītā*, popularly known as the *Gītā*, is one of the outstanding religious classics of the world. Hindus, irrespective of their sects and denominations, cherish great reverence for this book. A ceremonial reading of the book, or even a part thereof, is believed to confer great religious merit.

The book itself, comprising eighteen chapters, forms an integral part of a much bigger work, the great epic, *Mahābhārata* (*vide Bhīṣmaparva*, Chapters 25 to 42). It is a poetical work in the form of a dialogue between Śrī Kṛṣṇa and Arjuna, on the battlefield of Kurukṣetra. The setting of the battlefield contributes a dramatic element to the book and relates religion to the realities of life.

The *Bhagavadgītā* is one of the most translated religious classics of the world. The beauty and the sublimity of the work, its eternal relevance to the problem of human life and its universal approach that helps us view the whole of creation as one, may have prompted the scholars to undertake the task of translating it as a labour of love.

QUESTION: What is the reason for its popularity?

ANSWER: The greatness and the popularity of the *Gītā* can be attributed to several factors. It is a part and parcel of the epic *Mahābhārata* which itself has been highly venerated as the fifth Veda *(Pañcama-Veda)*. The teacher of the *Gītā* is Śrī Kṛṣṇa, who is regarded by the Hindus as an avatāra or incarnation of God Himself. An ideal friend, a great statesman, an invincible warrior, a wise preceptor and a yogi *par excellence,* he harmonizes in his life the various conflicting activities of life. It is precisely this that makes him the fittest person to preach such a religio-spiritual classic. Arjuna, the recipient of the teaching, though himself a great warrior, is a typical representative of the humans, liable to be upset or confused during periods of crisis. Hence, his predicament, very much represents ours, in a similar situation. The questions, doubts and misgivings he raises and the solutions that Śrī Kṛṣṇa offers are not only relevant but also valid even today.

There is an additional reason too. The Hindu Vedāntic tradition has always regarded the *Prasthānatraya* (the three foundational works) as its basis; and the *Gītā* is one of them, the other two being the Upaniṣads and the *Brahmasūtras.* That is why Śaṅkara (A.D. 788-820) and other ancient teachers have chosen to write commentaries on it.

QUESTION: Can we assign any date and authorship to Gītā?

ANSWER: Since the *Gītā* is an integral part of the epic *Mahābhārata*, its date and authorship are obviously those of the epic itself. Kṛṣṇa Dvaipāyana, better known as Vedavyāsa, is reputed to be its author. As per the Hindu oral traditions based on their notion of time as the yuga-system, the Kurukṣetra war must have taken place during 3139 B.C. The dates given however by the modern historians (mostly of the West) vary from 1424 B.C. to 575 B.C. At the present stage of the research, it may be difficult to clinch the issue on such chronological matters.

QUESTION: Tell us how the Gītā was delivered.

ANSWER: Dhṛtarāṣṭra, the blind king (father of the Kauravas) asks Sañjaya, his companion who had been endowed with divine sight to see and describe the war, to tell him as to what happened on the battle field. Sañjaya starts by telling how Duryodhana approaches Droṇācārya, the preceptor and describes the various warriors on both the sides. Just then, Bhīṣma, the grandsire and commander-in-chief of the Kaurava army blows his conch to indicate the commencement of the day's battle. This is followed by all the others including the Pāṇḍavas, blowing their respective conches. At the request of Arjuna, the Pāṇḍava hero, Śrī Kṛṣṇa, his charioteer, brings his chariot and stations it in between the two armies, but right in front of Bhīṣma and Droṇa! Seeing them and observing all the others assembled there for the war, Arjuna sinks in horror and sorrow. He describes his pitiable condition to Śrī Kṛṣṇa, argues against this fratricidal war by portraying its various evil consequences which will ultimately result in the total collapse of the socio-political system and sits down in the chariot abandoning his weapons.

QUESTION: *What is Śrī Kṛṣṇa's response to Arjuna's situation?*

ANSWER: Śrī Kṛṣṇa at first tries to rouse Arjuna from this stupor by strongly admonishing him for his psychological collapse at a critical moment, his un-Āryan and unmanly behaviour which does not befit a great warrior like him and urges him to bestir himself to action. Even such strong words fail to awaken him. He continues to sermonize, conveys his decision to retire, but in all humility, seeks his guidance. Then realising that Arjuna's confusion and delusion have gone too deep to be dispelled by cursory replies, Śrī Kṛṣṇa starts his immortal spiritual discourse aimed at curing his malady from the root itself by giving him a correct perspective of the whole picture, in fact, an entire philosophy of life. Arjuna is really sorrowing for those who should not be sorrowed for. All the people including those assembled on the battlefield are, in reality, immortal souls. Death or deterioration belongs only to the body and not to the soul or the spirit. Even supposing it is accepted that one is born with the body and dies with its death, there is no use lamenting it, since it is inevitable. Being a kṣattriya warrior on whose shoulders is cast the responsibility of defending dharma or righteousness, it is his sacred duty to fight and win, or, die for the cause on the battlefield. For a man like him, celebrated for valour, death is preferable to ignominy which will surely accrue to him if he withdraws from the battle now.

QUESTION: So, how should one fight the battle of life?

ANSWER: It is action motivated by selfishness that binds a man whereas when the same is performed without an eye to its fruits and with equanimity, it liberates. This is the 'buddhi' or 'yoga' or 'buddhi-yoga'. Then at Arjuna's request, Śrī Kṛṣṇa describes the characteristics of the sthitaprajña or the man of steady spiritual wisdom as a model for Arjuna's emulation. The sthitaprajña has abandoned all desires, and is ever contented in his own Self. He is unmoved by pleasure and pain. He is free from attachment, fear or anger. He has absolute mastery over his senses. He is ever awake to the Highest Truth and is indifferent towards the world. He is well-established in the state of Brahman, even at the last moment of his life.

QUESTION: What is the secret of right activity?

ANSWER: For most people, performance of one's duties with a controlled mind, for the good of the world, is the easier and the better path. The world-cycle as set in motion by the Creator needs everyone to do his allotted duties, so that it works smoothly. The path of work is in no way inferior since many great persons like Janaka in the ancient days, attained perfection through it alone. Leaders of society (like Arjuna) are expected to show the way to the less enlightened ones by doing their duties perfectly. By cultivating the right attitude towards work and by offering it to him (i.e., Śrī Kṛṣṇa, who is God Himself), one is not tainted by it even while working. Doing one's own duty, however imperfect it may appear to be, is far better than the performance of others' duties, relinquishing one's own. What normally spoils one's work and even impels one to evil ways of life, is selfish desire as also anger. These two have to be conquered by subduing the senses and raising the mind to the level of ātman or the soul.

QUESTION: How does an action take place?

ANSWER: Every action has five causes like the body and speech; and it is foolish to consider the ātman (the self) as the doer. One who does actions without the sense of doership and with an untainted mind is never bound by them.

QUESTION: 'Who' is God? How can we approach Him?

ANSWER: He is all—the various items of a sacrifice, the father, mother and sustainer of the universe, the goal and the Lord, the place of origin and dissolution. He is the sun that shines, the rain that pours. He is immortality as well as death. It is he who is propitiated through sacrifices. If people worship him only, are eternally devoted to him, then he will take over the responsibility of taking care of them. Those who worship other deities reach them, whereas those who worship him, come to him. However he is the Self of all these deities also. What really matters in worshipping him is devotion. He accepts even a leaf or a flower or water if offered with devotion and faith. He has no enemies nor friends. Even the worst sinner, once he realizes his mistakes and worships God with devotion, becomes transformed into a righteous soul.

QUESTION: Tell us something about the way God works.

ANSWER: God holds all beings and objects of the created world from within like a thread holding the beads. He is in fact the best and the essence in all beings and things. His māyā, comprising the three guṇas (sattva, rajas and tamas—which, incidentally is his aparā-prakṛti) can delude all and is difficult to overcome. Only those that totally surrender themselves to him can transcend it. The foolish and the evil ones do not surrender to him and hence will not attain him. As for his devotees, they are of four types: ārta (one afflicted), arthārthi (one desirous of worldly gains), jijñāsu (one interested in knowing him) and the jnāni (the knower). The last one is the best among them. People generally take recourse to different deities to fulfil their numerous desires. However, it is he (Śrī Kṛṣṇa, the Supreme Lord) that grants their desires, through those forms. He, the Supreme Lord, being enveloped by his own yogamāyā is not revealed to all. Only those who have performed good deeds and are sinless are devoted to him to get liberation.

QUESTION: What can we learn from this advice of Śrī Kṛṣṇa?

ANSWER: Arjuna is advised to remember the Lord always and fight his battles of life. Then he describes abhyāsayoga or yoga of repeated practice of thinking of the Lord. The yogi who practises it, especially at the last moment of his life, will reach the Supreme Lord. The repetition of the syllable Om at this juncture is a great help. If a person departs from the body in this way, he will not come back to this mundane existence. Attaining other worlds through meritorious deeds will be of no use since one has to return to this earth once again. Here Śrī Kṛṣṇa mentions about the two well-known paths— Arcirādimārga (path of light) and Dhūmādimārga (path of smoke)—mentioned in the earlier works like the Upaniṣads. The former leads to Brahmaloka (the world of Brahmā) from which there is no return, whereas the latter leads to Pitṛloka (the world of manes) from which one returns once again to the mortal world. A yogi who knows about these paths is never again deluded.

QUESTION: *How does one meditate?*

ANSWER: A person aspiring to meditate should sit in a clean place, keeping the body erect and steady. Controlling and gathering the forces of the mind, he should direct it towards Śrī Kṛṣṇa (who is God Himself). Thus he will attain peace. Such yoga is possible only for a person who leads a balanced life, avoiding all extremes. Such a yogi will be able to see all beings in God and God in all beings. He of an equanimous mind is the best of yogis. Here Arjuna raises two questions: How can one control this fickle mind? What will happen to a yogi who fails to attain the goal? Śrī Kṛṣṇa replies that though it is difficult to control the mind, it is not impossible. It can be achieved by vairāgya (renunciation) and abhyāsa (practice). As regards the yogi who has slipped from the ideal, he will be born once again in the family of yogis and, getting a conducive atmosphere, strives even harder, ultimately attaining the goal. A yogi, he concludes, is superior to men of austerity or knowledge or works; and exhorts Arjuna to become one.

QUESTION: *It is said that Arjuna actually had a vision of God. Is it so?*

ANSWER: Yes. Arjuna's curiosity being roused by what Śrī Kṛṣṇa said, he requests Lord Śrī Kṛṣṇa to show to him his divine form. The Lord endows him with a divine sight and reveals his Viśvarūpa or universal divine form. Decorated with divine garlands and garments, the wondrous cosmic form is more brilliant than a million suns. The whole world of variegated forms, constitutes only a small part of his being. Excited by wonder and joy, Arjuna starts praying to that Divinity. This beautiful prayer hymn of 17 verses gives a moving description of the Viśvarūpa or the cosmic form. All beings—divine, human and subhuman—are being seen in Him. He has several arms, bellies and faces. He is extraordinarily brilliant. He has pervaded the whole space. All beings like gods and sages, are praising Him with folded hands. The various heroes arrayed on the battle field are entering into Him and getting destroyed like moths in the fire. Gripped with fear and wonder, Arjuna prays to Him to reveal who He is. The Lord replies that He is Time, the eternal destroyer, come to annihilate the warriors in the enemy armies. Since this task will be achieved by Him even without Arjuna's involvement, the Lord advises Arjuna to fight, get victory and fame, and enjoy the kingdom.

QUESTION: *Who is a true devotee?*

ANSWER: Lord Śrī Kṛṣṇa describes the characteristics of a bhakta or an ideal devotee. He does not hate anyone. He is friendly to all. He is compassionate and free from egoism as also possessiveness. He is equanimous in pleasure and pain, ever forgiving and ever contented. Having mastered his passions he has dedicated his mind unto the Lord. He is never the cause of unrest for the world, nor can the world upset him. He is free from joy and anger, fear and anxiety. He is beyond pleasure and hatred, sorrow and desires, and has abandoned all actions, good or bad. He has devotion and looks upon friend and foe with an equal eye and is equanimous in honour and dishonour. Ever contented, having no particular place to lay his head, he has steadiness of mind. Such a devotee is ever dear to him.

QUESTION: *Tell us something about the 'three guṇas'?*

ANSWER: This *prakṛiti* [or Primordial Nature] gives rise to the three guṇas—sattva, rajas and tamas. Sattva is pure and bright, produces pleasure and knowledge, and binds the soul through them. Rajas is of the nature of passion, produces desire and attachment and binds the embodied soul through action. Tamas, born out of ignorance, deludes beings through inadvertence, sloth and sleep. Sattva creates attachment for happiness, rajas for actions, and tamas, covering knowledge, binds one to inadvertence. The three guṇas are constantly acting on one another. The rise of sattva can be inferred by the rise of jñāna or knowledge, of rajas by the rise of greed and activity and of tamas by the rise of inadvertence and delusion. Death at the time when sattva is on the ascendant takes one to the pure realms. Ascendance of rajas and tamas at the time of death leads one to birth in the families of those addicted to actions and in subhuman bodies. Anyone who realizes that it is the guṇas that act and knows the Self untouched by them, attains to my being.

QUESTION: *Can we go beyond the guṇas?*

ANSWER: Yes. Śrī Kṛṣṇa says that one who is unmoved by the effects of the three guṇas (like knowledge or action or delusion) is a guṇātīta (one who is beyond guṇas). He is equanimous in sorrow or happiness, looks upon a clod of earth or stone or gold as of equal worth, is unmoved by the pleasant and the unpleasant or by praise or blame. He is the same to enemies and friends. He abandons all undertakings. He serves me (the Lord) with undeviating love. Such a one is a guṇātīta and becomes fit to attain Brahman.

QUESTION: *In Gītā, divine versus demoniac traits are mentioned. What are they?*

ANSWER: The list of daivī-sampat (divine traits) comprises 26 qualities, the chief ones being: fearlessness, purity of mind, self-control, Vedic studies, austerity, non-violence, truth, spirit of renunciation, compassion, forgiveness and absence of pride. The other list, of the āsurī-sampat (demoniac traits), consists of six vices: hypocrisy, vainglory, egoism, anger, harsh speech and ignorance of higher values.

Gītā also gives a long but interesting description of the demoniac or evil persons and their way of life. They know neither the performance of good works nor the need to withdraw from the evil ones. They have neither purity nor truth. They consider kāma or lust as the sole cause of creation. Being addicted to it, they out of delusion, try to get unholy things. They boast about their wealth or works and exult in destroying their enemies. They dislike the Lord who is the Self of all beings. Such persons are thrown by me (i.e., Lord Śrī Kṛṣṇa) into abominable births.

The gateway to hell that ultimately causes self-destruction is threefold: lust, anger and greed. One who is free from these attains the highest abode. For this, one needs to act according to the Vedas and the śāstras (holy books) but with śraddhā or faith.

QUESTION: *What are the three types of food mentioned in the Gītā?*

ANSWER: Food is of three types. Food conducive to health, strength and purity of mind, and is pleasant is sāttvika. Foods that are very bitter, sour or saltish, pungent and produce diseases are rājasik. Old and stale food, the food that has lost its taste and flavour, petrified, spoiled and impure is tāmasic.

QUESTION: *What are the types of tapas?*

ANSWER: Tapas or austerity is of three types—śarīra, vāṅmaya and mānasa (pertaining to the body, speech and mind respectively). Worship of gods, brāhmaṇas and preceptors as also observing purity and continence, is tapas of the body. Truthful and unoffensive speech as also the study of one's branch of the Vedas is tapas of the speech. Peace of mind, control of thoughts and speech, and a pleasant demeanour is tapas of the mind. When this threefold tapas is performed with faith and without the desire for its fruits, it is sāttvik. If it is done in an ostentatious manner for name and fame, it is rājasik. If done without regard to one's capacity and for harming others it is tāmasik.

QUESTION: *And what are the types of dāna?*

ANSWER: Dāna or gifts given as a matter of duty to persons of the right type and in the right manner belong to the sāttvik type. If given with the desire for future rewards and not very willingly, it becomes rājasik. Gifts given in disdain to unworthy persons, transgressing the rules are tāmasik.

QUESTION: *What are the types of buddhi and dhṛti?*

ANSWER: Buddhi (intellect) and dhṛti (fortitude) are also of three varieties. Sāttvik buddhi is aware of bondage and liberation. Rājasik buddhi is that which is unable to understand dharma (righteousness) and adharma (unrighteousness) properly. Tāmasik buddhi understands everything in the wrong way. Sāttvik dhṛti helps in self-control. Rājasik dhṛti makes one to be selfishly attached to things. Tāmasik dhṛti impels one towards sleep, fear and vanity.

QUESTION: *What is Gītā's view about happiness?*

ANSWER: *Gītā* categorizes sukha or happiness, into three kinds. That which appears unpleasant in the beginning but gives happiness at the end, after a long practice leading to the mind being established in the ātman (Self) is sāttvik. Happiness got by sense-contact with sense-objects, which appears pleasant in the beginning but ends up in disaster, is rājasik. Tāmasik happiness causes delusion and induces laziness.

QUESTION: *So, how do we summarise Gītā's message?*

ANSWER: Though part of the *Mahābhārata,* it can as well stand on its own as an independent work. Though taught on the battlefield of Kurukṣetra, urging Arjuna to fight, it has nothing to do with wars or battles or bloodshed, but only with the discharging of one's sacred duties of life, however unpleasant they may be. Though given by Śrī Kṛṣṇa to Pārtha or Arjuna in the days of yore, its declarations like, 'Remember Me and fight!' (8.7) can help and inspire anyone of us, beleaguered with serious problems in life, even now. Though recognizing multiplicity here, its principle of unity in diversity as signified by the cosmic form (11.9-13) and the underlying divinity (as taught in 7.7), help us to cultivate a holistic approach to the whole universe of which the much talked of ecological balance too is only a small aspect.

སོ་ཅོ

Chapter Ten

Bhagavad Gita for the Commoners

SWAMI GAUTAMANANDA

A Common Man's Dilemma

The Gita begins with Arjuna not willing to wage the war and Sri Krishna exhorting him to the contrary. Hence the common man asks: 'Is indulging in violence or war right or wrong?' Gita's answer is that war certainly involves violence. But in this realistic world, at times the unrighteous capture power and position and create trouble for everyone—as in the case of Duryodhana, in the *Mahabharata*, who was not willing to listen to Sri Krishna's words of peace and reconciliation. In such cases, the only way to check the unrighteous is to put suitable righteous people in their place.

Thus Gita answers the question that violence is right when it is used in duty for the protection of the cultured, good and righteous people in the society. It says: 'Being killed you will attain heaven or being victorious you will enjoy earth. Therefore, Arjuna, arise and resolve to fight.'[1]

It assures the individuals who fight on the side of righteousness 'heaven', thus encouraging good people to be dynamic in fighting for right causes.

A common man wants to get everything imme-diate, be it solving his worldly problems or getting the experience God. He is willing to undergo hardships to gain material things, but when it comes to getting God-experience, he thinks that it is very easy and can be easily achieved through meditation. Soon he discovers that it is not easy. Meditation is not easy and it requires preparation by way of inner purification. Hence when he is advised that he should make his mind peaceful by gradually reducing selfish desires through working selflessly and dedicating all work as an offering to God (which is the essence of Karma Yoga), he becomes indecisive as to whether he should work as advised or should take to meditation.

Sri Krishna clears up this uncertainty thus: 'Two paths have been declared by Me—the way of seeking knowledge through meditation for Sankhyas (who have renounced all desires) and way of action for Yogis (Karma Yogis, who have yet to renounce desires).' This verse indicates that a Karma Yogi becomes a man of meditation by sincerely doing his work selflessly and offering them to God.[2]

To Own or Not to Own

Next question that assails the common mind is: What is the meaning of Gita which says, 'Do the works for the sake of God without any attachment?'[3] How can we work without attachment or expecting anything?

It means that we should have the attitude of a cashier working in a bank who has to handle a lot of cash but knows that he is *not* the owner or the enjoyer of that sum because it is owned and enjoyed by the bank, his employer. He is only entrusted a work which he should do earnestly and honestly.

If we feel that this creation is God's, and He is in the heart of everyone, making them do as they do, then we would feel that He is the doer and that the results of our actions are also His. We would then become free from ego and possessiveness. This is the real detachment, which would free us from the bonds of good or meritorious (*punya*) and evil or unmeritorious (*papa*) effects of our actions. Thus we would attain the desireless, calm mind. This is how Karmayoga leads one to Jnanayoga (meditation on Atman) or to Bhaktiyoga (meditation on God).

People who are given to a consumerist and materialistic way of life often wonder why Hindus always talk of the role of religion in every field of their activity—in education, social life, economic and ethical life.

Gita answers this by pointing that God incarnates whenever religion degenerates and irreligion grows.[4] The history records that God has incarnated Himself in India the highest number of times. This is why religion has become the backbone of India. This is the reason Hindus are the most religious and spiritually-inclined people. Even during the hard times of Mogul and British rule in India, the Hindus believed that they would be 'saved' by God Himself.

The common man hears that Jesus washes away the sins of sinners who take refuge in him. He asks does Hinduism have any such assurance? Gita says: Even if you are the worst sinner, you will cast off all your sins through the knowledge of your own Divine Self.[5]

This statement also refers to the potential divinity in every being and when it is awakened, this inherent Divinity washes away all sins and weaknesses.

Spiritual Life is for All

Another question that nags the common mind is which type of worship is superior—the one that is done with all pomp and show by offering large quantities of fruits, sweets, flowers, clothes, wealth, etc., to God or the one which is done with genuine prayers, charity, contemplation and meditation? Gita calls the first one as *dravyamaya yajna* (worship with various material objects) and the latter *jnanamaya yajna* (worship with knowledge and inner earnestness) and declares, 'The worship through knowledge is superior to worship performed with materials. All actions are included in knowledge.'[6] In other words, what matters in the spirit in which one offers one's worship to God.

The question of who is the right person who can be a guru and guide a common man in spiritual life is also an important one. The Gita makes it clear that only when an aspirant has attained to purity of mind through *dravya yajna* and *jnana yajna* as mentioned above that the Guru comes into a person's life. It is like the functioning of the law of demand and supply in the spiritual realm. Once the spiritual aspirant is ready, and approaches the guru with humility, prayerfulness and submissiveness, the guru would teach the highest knowledge out of pure love and compassion. The Gurus are beyond all desires and hence they teach only out of compassion to remove the miseries of this cycle of birth and death. Gita advises us: 'Learn that knowledge through prostration (humbleness), inquiry (prayerfulness) and service (submissiveness). The wise one, who are the knowers of Truth, will teach you.'[7]

It is common to hear that nowadays 'meditation' is being practised in business houses, factories and farms. What is true meditation? True meditation is when the mind, 'well-controlled and calm, becomes fixed on the inner Self alone, and one is free from craving for all enjoyments, then one is said to have attained Yoga (meditation).'[8] One attains this state when the mind becomes steady and fixed like 'a lamp kept in a wind-less place.'[9] Such a lamp does not flicker and that is the simile which describes the mind of a perfected yogi.

There is no loss of time and energy spent in this method of Yoga. If, for some reason, one dies before reaching this goal of perfect concentration, then one starts again in his next birth from where he had left his efforts in his previous birth. This goes on until he attains the goal of Self-Realization. Gita says, 'Verily, a yogi who practices assiduously being purified by all sins is perfected through many births and attains the supreme goal.'[10] This explains the question about how some people are inclined towards spiritual life from a very young age. It is because they have struggled hard in their previous lives.

The common man sees some people worshipping incarnations like Rama, Krishna, Buddha, Jesus, Chaitanya, Ramakrishna and some others worshipping gods like the sun, moon, *agni*, *vayu*, or their ancestors. Do they all attain the same goal? Gita says, 'Those who worship the gods (*devas*) attain to gods; those who worship ancestors (both states do not last long), attain to ancestors; those who worship Me (the incarnation or God Himself) attains Me (and that state is eternal and everlasting).'[11] Hence, the Gita suggests that one should only worship Divine Incarnations, if one wants to become Immortal which happens by the grace of God.

What about the people who worship places, rivers, hills, trees, etc., as holy? Why are they held sacred? The Gita says, 'Whatever thing is glorious, excellent or outstanding, verily know that it is born of a portion of God's splendour.'[12] By associating divine grandeur with material objects, one can remember Him constantly even though being amidst various mundane activities.

Answers to Some Common Questions

This is also an important issue: whether a person given to sense pleasures (generally called 'wicked') can come out of it? Is there any hope for him?

Gita points out that the inscrutable grace of God falls on such people also and redeems them.

Even if a very wicked person worships me with one pointed mind, he should be regarded as virtuous for he has rightly resolved. He soon becomes righteous minded and attains eternal peace.[13]

How can a wicked person become so pure as to worship with one-pointed mind? This is possible only by the power and grace of God and nothing else! Angulimala in Buddha's life and Girish Ghosh in Sri Ramakrishna's life are instances to the point.

Generally one hears that it is the laws of science on which universe goes on. One also hears that it is God's will that controls everything in the universe. The doubt arises whether these two sets of laws are separate? If so, which is superior? Gita says that God's will, with the omniscient God behind it, is supreme. If required, it can undo the physical laws. Sri Ramakrishna once showed flowers of two different colours on the same branch of a hibiscus plant which had yielded till then only single-colour flowers. Many times, due to the fervent prayers of devotees, many supernatural things too take place. All such cases are instances of the God's will setting aside physical laws. This is the reason that devotees of God do not fear because they are all under the will of God and whatever God does, being one's own father and mother, is good for them.

Again, some think of God as being with form, some others believe His as being without it. Which is superior? Gita says that embodied beings find it easy to worship God with form. Those who consider themselves as atman (i.e., not body), they can worship God without form. They also attain God but their path is very difficult. As Sri Krishna says,

> Those who worship Me fixing their mind on Me, ever devoted and endowed with supreme faith—them I regard as the best yogins.[14] The trouble of those whose minds are attached to the formless is greater; for the way of formless is attained with difficulty by the embodied soul (or the person attached to his body).[15]

But what about the idea of caste? Our society is divided into numberless hereditary castes and sub-castes. Are they sanctioned by God?

Sri Krishna in the Gita says: 'The four castes were created by me according to the differences in the aptitudes and actions of persons.'[16]

These four castes are actually to be seen from the idea of three *gunas* or qualities mentioned in the Gita. Those people who have more of sattva quality (serenity) in their personality and therefore are able to control their mind and the sense are Brahmanas. Those people whose mental make-up has the quality of rajas (activity) plus a little of sattva, are generally courageous and fit to wage war; they are called Kshatriyas. Those in whom one finds rajas together with a little of tamas (indolence), are good in agriculture and trade and thus are called Vysyas. And, those whose nature is full of tamas in addition to a little of Rajas, can only serve or assist others and are called Shudras.

It is to be noted here that the members of the same family can belong to different castes depending on their aptitudes. Thus castes are not hereditary but based on aptitude. It is also evident that the innumerable sub-castes in the Hindu society have no basis in Gita. They are only trade guilds, groupings of persons of same occupation such as weaving, carpentry and so on. Gita also says that 'all men are parts of God.'[17] Thus a spiritual equality runs across all the castes in spite of their outward difference in duties.

One more common question finally: we find some people gifted with good qualities even from their infancy whereas some are born with bad qualities. What does Gita say about them? Sri Krishna explains: 'Men are of two kinds, the divine and the demoniac.'[18]

The divine ones are fearless, pure, charitable, self-controlled, sacrificing, austere, upright, loving, truthful, calm, tranquil, friendly, kind, non-covetous, gentle, modest, strong-willed, bold, forgiving, forbearing and humble. They attain to supreme freedom in due course. The demoniacal ones are ostentatious, arrogant, self-oriented, angry, rude and ignorant. These are deluded birth after birth and fall into still lower conditions because of their excessive attachment to lust, anger and greed, the three gates to hell. These demoniacal people who do not obey the words of saints and scriptures do not attain happiness in this world nor attain the supreme goal. They are in a way doomed. Hence, the Gita warns us to be ever awake to the teachings of saints, seers and scriptures.

Modern man being materialistic in outlook thinks that there is no need for worship, charity or austerities prescribed as duty by our saints, seers and scriptures. But the Gita says worship (*yajna*), charity (*dana*), austerities (*tapas*) are essential to purify our mind and make us fit for spiritual progress. All these must be done in a spirit of worship of God. 'By performing one's ordained duties and dedicating their fruits to God, one attains spiritual illumination.'[19]

The ultimate message of Gita to the common man is this: 'Performing all works having Me as the supreme goal and not the heaven, etc., one attains to the supreme state of Vishnu through the grace of God.'[20]

Conclusion

Thus Bhagavad Gita answers most questions of the common man regarding God, man, the world, the way of bondage and the way to freedom. Finally it asserts that the essence of spiritual life is to realize our being, the Atman, and our eternal relationship of love with the Creator. Or as Sri Ramakrishna said, 'First God, then the world'. He used to say that the number increases if you put many zeros after the figure one; but the zeros don't have any value if the one is not there. The Bible too says, 'First seek ye the kingdom of heaven and all else shall be added unto you.'

In this age of materialism and information explosion, the best guidance the common man needs is the message of the Gita.

References

1. *Gita,* 2.37
2. *ibid.,* 3.3
3. *ibid.,* 3.9
4. *ibid.,* 4.7
5. *ibid.,* 4.36
6. *ibid.,* 4.33
7. *ibid.,* 4.34
8. *ibid.,* 6.18
9. *ibid.,* 6.19
10. *ibid.,* 6.45
11. *ibid.,* 9.25
12. *ibid.,* 10.41
13. *ibid.,* 9.30/31
14. *ibid.,* 12.2
15. *ibid.,* 12.5
16. *ibid.,* 4.13
17. *ibid.,* 15.7
18. *ibid.,* 16.6
19. *ibid.,* 18.45
20. *ibid.,* 18.56

☙❧

Chapter Eleven

True Happiness—Gita's Counsel
SWAMI BHASKARANANDA

What is Happiness?

In plain language, happiness is a feeling of well-being acquired through the fulfilment of a cherished desire. For example, the fulfilment of our desires for health, money, position, praise, appreciation, love, honour, fame, etc., gives us happiness. The Sanskrit counterpart of the word happiness is *sukham*.

The Bhagavad Gita uses the word *sukham* 17 times. Counting other variations of the word the number comes to 34.

Happiness and Bliss

To most people happiness is synonymous with joy. According to Hindu tradition, joy derived from sense objects is *sukham*. In this sense *sukham* is a state of sense-enjoyment. But super-sensuous joy is not *sukham*; it is *anandam*. In English it is called Bliss.

❖ *Anandam is 'true happiness'. Anandam,* in the highest sense of the word, is a state beyond enjoyment and suffering. To explain, let me suppose, I have a terrible headache. As long as my headache lasts, I am suffering. But after taking two tablets of Aspirin my headache is gone. Am I suffering now? No, I am neither suffering nor enjoying. I have gone beyond both. This state of relief from both suffering and enjoyment could be compared to *anandam*. It is this *anandam* which is 'true happiness.'

According to Hindu philosophers, this world of time, space and causation is a world of *dvandvas*—pairs of opposites. For example, darkness and light belong to a pair of opposites. They are inseparable; to know darkness we must also know light, and vice versa. Similarly, enjoyment and suffering form a pair of opposites. *Anandam* or 'supreme Bliss' is neither enjoyment nor suffering; it transcends both. This transcendental Bliss is one aspect of *Brahman* [*Brahman* is *sat-chit-anandam* or Existence-Consciousness-Bliss].

The Bhagavad Gita, however, does not use the word *anandam*. Nevertheless, it uses the words *sukham-atyantikam*, *sukham-uttamam*, as well as the expression *atyantam sukham* to indicate this supreme Bliss or *anandam*. The adjective *atyantikam* means 'absolute,' while the adjectives *uttamam* and *atyantam* mean 'absolute, supreme or unsurpassable.' All these expressions mean *anandam* or Bliss.

In this manner the Bhagavad Gita speaks about both *sukham* and *anandam*.

❖ *One cannot have only happiness, and not suffering*: The problem with sense-derived *sukham* is that it never comes alone. Along with it inevitably comes *duhkha* or suffering. As the story goes, a poor man petitioned to God with the prayer to become rich. He wrote to God, 'I am unhappy and miserable because I am extremely poor. Please make me rich.'

God wrote on his petition 'Prayer granted' and then returned it to him. Shortly thereafter the poor man won one million dollars in a lottery. He invested that money in real estate and the stock market. In a matter of years he became a multimillionaire. Keeping track of his investments kept him awfully busy. He hardly had any time to spend with his family. Aside from that, worrying about his money and investments all the time, he developed high blood pressure, an ulcer in his stomach and high blood sugar. To top the list of his problems, one day his wife threatened divorce.

Feeling totally helpless, he complained to God, 'Lord, to become happy I prayed to you for money, why then am I so unhappy? Why do I have all these problems?' Then he heard the voice of God.

God said, 'Find the petition that I granted, and read the fine print.'

The man took the petition out of his safe and carefully read the fine print with the help of a magnifying glass. It read: 'You'll be extremely rich, but along with it you will have worries, high blood pressure, an ulcer in your stomach, high blood sugar, and also a lot of family troubles.'

In spite of the moral contained in the above story one may think that while earthly happiness is accompanied by sorrow or suffering, the happiness or enjoyment in heaven must be unending and eternal. But Sri Krishna shows the flaw in that kind of thinking in chapter 9 (verse 21) of the Bhagavad Gita. He implicitly says that the enjoyment or happiness in heaven, which is the result of meritorious action performed during a person's lifetime on earth, can never produce eternal happiness or enjoyment in heaven. Action performed on earth, no matter how righteous, has to be finite. And common sense tells us that finite action can never produce infinite effect. That is why eternal and never-ending heavenly enjoyment is impossible. Eventually the merits of finite action will be used up and one has to be reborn on earth.

In the second chapter of the Bhagavad Gita (verse 38), Sri Krishna asks Arjuna to treat both *sukha* (happiness/enjoyment) and *duhkha* (sorrow/suffering) equally. In other words, he asks Arjuna to be indifferent to both because both of them come as a pair of opposites. This also is a secret to attaining true happiness or Bliss. The realisation that happiness and sorrow are only two sides of the same coin will eventually enable Arjuna to go beyond both, and thus attain transcendental Bliss or true happiness.

As long as a person considers himself to be a psychophysical being, he belongs to *prakriti*. *Prakriti* or 'Mother Nature' is composed of the three *gunas*—*sattva*, *rajas* and *tamas*. The mental states such as *sukha* and *duhkha*—happiness and sorrow—are caused by the *gunas*. Therefore, to have 'true happiness' one has to go beyond the three *gunas* of *prakriti*.

❖ *Sense-derived Happiness is caused by sattva-guna*: In verse 45 of the second chapter of the *Bhagavad Gita* Sri Krishna first asks Arjuna to go beyond the three *guna*s. But realizing the level where Arjuna stands, he comes down to that level and advises Arjuna to be established in *sattva guna*, because it is *sattva guna* which 'attaches one to happiness' (Gita, 14.9). This happiness, however, is sense-derived happiness; it is not 'true happiness.'

❖ *True happiness or Bliss can be attained through the yoga of meditation*: In verse 2.66 of the Bhagavad Gita we read: 'For the unsteady there is no wisdom, and there is no meditation for the unsteady man. And for an *un-meditative* person there is no peace. How can there be happiness for one without peace?' Peace is neither enjoyment nor suffering; it is neither sense-derived happiness nor sorrow. This peace is *anandam* or 'true happiness,' and it is attained through meditation.

In Gita (6.21), Sri Krishna says, 'When one experiences that absolute Bliss (*sukham-atyantikam*) which can be intuited by the intellect and which is beyond the senses, and being established thus, the person surely does not swerve from Reality.'

Again in 6.27, Sri Krishna says, 'Supreme Bliss (*sukham-uttamam*) comes to this *yogi* alone whose mind has become perfectly tranquil, whose (quality of) *rajas* has been eliminated, who has become identical with *Brahman*, and is taintless (free from vice).'

Also in 6.28 Sri Krishna says, 'By concentrating his mind constantly thus, the taintless *yogi* easily attains the absolute Bliss (*atyantam sukham*) of contact with *Brahman*, and is taintless (free from vice).'

'*True happiness*' can also be attained through the *Yoga of Devotion*: In 14.27, Sri Krishna says to Arjuna, 'And he who serves Me through the unswerving Yoga of Devotion, he, having gone beyond the *gunas* (of *prakriti*), qualifies for becoming *Brahman*.'

True happiness or Bliss is beyond the three gunas. In the second chapter of the Bhagavad Gita, Sri Krishna talks about the *atman* or our true Self. Our ego, which is none other than a thought born in the mind, is the false self. Being mental, it is a modification of *prakriti* or the three *gunas*. Birth, growth, decay, death and all such phenomena take place within the domain of the three *gunas*. The true Self or the *atman* is beyond such phenomena. It is beyond *prakriti* or the three *gunas*. The *atman* or the true Self is identical with *Brahman*. Then again, Brahman is infinite Bliss or *anandam*. So also is *atman* or the true Self. Therefore, the true Self in us is none other than infinite Bliss. Thus, 'true happiness' is our real nature. This is why in 2.45, Sri Krishna asks Arjuna to go beyond the three *gunas* to discover this 'true happiness' or Bliss that forms the very core of Arjuna's being.

❖ '*True happiness*' *or infinite Bliss* is indicated by expressions like *Brahma-nirvanam, Brahma-bhutam, etc.* The Gita use the expression *Brahma-nirvanam* to mean identification of the individual soul with *Brahman* in various places.

It also uses either the expression *Brahma-bhutam* or *Brahmabhutah* to indicate the identification of the individual soul with *Brahman*.

In 14.26 the expression *Brahma-bhuyaya* has been used to mean 'becoming one with Brahman.'

Conclusion

Thus we see that by the expression 'true happiness' only our Brahman nature is indicated throughout the Bhagavad Gita.

Note: The English translation of the verses of the Bhagavad Gita in this article is based on the English translation of the Bhagavad Gita by Swami Gambhirananda.

ॐॐ

Chapter Twelve

Gita's Description of Integrated Personality

SWAMI ADISWARANANDA

Inner integration, according to the *Bhagavad Gita,* is marked by the rise of the quality of *sattva* (spiritual balance) in an individual over the qualities of *rajas* (restlessness) and *tamas* (inertia). *Sattva* manifests itself as honesty of conduct, promptness, freedom from dependence and anxiety, discrimination between right and wrong, skill in action, fortitude and forbearance in the face of unfavourable circumstances, even-mindedness, firm faith, and contentment. Opposed to *sattva* are *rajas* and *tamas*: *rajas* is characterized by greed, overactivity, overambition, enterprise, unrest, and longing; *tamas* by darkness, indolence, inadvertence, and delusion.

The three qualities, or *gunas,* are present in every individual in differing proportions, and these differing proportions of the *gunas* make for the difference between one personality and another.

An individual in whom *sattva* prevails over *rajas* and *tamas* is said to be *sattvika;* an individual in whom *rajas* prevails over *sattva* and *tamas* is said to be *rajasika;* an individual in whom *tamas* prevails over *sattva* and *rajas* is said to be *tamasika*. The rise of *sattva* leads to inner integration, the rise of *rajas* to tension, and the rise of *tamas* to disintegration and destruction. In keeping with these three divisions, all personalities come under three broad categories of *sattvika, rajasika,* and *tamasika.*

The *Bhagavad Gita* describes in detail the characteristic behaviour patterns of the three types of personalities in regard to their faith, food preferences, worship, practice of austerity, making of gifts, knowledge of reality, performance of action, character pattern, sense of discrimination of right and wrong, firmness of mind, and sense of happiness:

❖ *Faith.* The *sattvika* person worships the gods; the *rajasika* person worships demigods and demons; and the *tamasika* person worships ghosts and disembodied spirits.

❖ *Food Preferences.* The *sattvika* person favours food that promotes longevity, vitality, strength, health, pleasure, and appetite, and that is succulent, oleaginous, substantial, and agreeable. The *rajasika* person prefers food that is excessively bitter, sour, salty, hot, acrid, dry, and burning. The *tamasika* person likes food that is poorly cooked, tasteless, putrid, stale, unclean, and left over.

❖ *Worship.* The *sattvika* person follows scriptural rules and orthodox observances and worships for the sake of worship; the *rajasika* person's worship is desire-prompted and ostentatious; and the *tamasika* person's worship is whimsical and devoid of faith.

❖ *Practice of Austerity.* The *sattvika* person is steadfast, full of faith, thorough, and not prompted by any desire for worldly gain. The *rajasika* person practices austerity for display and in order to gain respect, recognition, and honour. The *tamasika* person's practice of austerity is self-torture, based on foolishness, and for the purpose of doing harm to others.

❖ *Giving Gifts.* The *sattvika* person gives gifts expecting no return and from a sense of duty, giving at the right place, at the right time, and to worthy person. The *rajasika* person makes gifts in a grudging mood, expecting results, and for the sake of recompense. The *tamasika* person gives without respect, at an improper place and time, and to an unworthy person.

❖ *Knowledge of Reality.* The *sattvika* person sees undivided unity in the midst of diversities; the *rajasika* person sees only diversities; the *tamasika* person's knowledge of reality is trivial, meaningless, and not founded on truth.

❖ *Performance of Action.* The *sattvika* person acts with non-attachment, desiring no gain; the *rajasika* person acts in order to gratify his own egotistical desires and with much effort; the *tamasika* person is indiscriminate, irresponsible, and careless in regard to the consequences and results of his actions.

❖ *Character Pattern.* The *sattvika* person is free from attachment and aversion, is endowed with fortitude and zeal, and is unaffected by success and failure. The *rajasika* person is passionately attached to his action; hankers after its fruits; is greedy, violent, and impure; and is easily carried away by joy and sorrow. The *tamasika* person is vulgar, unsteady, arrogant, deceitful, malicious, indolent, despondent, and procrastinating.

❖ *Discrimination between Right and Wrong.* The *sattvika* person is always guided by spiritual consideration; the *rajasika* person's sense of discrimination is distorted and faulty because it is heavily coloured by personal desires and attachments; the *tamasika* person's sense of discrimination is enveloped in darkness and delusion.

❖ *Firmness of Mind.* The *sattvika* person shows unswerving concentration and self-control; the *rajasika* person exhibits firmness of mind in his pursuit of pleasure, wealth, and fulfilment of desires; the *tamasika* person's firmness is a form of rigidity that will not give up stupidity and delusion, sleep, fear, grief, despondency, and sensuality.

❖ *Sense of Happiness.* The *sattvika* person's happiness is an inner state born of the clear knowledge of the Self, which may be like poison at first but like nectar in the end. The *rajasika* person's happiness is born of the contact of the senses with their objects, and it is like nectar at first but like poison in the end. The *tamasika* person derives happiness from sleep, sloth, error, and inertia.

In brief, a *sattvika* person is guided by spiritual consideration, a *rajasika* person by self-interest, and a *tamasika* person by inertia. Integration is thus an inner movement, a progression from the state of inertia *(tamas)* and self-affirmation *(rajas)* toward the state of spiritual balance *(sattva)*. An individual may be said to be attaining inner integration and progressing well in his path of meditation when a *sattvika* behavioural pattern becomes more and more evident in him. No matter what path the aspirant follows, the quality of *sattva* is vital to him. It is the precursor of all spiritual success and, therefore, of success in meditation. Inner integration paves the way for concentration of mind and meditation. As Sri Ramakrishna says: 'Sattva is the last step of the stairs; next is the roof.'

ॐ

Chapter Thirteen

'I Take Care of Their *Yogakshema*'

C S RAMAKRISHNAN

A Fascinating Story

The story goes that a poor devotee was doing *parayana* [ritualistic recitation] of the Bhagavad Gita regularly. One day when he came to the following verse (Gita, 9.22)

ananyaschintayanto mam ye janah paryupasate
tesham nityabhiyuktanam yogakshemam vahamyaham

['Persons who, meditating on Me as non-separate, worship Me in all beings, to them thus ever zealously engaged, I carry what they lack and preserve what they already have.']

He thought there was a mistake here. Is the Lord supposed to—*yogakshemam vahamyaham* i.e., 'I carry the material for welfare on My head to the devotee'? The scholar-devotee felt that this is not appropriate. He took a red ink pen and cancelled in two strokes the phrase *vahamyaham*. Instead he wrote *dadamyaham* i.e. 'I *give* yogakshema to My devotees.'

Now, his wife came to him and told him that there was nothing in the kitchen for cooking. She implored him to meet one of his devotees and get some grant. The scholar accordingly went out and tried to meet some of his rich trusted disciples but was unlucky. Even after two hours he had to return empty handed.

To his surprise he found that the home had been well decorated with garlands and the fragrance of many dishes was wafting. His wife asked him to hurry and do the puja so that they could all partake of the sacred food that had been offered to God (prasada). The scholar was stupefied and asked who brought all these delicious dishes. The wife said that it was his young disciple, a dark boy, who brought these things. When the scholar said he did not meet any dark boy that day, the wife told him that as an identification mark the boy had two red strokes on his back. Red marks! The scholar was aghast. The Lord himself had come carrying on his head the offerings! He was insisting that the phrase *vahamyaham* was the correct one and not *dadamyaham*. The red marks were the two strokes he had scored on the word *vahamyaham*! The story illustrates how much the Lord takes care of the devotees.

Understanding *Yogakshema*

The term *yogakshema* can be interpreted in two ways. *Yoga* is getting or acquiring and *kshema* means maintaining. Therefore any effort we make to get something and then taking steps to maintain that is *yogakshema*. A second way of interpretation is *yogena kshema,* welfare through proper yoga.

The first interpretation summarises our worldly life. We spend all our life trying to get many things. We try to fulfil one desire after another. But we find that there is no end to such seeking. Getting one desire fulfiled only leads to another desire nudging us. Either the desire we seek is not fulfilled or it gives place to a still stronger desire. This goes on endlessly. So in the worldly life we may work sincerely to get a desire fulfilled but may not get the corresponding *kshema*. We find we may have to take many more steps for maintaining intact the desire already obtained. *Kshema* becomes a mirage—tempting us but not fulfilling us.

This principle haunts us in all aspects of life. Not only wealth, we want to secure more and more. We are also in need of keeping ourselves healthy. Maintenance of health becomes a great problem. Likewise we earn a place in society by doing certain appropriate things, and in order to maintain that status we have to work still harder, very often with no corresponding benefits. Not only one's position in society but also one's relationships in the family are governed by this path of establishing good relations and enjoying peace of mind. All the other aspects of life like in business, politics, social status and so on are subject to this pursuit of fulfilling desires non-stop.

Thus it looks as if while yoga is un-avoidable *kshema* does not necessarily follow. Therefore the second interpretation of *yoga-kshema* has to be carefully examined. *Kshema* or welfare is to be obtained through proper yoga—*yogena-kshema*. In spiritual life we have the four yogas of *bhakti, jnana, karma* and *dhyana*. They are royal paths by means of which we can walk along the highway of *kshema*.

A more appropriate elucidation is the statement *yoga karmasu kausalam*—Yoga is dexterity in action i.e., whatever work we do, be it small or big, it should be as dexterous as possible. It is not the amount of work we do that matters but the skill with which we do it. It should be noted that *kausalam* has also another derivation namely *kausalya idam* i.e., this work is for the welfare not only of myself but also of every one else connected with it. This is an underlining of the fact that the work we do should be unselfish and beneficial to all around. This is what is known as *nishkama-karma* or selfless work.

Wider Meaning of *Kshema*

In order that the yoga or the path yields good results we should try to fill our mind with positive ideas. What is called the ego is only wallowing in negative ideas like anger, greed and hate. If we fill our mind with the corresponding positive ideas we can clearly account and attain *kshema*. Therefore, yoga is not a formidable undertaking but an orderly, harmonious positivistic approach to every problem in life. It is here that Swami Vivekananda's *mahavakya* reminds us that 'each soul is potentially divine' and this divinity can be brought out through proper yoga. Therefore *yoga* and *kshema* need not be considered as two different things. They are merely the obverse and reverse of the same coin. All the efforts we make to attain *kshema* really form *yoga*. For instance there is the instruction that we should be *samadarshis* i.e., equal sighted. If we are not narrow-minded we can treat every one as equal.

Of course this requires a lot of practice, for we are born with a heavy load of *samskaras* [past impressions] that separate the 'I' from the 'you'. It is not difficult but it takes a lot of practice. We can be happy in any circumstance if we are able to treat everything that comes to us as God given. The mother may give bitter medicines or chocolate for the welfare of the child. It is foolishness on the part of the child to think of the mother as kind or cruel to it. God gives us what is necessary for our real *kshema*. In our narrow mindedness we may not understand the manner in which God sends us the *yogakshema*. Any work done without selfishness and with perfection is yoga that will lead us to undisputed *Kshema*.

৪০উ

Chapter Fourteen

Meditating on the Message of the Gita

SWAMI DAYATMANANDA

Being the most popular of Hindu scriptures, hundreds of commentaries have been written on the Bhagavad Gita. Of these the shortest is the commentary by Sri Ramakrishna. He says:

> What is the significance of the Gita? It is what you find by repeating the word ten times. It is then reversed into 'tagi', which means a person who has renounced everything for God. And the lesson of the Gita is: 'O man, renounce everything and seek God alone.' Whether a man is a monk or a householder, he has to shake off all attachment from his mind.[1]

The Gita is one of the most practical books, giving down-to-earth solutions to all problems of life—spiritual or secular. It is not just a book to be read but also a book to be meditated upon. Swami Turiyananda, a direct disciple of Sri Ramakrishna, used to say that he meditated on each and every verse of the major Upanishads until he realised their purport. This is what every spiritual aspirant should also do, whatever scripture he follows.

The Practice of Meditation

The practice of meditation has become much popular these days. People, of course, meditate for various reasons—for peace of mind, stress-relief, to improve relationships, and even to gain material benefits. No doubt, meditation helps in attaining all these but they are mere trifles. The real purpose of meditation is to *experience* God or attain Self-knowledge.

When we hear the word meditation, it brings before us the picture of a person sitting in a posture—usually *padmasana*—with his eyes closed and lost in some deep thoughts. Though this is what meditation looks from outside, meditation is more than this, and we should have a clear idea of what meditation is.

Meditation is a mental activity. In this inner act we meditate on an ideal and internalise it, making it our very nature. In the ideal state of meditation, the meditator becomes one with the *Ishta devata* [the chosen form of God] or the idea he is meditating upon. In other words, the meditator's whole nature or behaviour must undergo change; all the old habits (mental and physical) must be replaced by newer and better habits. Meditation cannot be considered a success unless this transformation takes place, however long a person might be practising Japa or meditation.

The process and the results of meditation are described in the sixth chapter of the Gita. Yoga is a state in which the disciplined mind becomes perfectly still like a lamp placed in a windless place. Yoga means utterly losing of oneself in Atman, the inherent divine core of our personality. This state of perfect absorption is the highest state and no other gain is considered equal to it. A person, who becomes established in this state is called a Yogi, becomes free from all suffering and swims in unequalled bliss. Being one with God, he becomes one with all beings.

Since all beings long to be free from suffering and attain unending happiness, even from a utilitarian point of view, meditation is a worthwhile pursuit. What can we expect from meditation? Here are some of the immediate benefits of practising meditation:

❖ Greater concentration, and improved ability to comprehend, specially the teachings of the scriptures.

❖ Deepening of our faith (*shraddha*) in the truths taught in the scriptures.

❖ Increased self-awareness, which helps to identify and overcome our weaknesses.

❖ Self-acceptance and acceptance of the realities of life in general. This sense of acceptance makes one more responsible for all that life brings.

❖ Goal-orientation and thoughtfulness in our dealings.

❖ Greater chances of development of our latent possibilities.

❖ Enhanced patience, forbearance and calmness of mind.

Meditation on the Gita

This is what the practice of mediation promises us. Now, with this in mind, let us meditate on a few salient teachings of the Gita in order to make them a part of our life.

1. *Life is a battlefield.*

Life is not a bed of roses but a battlefield. No one can escape suffering. Sri Ramakrishna used to say that, caught in the net of the five elements, Brahman weeps. Incarnations of God are also seen to undergo much suffering. Hence it is useless to try escaping from the inevitable. Heat and cold, loss and profit, pleasure and pain—dualities of life—always come together. A devotee fully accepts this fact and remains calm, and turns his mind towards God.

Life is not a mere battlefield; it is both a *dharma-kshetra* [the field of righteousness], and also a *kuru-kshetra*, [the field of action]. This field of life yields the faithful result of whatever we do. No one can cheat the divine Lord who is *Viswatomukha*, the All-pervading One, a silent witness to all our thoughts, words and deeds. We reap what we sow. Hence, we alone are responsible both for our suffering and our happiness, our progress as well as our failure. This is the basis of the law of Karma.

2. *Our battle is with the enemy within*

Our battle is not with an external enemy—external elements and circumstances are mere expressions of our

inner state. Arjuna was not frightened of the Kauravas—
he had defeated them many times in the past. He was
overcome by *moha* or delusion. At the end of his teachings,
Sri Krishna asks Arjuna if he has rid himself of his *moha*.
He replies emphatically, 'Yes, by your grace I am rid of
this delusion and my *smriti* or memory of my real nature,
is obtained.' [that is, 'now I know that I am not the body
or mind, but I am the Atman'].[2]

Our enemy is *ajnana* or ignorance of our real nature.
This ignorance deludes us all. Vedanta tells us that we
suffer this forgetfulness. Though we are the ever-blissful
atman, we identify ourselves with matter and that is what
causes suffering. This identification is what is called
ignorance and is expressed in the ideas 'I' and 'mine'. We
mistake the un-real for the real and that is how we perceive
the world and undergo all its relative experience.

Specifically, this ignorance manifests in the form of
our inner enemies of negative and harmful tendencies.
Speaking of the three most powerful ones, Sri Krishna
says:

Triple is this gate of hell, destructive of the self—lust,
    anger and greed; therefore one should forsake these
    three.[3]

Sri Ramakrishna too summed up worldliness as 'lust,
and gold' (*kama-kanchana*). Only a hero can conquer these
powerful enemies. Once one conquers them, one attains
Self-knowledge and becomes wholly fulfilled and happy.
'He who can withstand in this world,' tells Sri Krishna,
'before the fall of the body, the impulse arising from lust

and anger, he is steadfast [in yoga], he is a happy man.'[4] One who is free from these three is a *jivan-mukta*—free while living.

3. The Goal of life

We are all [potentially] divine. Nothing can alter this fact. We come from God, live in God, and go back to God. However much this divinity might be obscured, it manifests itself in the end. Gita states this truth succinctly:

The unreal never is. The real never is not. Men possessed of the knowledge of the Truth fully know both these.[5]

If we are all divine then the goal of life is clear. Says Sri Ramakrishna: 'The goal of life is God-realisation, to see God in everything, in everyone at all times.' It may seem to take a long time, but in the end all of us are going to reach God. Evolution presupposes involution. Life and nature are gradually but inevitably leading us back to where we came from—God. The dualities of life such as pain and pleasure, good and evil are there only to make us realize and unfold our divinity and lead us to God.

After undergoing all the experiences in life, we get spiritually educated and then realise our real nature and learn to see the same divinity everywhere, in all things.

The Yogi, striving assiduously, purified of taint, gradually gaining perfection through many births, then reaches the highest goal.[6] At the end of many births, the man of wisdom takes refuge in Me, realising that all this is Vasudeva (the innermost self).[7]

4. 'My devotee will not perish'

Twenty-five centuries ago, the Buddha, the Enlightened One, declared, 'Life is full of suffering.' Indeed, no one can escape suffering; no one became a saint enjoying the comforts of life. There are many things that can happen in life: our near and dear ones may desert us; we may have to go through terrible trials (we may recall here the hardships which Harischandra and the Pandavas underwent for the sake of keeping truth.) But we should not fear difficulties. Sri Krishna assures us that if a devotee sincerely leads a spiritual life relying on Him, He will not abandon him; He will look after him. 'Soon does he become righteous, and attain eternal Peace, O son of Kunti; boldly can you proclaim, that My devotee is never destroyed.'[8]

Not only is the devotee protected, God stands by him under all circumstances. Sri Krishna says,

> Persons who, meditating on Me as non-separate, worship Me in all beings, to them thus ever zealously engaged, I bring what they lack and preserve what they already have.[9]

Indeed whatever we do to improve ourselves remains with us. No effort in this direction goes vain. Its results may be slow to come, they never go waste.

5. The purpose of spiritual practices

All spiritual practices are aimed at getting rid of delusion about our real nature. It is possible to reach this state of disillusionment only by the grace of God, Guru and by earnestly working for it.

In a practical sense, all spiritual practices aim at gaining, controlling and purifying the mind. As the Gita says, 'a controlled mind is one's greatest friend, and an uncontrolled mind is one's worst enemy.'[10] Though mind-control is a very difficult task, it can be done though practice. Sri Krishna says that through practice and dispassion the mind comes under control. This is what all aspirants have done in the past and will do in the future. What is needed is constant effort. To always work for purification and control, that is primarily our own responsibility. To bestow grace is God's responsibility.

5. *The two paths*

There are two main pathways to realise God—the path of devotion and the path of knowledge. Both the paths lead us to God; there is no question of superiority or inferiority about the paths. A spiritual aspirant should choose the path suitable to his or her temperament. Since most of us are body-bound and are quite emotional and bound to ego, the Gita tells us to take up the path of devotion. Declares Sri Krishna in the Gita:

> Greater is their trouble whose minds are set on the Unmanifested; for the goal of the Unmanifested is very hard for the embodied to reach.[11]

6. *Surrendering to God*

Sri Krishna advises Arjuna, and through him all spiritual aspirants, that the only sure way of realising God is through total self-surrender to God. It is through the will of God or the Divine Mother that one becomes great or small, becomes enlightened or remains ignorant. Happiness depends entirely on the will of God. In Sri Ramakrishna's life we read that even the great Totapuri, a knower of Brahman, had to undergo hard experiences in order to finally learn to surrender to the Divine Mother. So also Narendernath had to acknowledge Divine Mother's grace.

Surrendering to the Divine is the only way for worldly achievements (*bhoga*) and spiritual advancement (*yoga*). In all centres of the Ramakrishna Order during the evening *arati*, the hymn composed by Swami Vivekananda is sung. It says: 'Therefore I take refuge, O friend of the helpless,' and 'I take refuge O Saviour of the helpless.' This idea of self-surrender is the central teaching of Christ, Rama, Krishna, Chaitanya Mahaprabhu, Sri Ramakrishna, Holy Mother and Swami Vivekananda. This is in accordance with the teaching of the Upanishads:

> The Self is not attained through discourse, nor through intellect, nor through learning. It is gained only by him who is accepted by the Self. To such a one the Self reveals its true nature.[12]

Sri Ramakrishna echoes this succinctly thus: 'The police sergeant walks his rounds in the dark of night with a lantern in his hand. No one sees his face. If you want to see the sergeant, you must pray to him: 'Sir, please turn the light on your own face. Let me see you.'[13] This is the essential and final teaching of the Bhagavad Gita.

Conclusion

The Bhagavad Gita is a treasure-house of spiritual insights. In order to truly benefit from these, one should meditate on these and make them a part of their thinking. As the aspirant gains fresh insights and progress towards the highest of life—God—he realises the greatness of Gita evermore.

References

1. *The Gospel of Sri Ramakrishna*, p. 104-105
2. *Gita*, 18.73
3. *Gita*, 16.21
4. *Gita*, 5.23
5. *Gita*, 2.16
6. *Gita*, 6.45
7. *Gita*, 7.19
8. *Gita*, 9.31
9. *Gita*, 9.22
10. *Gita*, 6.5
11. *Gita*, 12.5
12. *Katha Upanishad*, 1.2.23
13. *The Gospel*, p.174

৪০ ০৪

Chapter Fifteen

The Bhagavad Gita—its Relevance to Teachers

SWAMI ATMARAMANANDA

The *Bhagavad Gita* is one of the few books which have remained universally relevant irrespective of language, gender, religion, nationality and profession. Its objectivity, rationality, practicality, and comprehensive insights into life, both in its microcosmic and macrocosmic dimensions, have invited many serious studies. There have been, and are coming up, so many writings, interpretations and commentaries on the *Gita*. Each of them is suited to the times, written from different, and sometimes divergent viewpoints determined by the extent to which the authors have imbibed its many-sided profound teachings. Monks and royalty, warriors and peace-makers, consumers and traders, leaders and the led, spiritual seekers and teachers, rationalists and devotees, the rich and the poor, activists and pacifists, men and women, time-managers and personnel managers, scientists and philosophers, and those trying to make sense of life—all of them have drawn from this wonderful book their inspirations and understanding of life.

Does the *Gita* contain anything relevant to teachers in today's society? If so, is it only to teachers in India or just anywhere in the world? Is the *Gita* useful to them only in their personal lives or in their profession also?

Gita: Its Relevance

The *Bhagavad Gita* has an immense and timeless relevance to teachers—no matter to which country they belong—both in their private lives and in their professions as special human beings holding the all-important responsibility of sculpting well-balanced citizens. This is because most of the *Gita* concerns human situations. Obviously, a good teacher has to be first a good human being. The *Gita* helps teachers better understand themselves and others, including their students. It provides a large well-structured perspective with which as the background teachers may be able to put the bewildering aspects, turns and twists of life in their right places which goes a long way in dealing with a variety of students.

Some of the dilemmas that teachers face are—is one's family responsibility more important than the profession? Should dilemmas and intense conflicts, unavoidable in life, be resolved by ignoring them; or by escaping from them by changing one's lifestyle or profession or by facing and resolving them after understanding them?

How to face joys and sorrows, successes and failures in life? Is faith in God necessary to live meaningfully? How to overcome death, anxiety and stress? Is there a method to enhance creativity, alertness of mind, and enthusiasm?

G10

Without satisfactory answers to such questions, a teacher may not be able to sustain a good level of self-motivation, creativity, and love for knowledge, which are so important in the teaching profession. Nor would he or she come to feel oneself as a complete integrated human being.

Framework for a Philosophy of Education

Those who want to be good teachers and better human beings would do well to study the *Gita*. It provides a framework for a philosophy of education. It answers, indirectly though, such questions as: What is education? What are the aims of education? What is the nature of the person who is to receive education? How is education to be transmitted by a teacher to a student? What should be the relationship between a teacher and a student? Does education involve education in moral standards to live by? Who is an efficient teacher? Is it central to education that training in critical thinking be imparted to a student? Can all knowledge be taught? Can or should ethics and morality be taught in the same way as, for instance, mathematics or chemistry? Should spiritual practices such as meditation, prayer to God, and so on be a part of education? Should a teacher show a student the links between education and society, that is, the social responsibilities of an educated person?

Answers to such questions can be found in the *Gita* itself, as also in the commentaries on the *Gita* where the interconnections among the verses and among the chapters, as also the significance of the use of certain words and adjectives have been highlighted by the authors. Of course, considering the context in which the *Gita* was taught, its answers to the above questions are not elaborate, but succinct and lucid.

Do Teachers Feel the Want?

Before we discuss what can today's teachers get from the *Gita*, it is necessary for *teachers to accept* that there is something lacking in the current models of education. Do the *teachers* feel that, as a result of the present understanding of education, the end-results of education are far from edifying? That neither do most teachers and students get uplifted through education, nor is there harmony and peace in the minds of people or in families or societies, nor a sense of fulfilment at the end of their lives. Do *teachers* agree that the system of education that has been prevailing for decades now has given mere information and knowledge but not wisdom? That education has generated power but not self-discipline? That education has failed to subdue fanaticism and violence, unfair competition, exploitation, racial prejudices, etc., and increase compassion, sharing and acceptance of diversity? That the teacher-student relationship has become impersonal, commercial, and irreverent?

If teachers do feel lag, then the *Gita* has many ideas to offer. To begin with, take the question, 'What is education?' Sri Krishna has provided the answers: Education is a training of the body and mind of a person to help him gain through lawful means, work-efficiency, prosperity, self-esteem, self-possession, objectivity, and clear thinking, gradually leading the person towards gaining a sense of fulfilment and abiding love for God.[1] The next question naturally is, what is the goal of education? Is it not just a process for enabling a student to get a job, build a career, and live comfortably (and die choicelessly as do all living beings)? It is a process through which one is enabled to gain knowledge and then use it for the benefit of others also and also for finally gaining wisdom, a special kind of inner joy, peace, and philosophic perspective as one progresses in life? Or is it all these, depending on the stage of a person's life?

Gita on Aspects of Education

We learn from the *Gita* that education (*vidya*, *jnana*) is sacred and sanctifying[2]; hard-earned prosperity is not bad[3], but that it cannot be the final goal of life[4]; that it liberates a person from the compulsions of the body, senses, bias, fear, sorrow, stress, anxiety, and egotism.[5] At its best, it gives perfect self-knowledge, inner poise and harmony with all forms of diversities.[6]

In the *Gita* a teacher will find an excellent way to regulate and channelise into nobler goals one's natural and powerful human urges of desire[7], ambition and career through the ideal of *dharma* and *svadharma*. *Dharma* is that which, being in harmony with the truth of the divine nature of human beings, brings about integration of human personality, of all one's faculties, of all the dimensions of one's being. *Svadharma* is all that a person is best capable of doing—physically, mentally, emotionally—according to his natural characteristics and intrinsic capabilities, in consonance with *dharma*. The ideas of *dharma* and *svadharma* help one even to resolve work-related disappointments, dissatisfactions, doubts, confusion, conflicting choices and depression as and when they arise in one's life.[8] A teacher who has assimilated these ideas of *dharma* and *svadharma* can easily help his or her students both in their personal and professional lives.

Qualities of a Good Teacher

The *Gita* also indicates some characteristics of a good teacher, as personified by Sri Krishna, which are in keeping with the traditional or time-tested views: a good teacher is one who is straight-forward, frank, guileless; contented, not greedy, impossible to be swayed by worldly ambitions and desires; who is trustworthy, has mastered his subject, has insight and perspective, commands respect, is open to constructive questions and discussions, and has both theoretical knowledge and practical wisdom.[9]

A good teacher is one who understands what a student is thinking or his level of comprehension, and so does not rush to simply pour his own learning into the student, leaving no time for the student to *assimilate* information.[10] We can see in the *Gita* how Sri Krishna succeeded in making Arjuna open up his mind and unhesitatingly ask questions, and thus reveal his level of comprehension of what was being said by Sri Krishna.

For example, up to the moment of crisis that overwhelmed Arjuna at Kurukshetra, Sri Krishna was to Arjuna an unfailing friend and an expert charioteer, with whom he could take liberties (*prasabham yaduktam maya, ajanata mahimanam tavedam*, 11.41). It was on account of Sri Krishna's wisdom the complete teacher that he was, that he could build up that kind of informal relationship with his student Arjuna. At no time before the war did Sri Krishna prematurely overawe Arjuna with a display of his knowledge and power. It was only when Arjuna surrendered to him completely with absolute trust[11] that Sri Krishna taught him how to handle self-doubt, dilemma, conflicting ideas, and acquire clarity of thought.

Sri Krishna shows that a teacher can and should teach only after winning the confidence of one's students; then try to assess their intellectual stage; and then impart knowledge gradually. A would-be good teacher must have a first hand mastery over the subject, clarity of thought, an ability to present a subject in a systematic way, avoiding redundancy and unnecessary digression merely to show off scholarship.

The *Gita* also tells us that a good teacher should have great patience and self-control, at no time getting annoyed or disappointed with a student, no matter how ordinary or challenging a student's questions. We find Sri Krishna often using such encouraging and self-confidence-enhancing epithets with regard to Arjuna as *bharatarsabha* (O mighty bull among the Bharatas), *gudakesa* (conqueror of sleep, i.e. always alert and energetic; not given to lethargy), *parantapa* (vanquisher of enemies), *anagha* (blemishless), *bharata* (given to cultivating discrimination, knowledge, and wisdom), and so on.[12]

Apart from all the above ideas that a teacher may find useful, one all-important message of the *Gita* for the teachers is: The best teacher is one who, besides imparting to the students temporal life-skills, secular knowledge and means to mundane success, deepens their vision to perceive the existence of the one all-pervading, all-embracing, all-unifying spiritual reality, of which all things, including themselves, are organically related parts, and also shows them how to realize it through intuition.

Critical Thinking

Basic to the methods that lead to that vision is the power of discrimination or critical thinking. Without this power, education is incomplete. This is the power that gives each person an individuality, a uniqueness. That is why we see Sri Krishna inducing Arjuna to ask pertinent questions, thereby arousing Arjuna's power of critical thinking and desire to know more.[13] As a result, we find that though Arjuna's initial questions concerned the immediate mundane world of relatives, enemies, success, failures, wealth, dominion, etc., later on his questions became philosophical. Once this power of discrimination is aroused in a student, the teacher may as well stand back and watch a new 'ship' sail out to its human or spiritual destiny. For, that ship has got a pathfinder compass installed on it.

Education, Ethics and Morality

In addition to the power of critical thinking, a student should also imbibe the ideals of ethics and morality. Sri Krishna often uses the two words *dharma* and *svadharma*, which are suggestive of ethics and morality also. The *Gita's* description of the divine (*daiva*) and demoniac (*asura*) characteristics of human beings, the ethical and moral consequences of possessing either of them, the importance of increasing one's *sattva* (uplifting) quality (*guna*), and the means of freeing oneself from the influences of the qualities of *rajas* (extroversion) and *tamas* (debasing, dehumanising behaviour) point to the duty of a teacher to forewarn one's students of the dangers of not cultivating the ability to discriminate. Though a teacher can and should teach students the value and power of critical thinking, still, that teaching is best done by one possessing and practising that power of unbiased, rational or objective examination. Critical thinking, power of discrimination, or power of making right choices become easy to practise when one has control of over one's emotions such as personal ambitions, jealousy and egotism.

Such personal traits allow concentration and sharp insight, for, uncontrolled emotions, passion, greed, etc., cloud the mind.[14] Then goal setting, which is a primary and crucial need of all students, becomes possible. After all, critical thinking, discrimination etc., cannot be ends in themselves.

Education through Prayer and Meditation

Those vitiating obstructive emotions, says the *Gita*, are effectively neutralized through prayer to God, meditation, and so on.[15] The goals set by minds that have undergone the disciplines of prayer and control of self-centred emotions and similar practices, be those goals temporal or spiritual, are always conducive to personal and universal good. Education should be able to shape that kind of individuals, who feel responsible towards society. Sri Krishna has said several times in the *Gita* that persons who are famous and powerful should remember they are socially responsible.[16]

Teachers should therefore emphasize this aspect of education to their students, besides enthusing them towards skill-development, personality-development, career-building, job-placements, pay-prospects-promotion, getting mentioned in the Limca Book or Guinness Book or Forbes List. Too much of self-or ego-pampering has released into society thousands of self-centered educated individuals, racists, fanatics and compassionless 'clashing billiard balls' incapable of humanistic impulses.

Conclusion

When teachers, themselves self-made venerable heroes, embodying as many of the characteristics of a complete teacher as suggested in the *Gita* by Sri Krishna, create such wonderful well-balanced, courageous, modest, efficient and educated students as Arjuna, the gains for humanity will be immense. As immense as were the gains from the Sri Krishna-Arjuna combination:

Wherever is Krishna, the Lord of Yoga, wherever is Partha, the wielder of the bow, there are unfailing fortune, victory, prosperity, and prudence. Such is my conviction.[17]

As immense are the gains from the ideal of the Ramakrishna-Vivekananda combination: *Atmano moksartham jagat-hitaya ca:* For one's own spiritual freedom from worldliness, and for the good of the world.

Notes and References

1. We can compare this with the current understanding of what education is, which in our view is shallow or partial: 'Education is the art or process of imparting skill and knowledge. . . . The success of education lies in harnessing the latent potential of an individual ... Informal education happens subconsciously when the values and behaviour of an individual are shaped due to constant interaction with his environment. Formal education on the other hand is a deliberate effort by a person to learn the skills considered important for a particular job or activity.' 'Good education is an ability to understand life.'
    Compare this, again, with Swami Vivekananda's definition of education: 'Education is the manifestation of the perfection already in man.' 'We want that education by which character is formed, strength of mind is increased, the intellect is expanded and by which one can stand on one's own feet. What we need is to study the different branches of knowledge that is our own and with it English language and Western

science; we need technical education and all else that will develop industries, so that men instead of seeking for service may earn enough to provide for themselves and save against a rainy day.' 'The end of all education all training, should be man-making. The end and aim of all training is to make the men grow. The training by which the current and expression of will are brought under control and become fruitful, is called education.' 'Without the personal life of the teacher, there would be no education.' 'Education is not the amount of information that is put into your brain and runs riot there, undigested, all your life. We must have life-building, man-making, character-making assimilation of ideas.' Clearly, most of the *present* views on education are silent on the ultimate ends of education, and are concerned with 'bread-earning', 'skill-learning', and secular 'knowledge-gathering'.

Note: *Translations of the Sanskrit references are based on* The Bhagavad Gita *translated by Swamis Swarupananda and Gambhirananda.*

2. i. न हि ज्ञानेन सदृशं पवित्रमिह विद्यते । There is nothing in this world purifying like knowledge (4.38).
    ii. ज्ञाननिर्धूतकल्मषाः । Those whose impurities have been removed off by knowledge (5.17).

3. i. हतो वा प्राप्स्यसि स्वर्गं जित्वा वा भोक्ष्यसे महीम्। By being killed you will attain heaven, or by winning you will enjoy the earth (2.37).

4. i. भोगैश्वर्यप्रसक्तानां तयापहृतचेतसाम् । व्यवसायात्मिका बुद्धिः समाधौ न विधीयते ।। No set determination is formed in the minds of those that are deeply attached to pleasure and power, and whose discrimination is stolen away. (2.44).

ii. निस्त्रैगुण्यो भवार्जुन ... आत्मवान् । O Arjuna, you be free from the triad of the gunas, and be established in the Self (2.45).

iii. यः . . .वर्तते कामकारतः । न स सिद्धिमवाप्नोति न सुखं न परां गतिम् ।। He who acts under the impulse of desire, attains not to perfection, nor happiness, nor the Goal Supreme (16.23).

iv. कामोपभोगपरमा एतावदिति निश्चिताः । (They work) regarding gratification of lust as the highest, and feeling sure that that is all... (16.11).

प्रसक्ताः कामभोगेषु पतन्ति नरकेऽशुचौ ।। Addicted to the gratification of lust, they fall down into a foul hell (16.16).

v. कामकारेण फले सक्तो निबध्यते । (The unbalanced one,) led by desire, is completely bound on account of being attached to the fruit (of action) (5.12).

5. i. त्रायते महतो भयात् । Saves from great fear (2.40).

ii. विधेयात्मा प्रसादमधिगच्छति । The self-controlled person, attains to serenity (2.64).

iii. स शान्तिमाप्नोति न कामकामी । That person, not the one who hankers for objects of pleasure, attains to peace (2.70).

iv. निर्द्वन्द्वः... बन्धात्प्रमुच्यते । The one who is free from the pairs of opposites is set free from bondage (5.3)

v. समदुःखसुखम् । Same in pain and pleasure (2.15).

vi. एनम् एवम् विदित्वा नानुशोचितुमर्हसि । Knowing this to be such, you ought not to grieve (2.25).

न एनम् शोचितुमर्हसि । You ought not to grieve thus (2.26).

न त्वं शोचितुमर्हसि । You ought not to grieve (2.27).

vii. अध्यात्मचेतसा ... विगतज्वरः । With your mind spiritually imbued and free from (mental) fever (3.30).

viii. कर्मबन्धं प्रहास्यसि । You will totally get rid of the bondage caused by actions (2.39).

कर्मभिर्न स बध्यते । He is not fettered by actions (4.14).

जहाति सुकृतदुष्कृते । He casts off virtue and vice (2.50).

6. i. ज्ञानं लब्ध्वा परां शान्तिम् ... अधिगच्छति । Having achieved (spiritual) Knowledge, one attains Supreme Peace (4.39).

    ii. सुखमक्षयमश्नुते । He acquires undecaying happiness (5.21).

    iii. प्रशान्तमनसं एनं ... शान्तरजसं To this yogi, whose mind has become perfectly tranquil, and whose passions are quieted... (6.27).

7. बलं बलवतां ... कामरागविवर्जितम् । धर्माविरुद्धो भूतेषु कामोऽस्मि ।। Of the strong, I am the strength that is devoid of desire and attachment. I am, O bull among the Bharatas, desire in beings, unopposed to dharma (7.11).

8. i. श्रेयान्स्वधर्मो विगुणः ... परधर्मो भयावहः ।। Better is one's own dharma, though defective. (But) the dharma of another is fraught with fear (though it may appear attractive) (3.35).

    ii. स्वे स्वे कर्मण्यभिरतः संसिद्धिं लभते नरः । स्वकर्मनिरतः सिद्धिं यथा विन्दति तच्छृणु ।। Devoted each to his own duty, man attains the highest perfection. Hear how one devoted to his own duty achieves success (18.45).

    यतः प्रवृत्तिर्भूतानां येन सर्वमिदं ततम् । स्वकर्मणा तमभ्यर्च्य सिद्धिं विन्दति मानवः ।। From whom is the evolution of all beings, by whom all this is pervaded, worshipp-

    ing Him with his own duty, a man achieves success (18.46).

    श्रेयान्स्वधर्मो विगुणः परधर्मात्स्वनुष्ठितात् । स्वभावनियतं कर्म कुर्वन्नाप्नोति किल्बिषम् ।। Better is one's own dharma, (though) imperfect, than the dharma of another well performed. He who does the duty ordained

    by his own nature incurs no evil (18.47).

सहजं कर्म कौन्तेय सदोषमपि न त्यजेत् । सर्वारम्भा हि दोषेण धूमेनाग्निरिवावृताः ।।
One should not relinquish, O son of Kunti, the duty to which
one is born, though it is faulty; for, all undertakings are
enveloped by evil, as fire is by smoke (18.48).

iii. स्वधर्मम् ...अवेक्ष्य न विकम्पितुमर्हसि । (Even) considering your own
dharma, you should not waver (2.31-2).

इमं धर्म्यं संग्रामम् । This righteous battle... (2.33).

iv. एवमुक्त्वार्जुनः संख्ये रथोपस्थ उपाविशत् । ... शोकसंविग्नमानसः ।। Speaking
thus in the midst of the battle-field, Arjuna, sat down on his
chariot, with his mind distressed with sorrow (1.47).

v. कृपयाविष्टमश्रुपूर्णाकुलेक्षणम् । विषीदन्तम्... (To him) who was thus
overwhelmed with pity and was sorrowing, and whose eyes
were filled with tears and showed distress... (2.1).

vi. न योत्स्य इति ...उक्त्वा तूष्णीं बभूव । Having spoken thus, (Arjuna)
became silent, (telling Govinda,) 'I shall not fight' (2.9).

vii. क्षुद्रं हृदयदौर्बल्यं Petty faint-heartedness (2.3).

viii. कार्पण्यदोषोपहतस्वभावः...धर्मसम्मूढचेताः । With my nature
overpowered by the taint of weak commi-
seration, and with a mind in confusion about dharma (duty)...
(2.7).

ix. शोकमुच्छोषणमिन्द्रियाणाम् Sorrow which is blasting my senses
(2.8).

x. धर्म्याद्धि युद्धाच्छ्रेयोऽन्यत्क्षत्रियस्य न विद्यते । Because there is nothing
higher for a Ksatriya than a righteous war (2.31).

xi. कर्माणि प्रविभक्तानि स्वभावप्रभवैर्गुणैः । The duties... have been fully
classified by the gunas which are the sources of dispositions
(18.41).

xii. स्वे स्वे कर्मण्यभिरतः संसिद्धिं लभते । Devoted each to his own duty,
(man) attains the highest perfection (18.45).

xiii. स्वभावनियतं कर्म कुर्वन्नाप्नोति किल्बिषम् । He who does the duty ordained by his own nature incurs no evil (18.47).

xiv. नष्टो मोहः स्मृतिर्लब्धा...गतसन्देहः । Destroyed is my delusion, I have regained my memory (through Your grace). I stand with my doubt removed (18.73).

9. ii. उपदेक्ष्यन्ति ते ज्ञानं ज्ञानिनः तत्त्वदर्शिनः । Those who have realized the Truth will instruct thee in that knowledge (4.34).

10. A child receives a quarter of its knowledge from its parents, the second from its teachers, the third through experiences as it grows, and the last with the passage of time.

11. i. शिष्यस्तेऽहं शाधि मां त्वां प्रपन्नम् । I am your disciple; instruct me who have taken refuge in You (2.7).

ii. त्वदन्यः संशयस्यास्य छेत्ता न हि उपपद्यते । For, none other than You can be the dispeller of this doubt (6.39).

12. i. अनार्यजुष्टम्...अकीर्तिकरम् । (Doubt) entertained by unenlightened people, ... and which brings infamy (2.2).

ii. कीर्तिं च हित्वा पापमवाप्स्यसि । Forfeiting honour, thou shalt incur sin (2.33).

iii. सम्भावितस्य अकीर्तिः मरणादतिरिच्यते । To an honoured person infamy is worse than death (2.34).

iv. भयाद्रणादुपरतं मंस्यन्ते त्वां महारथाः । येषां च त्वं बहुमतो भूत्वा यास्यसि लाघवम् ।The great chariot-riders will think of you as having desisted from the fight out of fear; and you will earn the contempt of those to whom you had been estimable! (2.35).

iv. अवाच्यवादांश्च बहून्वदिष्यन्ति तवाहिताः । निन्दन्तस्तव सामर्थ्यं ततो दुःखतरं नु किम् । And your enemies will speak many indecent words while denigrating your might. What can be more painful than that? (2.36).

13. i. For example, see Madhusudana Saraswati's introduction: to verse 2.54; to Chapter 5, last paragraph, and to the eighth chapter of the Gita.

ii. विमृश्यैतदशेषेण यथेच्छसि तथा कुरु ।Pondering over this as a whole, do as you like (18.63).

14. i. ध्यायतो विषयान्पुंसः सङ्गस्तेषूपजायते । सङ्गात्सञ्जायते कामः कामात्क्रोधोऽभिजायते ॥ In the case of a person who dwells on objects, there arises attachment for them. From attachment grows hankering, from hankering springs anger (2.62).

क्रोधाद्भवति सम्मोहः सम्मोहात्स्मृतिविभ्रमः । स्मृतिभ्रंशाद् बुद्धिनाशो बुद्धिनाशात्प्रणश्यति ॥ From anger follows delusion; from delusion, failure of memory; from failure of memory, loss of understanding; from loss of understanding he perishes (2.63).

रागद्वेषवियुक्तैस्तु विषयानिन्द्रियैश्चरन् । आत्मवश्यैर्विधेयात्मा प्रसादमधिगच्छति ॥ But the self-controlled man, by perceiving objects with the organs that are free from attraction and repulsion and are under his own control, attains serenity (2.64).

प्रसादे सर्वदुःखानां हानिरस्योपजायते । प्रसन्नचेतसो ह्याशु बुद्धिः पर्यवतिष्ठते ॥ When there is serenity, then follows eradication of all his sorrows, because the wisdom of one who has a serene mind soon becomes wholly established (2.65).

नास्ति बुद्धिरयुक्तस्य न चायुक्तस्य भावना । न चाभावयतः शान्तिरशान्तस्य कुतः सुखम् ॥ For one who has not controlled his mind there is no Wisdom, and there is no meditation for the unsteady man. And for an unmeditative man there is no peace. How can there be happiness for one without peace? (2.66).

इन्द्रियाणां हि चरतां यन्मनोऽनुविधीयते । तदस्य हरति प्रज्ञां वायुर्नावमिवाम्भसि ॥ Among the wandering organs, since that (organ) with regard to which the mind is impelled carries away the Wisdom of this one, as wind (diverts) a boat on the waters... (2.67).

ii. शक्नोतीहैव यः सोढुं प्राक्शरीरविमोक्षणात् । कामक्रोधोद्भवं वेगं स युक्तः स सुखी नरः ॥ One who can withstand here itself, till liberation from the body, the onrush arising for desire and anger, he is a yogi, he is happy, and he is a man (5.23).

iii. कामः क्रोधस्तथा लोभः...एतत्त्रयं त्यजेत् । One should forsake these three: lust, anger, and greed (16.21).

ततो याति परां गतिम् । Thereby attains the Goal Supreme (16.22).

15. i. तमभ्यर्च्य सिद्धिं विन्दति । By adoring Him, (a human being) achieves success (18.46).

ii. आत्मानं नियम्य...ध्यानयोगपरो... अहंकारं बलं दर्पं कामं क्रोधं परिग्रहम् विमुच्य... समः सर्वेषु भूतेषु । By controlling the aggregate of body and organs... who is ever engaged in dhyana and yoga... having discarded egotism, obstinate evil inclination, pride, desire, anger, hatred, external accessories (for the maintenance of the body brought in by others)... becomes the same towards all beings (18.51 to 54).

iii. मच्चित्तः सर्वदुर्गाणि मत्प्रसादात्तरिष्यसि । Having your mind fixed on Me, you will cross over all the difficulties through My grace (18.58).

iv. सर्वधर्मान्परित्यज्य मामेकं शरणं व्रज । अहं त्वा सर्वपापेभ्यो मोक्षयिष्यामि मा शुचः ॥ Abandoning all forms of rites and duties, take refuge in Me alone. I shall free you from all sins. (Hence) do not lament (18.66).

16. i. लोकसंग्रहमेवापि सम्पश्यन्कर्तुमर्हसि । You surely ought to perform (your duty) simply with a view to making people undertake their duties, and preventing them from taking the wrong path (3.20).

ii. यद्यदाचरति श्रेष्ठस्तत्तदेवेतरो जनः । स यत्प्रमाणं कुरुते लोकस्तदनुवर्तते । Whatsoever the superior person does, that (very thing) is followed by others! What he demonstrates by action, that the ordinary people follow (3.21).

iii. यदि ह्यहं न वर्तेयं जातु कर्मण्यतन्द्रितः । मम वर्त्मानुवर्तन्ते मनुष्याः पार्थ सर्वशः ॥ If ever I did not continue in work without relaxation, O son of Pritha, men would, in every way follow My path (3.23).

iv. जोषयेत्सर्वकर्माणि विद्वान्युक्तः समाचरन् । While himself remaining alert the enlightened person should, by duly performing all the duties, make them do these (3.26).

17. यत्र योगेश्वरः कृष्णो यत्र पार्थो धनुर्धरः । तत्र श्रीर्विजयो भूतिर्ध्रुवा नीतिर्मतिर्मम ॥ (18.78)

Chapter Sixteen

Keeping Calm—the Gita Way

SWAMI NITYASTHANANDA

The Milky Nectar of the Gita

The Bhagavad Gita is a manual on all practical issues related to spiritual life. A popular verse used for meditation on the Gita says that while the Upanishads can be likened to a milch cow, the Gita is its milk. Arjuna is compared to the calf, and Sri Krishna as the person who milks the cow. The people who drink this milk are called men of wisdom. Obviously, the milk is meant to be consumed; the content-analysis of the milk is secondary. So is the case with Gita. It's primary utility lies in its practical application; its philosophical analysis is secondary.

It is, however, unfortunate that in order to popularize Gita through various ways such as speeches, books, different competitions, memorizing the text and so on, its central message is often overlooked. There are, again, people who just worship a copy of the Gita, place flowers on it and sing its glories. They forget that real worship of the Gita lies in installing its messages on the altar of our heart and worship it through working without attachment and the real glory lies in being devoted to its ideals.

But, it is not easy to place the message of the Gita on one's inner altar and follow it in life. This requires constant efforts in training our senses and mind. Of course, the Gita provides various methods to do it. The Gita's central idea is to divert all our energies towards Divine. The very meaning of the word 'Bhagavad Gita' refers to this. The literal meaning of the Gita is *song* of God or a divine song. When our whole life becomes God-oriented, then our life itself gets transformed into a living Bhagavad Gita. This inner transformation is the true aim of understanding this divine song.

Music of the Gita

If 'Gita' means song, then the song should be accompanied by instrumental music. A good music, everyone knows, is a harmony of sounds. In Indian classical music concert, the singer is accompanied by various musical instruments such as violin, *tanpura*, harmonium, *tabla* and so on. All these instruments, though producing different sounds, become a part of harmony called concert. Then there is no discordant note in the concert. This melodious blend of notes happens when all the instruments tune in to produce the same note in consonance with the singer. Different sounds, thus, become a melodious harmony. If this oneness of tune is not followed, then the whole concert ends up as a disgusting cacophony, however good be the singer or instrument players.

Taking this illustration further, let us think of our own personality. Our personality, as we all know, consists of so many factors such as senses, mind, emotion and so on. The nature and function of these aspects of our personality are also distinct. However, when they all attune themselves with the Divine Note of our life, and function accordingly, then our whole personality becomes a song of God, the Bhagavad Gita. So the life, attuned with God is Bhagavad Gita. There are a number of passages in the Gita which corroborate this idea. For example, there is a famous passage that occurs both in ninth (34) and eighteenth (65) chapters of the Gita, which says:

> Fill thy mind with Me, be My devotee, sacrifice unto Me, bow down to Me; thus having made thy heart steadfast in Me, taking Me as the Supreme Goal, thou shalt come to Me.

Here Sri Krishna indicates that the mind i.e., the thinking faculty, should get attuned with Divine ('Fill thy mind'); the emotional aspect must function in harmony with Divine ('Be My devotee'); the will also must concord with Divine rhythm ('Sacrifice unto Me'); and lastly the ego must be surrendered to God ('Bow down to Me'), shedding its discordant note of self-seeking. Similarly, all the factors of our personality must work in harmony, attuning themselves with Divine Note. All the spiritual practices, such as prayer, Japa and meditation are nothing but this process of tuning our personality—making the mind work in harmony with the Divine. This is the Gita's way of calming the mind—not violently suppressing the unrest of mental faculties, but quietly directing their energy toward the Divine.

Two Approaches

There are two kinds of way to control the mind: through the active will and through the passive will. In the first case, the will is used with force in order to make the mind quiet. This, at times, has a negative result. In contrast to this, passive willing means controlling the mind quietly, but strongly—*willing* the mind itself to get controlled. The Gita way of mental control is that of passive willing. Here it is worth recalling what Swami Brahmananda, a direct disciple of Sri Ramakrishna, says regarding this:

> 'I will conquer lust, I will conquer anger and greed'—if you try in this way, you will never conquer them. But if you concentrate your mind on God, the senses will of themselves be curbed without much effort on your part.[1]

As noted above, our personality itself can be compared to a musical instrument consisting of different strings such as thinking, feeling, willing and other aspects of mind. Many times, this instrument is not properly tuned—the strings being either too tight or too loose. We allow various persons, events and thought currents to play with this instrument. And this damages the instrument itself. Emotional storms and insatiable desires weaken all our efforts to keep this instrument reasonably sound. The inharmonious sound of our instrument, with all its discordant notes like misunderstanding, resentments, irritability and so on, make our personality unbearable to others. The best remedy is to allow God to play this instrument Himself. He will, then, tune it properly and produce a soul-enthralling music from it. When God starts playing this musical instrument, our personality, our life itself becomes divine music—a Bhagavad Gita and not a *jada gita* or the worldly song. This is what Sri Krishna hints when he says, 'Giving up all concerns, take refuge in Me only.'[2]

In fact, God Himself is actually playing this instrument. Sri Krishna says in the Gita itself: 'The Lord of the universe dwells in the hearts of all beings, moving them all by His mysterious power as if they are geared to a machine.'[3]

However, our ego sneaks into the picture unnoticed and spoils the whole music. As a computer virus spoils the whole system, this ego too harms the music of not only our personal life, but also of family and social life. So we must have always with us, to use a modern term, an anti-virus—the will to surrender to God in the midst of all our activities and events. This alone will make us free from all stress and strain and keep the music of our personality unharmed. It is indisputably true that good music is the best antidote for stress. But we do not have to go out in search of good music, spending money and, again, straining ourselves. We have only to go within and locate the discordant note, the ego, and silence it. Once the ego is silenced mind is also silenced. It is then that we listen to divine music within. Hence, self-surrender or silencing the ego is the Gita's way of keeping calm and joyful.

Two More Similes

A song is a piece of poetry. The use of right figures of speech is fundamental to good poetry. When a poet has deep thinking and a sense of genuineness, it gets reflected in his compositions. He then does not have to indulge in verbal jugglery or ornamentations. If one considers life as poetry, there also this holds true. When the mind is full of excessive desires, one tends to lead false life, full of external pomp and glory. On the other hand, if one is inspired by higher ideals, filled with inner richness, his life becomes meaningful and joyful. Life with inner richness is what is called true life.

Sri Krishna deplores the life of pomp and vanity. He says that in case of people who indulge in ostentatious life-style, 'no set determination is formed in the minds of those that are deeply attached to pleasure and power.'[4] 'Bound by a hundred ties of hope, given over to lust and wrath, they strive to secure by unjust means hoards of wealth for sensual enjoyments.'[5] On the other hand, one's life becomes a piece of wonderful poetry with external simplicity but inner richness for one, 'who finds delight, satisfaction and light within himself.'[6] Hence, in order to find the higher meaning in life—to lead a really meaningful life—one must control one's desires and negative emotions. Conversely, the search for higher meaning in life itself controls the mind naturally, and this is the Gita's way of calming the mind.

When we achieve inner harmony and inner rhythm, we find the same rhythm and harmony in the outer world also. There is already a great symphony in God's world going on. Even the particles in an atom follow a pattern. So do the various seasons such as summer, winter and spring, and daily cycle of day and night have an inherent rhythm—producing their note in the universal orchestra of Nature. We often fail to listen and understand this music because of our preoccupation with the world of chaos, discord and doubt that we build around us.

Generally, those who are used to only light music cannot appreciate the classical music. However, they can develop the taste for classical music by frequent listening to it and understanding its inner harmony. In the same manner, we must develop divine faculty (though Sri Krishna calls them as 'divine eyes', we could also call them as 'divine ears') to appreciate and enjoy the universal music that goes on beneath the noise and activity of everyday life. If we can identify ourselves with cosmic consciousness, go beyond the little dimensions of our personality, then the mind comes completely under our control. Then it can tune to the cosmic vibration and we get to hear and enjoy the eternal cosmic music. The modern science also testifies this cosmic musical dance. Fritjof Capra, the well-known writer on this subject, says:

The modern physics has shown us that movement and rhythm are essential properties of matter; that all matter, whether here on earth or in outer space, is involved in a continual cosmic dance. . . . According to field theory, each particle does indeed 'perpetually sing its song', producing rhythmic pattern of energy (the virtual particles) in 'dense and subtle forms.[7]

God is the great universal master of music, who composes and directs the cosmic orchestra of infinite dimensions. It is he who makes everyone speak, hear, move and do things according to His tunes. In this sense, the whole universe is a Bhagavad *Gita* or Lord's Song. When our own life gets attuned to Lord's Song, our life too becomes a divine life. This is the true meaning of keeping the mind calm, always.

References

1. *The Eternal Companion*, Sri Ramakrishna Math, Chennai, p.293
2. *Gita*, 18:66
3. *ibid.*, 18.61
4. *ibid.*, 2:42
5. *ibid.*, 16:12
6. *ibid.*, 5.24
7. The *Tao of Physics*, Fritjof Capra, Flamingo, 1982, pp. 268-69

೮೦ಜಿ

Chapter Seventeen

The Spot Where the Gita was Delivered

Jyotisar is the place in Kurukshetra (some 120 km from New Delhi) where Bhagavad Gita is said to have been delivered by Sri Krishna. The belief is that the whole place was part of the battleground where Mahabharata War was fought. The word Jyotisar means 'the lake of light'—referring to the small lake that flanks the marble platform which marks the place where the Gita was delivered. Two banyan trees, a marble model of the Gita Ratha and a few shrines dedicated to various deities is

what the whole place consists of. These little shrines were constructed centuries ago by some of the erstwhile Kings of north India. *Gita Upadesha Sthal* [*the spot where the message of Gita was delivered*] is written on a stone plaque nearby. The historicity of the place is lost in the march of events over the years but the place is revered and visited by countless devotees every year. The Government of Haryana through its Kurukshetra Development Board looks after its upkeep and maintenance.

Chapter Eighteen

'Grieve not—
the Lord is with Us'
Gita's Lessons for Fearlessness

PREMA NANDAKUMAR

The Message of Fearlessness

Some years ago I was at a meeting addressed by some eminent scholars. The subject was the Bhagavad Gita. When it was the turn of Dr. Karan Singh, he put us all at ease in a moment by affirming that the gist of the *Song Celestial* was very simple: *Sri Bhagavan Uvacha*: *maa sucha*! 'The Lord said: Don't worry.' The rest of his speech was about the need for faith in the Lord whom we cannot easily describe. To drive home this point, Dr. Singh concluded by reciting in its entirety, a great poem by Sri Aurobindo, 'Who?'

In the blue of the sky, in the green of the forest,
Whose is the hand that has painted the glow?
When the winds were asleep in the womb of the
ether,
Who was it roused them and bade them to blow?

The message for the audience was clear. The Gita gives us the message of fearlessness. And the giver of the promise is no ordinary person but the creator himself. If we approach the Bhagavad Gita with these twin concepts firmly imbedded in our mind, all will be well.

When I was ten years old, my father gave me a copy of Swami Swarupananda's edition of the Gita. Though today I have nearly thirty editions and commentaries, Swami Swarupananda takes precedent. The one given by father became too brittle for use and so I got another one in 1975. Swami Swarupananda has a direct, clear way of presenting the slokas [verses] and today I realize how helpful this work has been to overcome many a mental and emotional quandary with electrical ease.

Though, it is not uncommon to see retired, old people being presented with copies of the Gita, I think it is the youngsters who should get it. This is the lesson about gifting books that I have learnt. For, the first lesson comes from the very first sloka!

Tell me, O Sanjaya! Assembled on Kurukshetra, the centre of religious activity, desirous to fight, what indeed did my people and the Pandavas do?[1]

Absence of egoism, ahankara, is the first lesson we need to learn if we wish to sculpt ourselves into an ideal person. Look at Dhritarashtra's saying *maamakah* first! After all Kauravas and Pandavas belong to the same group and yet, Dhritarashtra considers the Pandavas to be outsiders. And, we are told, this egoistic attitude ultimately led to the ruin of Kauravas. Where the 'mine' (*maamakah*) comes, the Lord destroys it ultimately. In this land which has always ended its prayers with *sarve janah sukhino bhavantu* ['May all be happy'] from times immemorial, for Dhritarashtra to compartmentalise himself and the Kauravas was unbecoming.

Each of the verses of the Gita has been couched in purposeful language, aimed at creating the ideal man. As indicated earlier, fearlessness and freedom from ego apart, as the boy or girl enter their teens and then pass through their adolescence, chanting the Gita verses percolates into the consciousness, and remains within as an unheard melody, *'anahata nada'* [the unstruck sound]. Suddenly someone explains a familiar verse or one goes through an experience which reminds one of a Gita couplet; and what has been dark in our mind gets illumined suddenly.

It is in Giving that We Receive

Do we not come across daily the spectacle of bandhs and processions and poster-splashing to press our 'rights'? I have this 'right' for reservation, I have that 'right' for enhanced dearness allowance, we have this 'right' for a holiday and so on. When we see such a demonstration, all we have to do is to touch the memory button in our brain and there splashes on our mental screen the verse,

The devas, cherished by Yajna, will give you desired-for objects'. So, he who enjoys objects given by the devas without offering (in return) to them, is verily a thief.[2]

Chanting this verse with an attention to its meaning would make us be mindful in discharging our duties. The young man should think: Do I care to be known as a thief?

After all, even if one does not discharge one's duties well and others do not know about it, there is something called 'conscience' within each one of us. That inner voice, verbalized by this sloka would tell us that we have been lax in discharging our duties. Next, we are to be more anxious in performing our duties than in pressing for our rights. Gradually, performing one's duties well would become a second nature and the ideal man would be getting sculpted as a handsome personality. For what is beauty but the joy in one's face at having done the right thing in life?

Life's experience would also teach us that the Devas and the Yajna are not mere Puranic concepts. They are the symbolic representations of the wise men, the good men, the elders of the family and the society. These elders have given us so much; these parents have sacrificed so much to bring us up. Their blessings have never failed us. It is but appropriate that we seek to return to our parents in at least a small measure what we owe to them. Our own services will be one of gratitude and *ananda* or joy. Serving the parents and elders itself is ananda. To think that we are serving the devas in their person makes the ananda a thousand-fold. And to know that whatever we do—service to our parents, our family, our society, our country, this humanity—is itself a *yajna*, gives a sacred feeling to whatever we do. And when we think of something sacred and consecrated, we cannot be careless, flippant or irreverent. Or unclean either!

The Gita teaches us to engage ourselves in action, an important teaching for the growing mind. I love to remember an incident connected with the verse,[3]

I have, O son of Pritha, no duty, nothing that I have not gained; and nothing that I have to gain, in the three worlds; yet, I continue in action.

It was given to me to be in close touch with a great scholar for decades. He would always be writing, reading, typing or teaching. One day I was astonished to see him bring down all the books from a huge shelf. Was he searching for any book? No, he said. Then he went about dusting the books and putting them back in the shelf. Did he not have assistants to do his work? Oh, yes, there were a couple of them, he said. 'It is true I need not do this work. But unless my assistants see me do it, and the way I dust the books, each one with care, they may not understand the value I attach to my books. And in any case, physical work of any kind should be welcomed to keep our limbs active. Yes, it helps the mind too!'

I realized that the manner in which this child of Goddess Saraswati was working demonstrated Sri Aurobindo's description of the goddess in his book, *The Mother*:

Carelessness and negligence and indolence she abhors; all scamped and hasty and shuffling work; all clumsiness and *a peu pres* and misfire, all false adaptation and misuse of instruments and faculties and leaving of things undone or half done is offensive and foreign to her temper. When her work is finished, nothing has been forgotten, no part has been misplaced or omitted or left in a faulty condition; all is solid, accurate, complete and admirable.

Yoga of Skilfulness

This directly takes us to the sloka in Gita which should always be kept glowing in our heart:

Endowed with this evenness of mind, one frees oneself in this life, alike from vice and virtue. Devote thyself, therefore, to this Yoga. Yoga is the very dexterity of work.[4]

Yogah karmasu kausalam! There are yogas and yogas: Karma, Jnana, Bhakti, Prapatti, Hatha, Tantra yogas and their like. In truth, all life becomes yoga if we approach it in the Gitaesque methodology. If yoga is an aspiration towards uniting with the Supreme, any work undertaken can become a yoga. Aspiring for perfection in that work, one gets engaged in yoga. Can we dismiss as mere artisans and sculptors the ancients who were absorbed in creating a Yoga Narasimha at Hampi, a Gomateshwara at Shravanabelagola, or envisioning the dancing Shiva thousands of years ago? They were yogis too, for they sought perfection in the works undertaken by them. I have been absorbed watching a clerk in a government office tie the files so well that not a paper can get away and at the same time the files never look ungainly or ugly. Such natural tendency towards perfection in his area of work in an office which seems to be a muddle of chairs and half opened shelves with papers strewn here and there and half a dozen upturned waste paper baskets! This clerk has taken to his job with the attitude of a yogi! The Gita is worthy of being cherished even if this single lesson is soaked up by the young mind. That person's life would be beautiful in every way. He has made his life meaningful, and that is the aim of an ideal life.

We do have reams and reams of ethical texts and dharma shastras. There are the *Mahabharata* and the *Ramayana* which have long cantos on the practicalities of day-to-day living. However, it is the Gita (which is a part of the Mahabharata and yet stands out by itself as the *Vishnu Sahasranama*) that has verses which explain in unambiguous terms all about the three gunas, the godly and ungodly natures, the important yogas and the need to surrender. It is this work that puts unambiguously the command-cum-assurance:

Relinquishing all dharmas take refuge in Me alone; I will liberate thee from all sins: grieve not.[5]

Back to the beginning, then. Today the biggest enemy of youth is 'fear'. Fear of failure, of not being able to get a job, of not being able to go on and on and up and up; fear of being branded a failure. In a world of fast-forwarded technology and information revolution, the constant worry that plagues youth is whether he is taking the right decision. Worry! Worry! Worry! Tension is the 'in' word today, and the physicians are having a bonanza out of it. But why fear, asks the Lord: why should you be sad? If one is able to feel close to the Lord, to the divine, to one's Guru, what is it that can sway you and make you helpless?

Ma sucha! [Grieve not!] Nectarean words. Keep the smile on! The Lord is with us!

Interestingly enough, for such people who give up fear by turning to the Lord, the Divine turns up with his help.

Persons who, meditating on me as non-separate, worship Me in all beings, to them thus ever zealously engaged, I carry what they lack and preserve what they already have.[6]

God helps those who help themselves is a familiar proverb. There is a reassuring belief in the famous temple of Goddess Ranganayaki in Srirangam. The sanctum is a little away from the main entrance. The knowledgeable say: 'If you walk four steps towards Mother's sanctum, she will take eight steps towards you!' We have the Upanishadic dictum: *tapah prabhaavaat deva prasaadaascha*: with the help of tapasya *and* with the Grace of the Divine! Swami Vivekananda reiterated this when he said: 'Faith, Faith, faith in ourselves, faith, faith in God, this is the secret of greatness.' If this assurance is buried deep into the psyche of the youth, there will be no need to worry. While performing their work with zeal to attain perfection, they will also take up new activities for the good of fellow-human beings. For they would know help and resources will come to them of their own, once their sincerity and hard work is recognized by the society.

We have a number of happenings to attest this promise of the Lord. Each and every success story of the children brought up in the Homes run by the Sri

Ramakrishna Mission is a practical demonstration of this verse. It is a humbling lesson for why should we always worry about what we lack? Have we put to good and full use the talents we do possess? The Lord assures us that we are all born with talents: we 'already have'. These talents are brought out by the Lord.

Such was the philosophy of Swami Vivekananda who said education is the act of bringing out the capacities within us. Faith is all. Faith makes the dumb person a scholar. The lame can climb up the mountains. Faith and perseverance are the two wings that carry such a person towards his goal. When Krishna, Madhava of Supreme *ananda*, Paramananda Madhava is the guide of youth times, the future is assured. All we need to do is to place a copy of Gita in a ten-year old's hands and encourage him or her to read it. Sixty years after, the one-time child would look back on the past with a sense of fulfillment and *ananda*, and would have come somehow close to understanding the Song Celestial.

References

1.	Translations from the Gita used in this essay are by Swami Swarupananda, published from the Advaita Ashrama, Kolkata, 1.1	2.	*ibid.*, 3. 12
		3.	*ibid.*, 3. 22
		4.	*ibid.*, 2. 50
		5.	*ibid.*, 18. 66
		6.	*ibid.*, 9. 22

Chapter Nineteen

Ten Principles of Work Ethic in the Bhagavad Gita

SWAMI ABHIRAMANANDA

The Bhagavad Gita is an immortal work. Hundreds of commentaries and explanations have been written on each of its verses through the centuries, yet it is amenable to many more interpretations. Such is the genius of its author, Sri Krishna that the more we study the verses of the Gita, the more joy and knowledge we derive, and clearer becomes our understanding of life. We shall take up a few verses of the Gita that expound the philosophy of work in three stages.

Four Principles of Work:

Duties and Responsibilities versus Rights and Privileges

In the first stage, we enter the Kurukshetra war-field. The Pandavas and the Kauravas are arrayed against each other. Arjuna, the greatest hero among the Pandavas, asks his charioteer, Sri Krishna, to place his chariot in between the two armies so that he can have a clear view of them.[1] On being placed in the middle, and seeing his gurus and relatives in the rival camp, Arjuna becomes dis-spirited; the arrows and bows fall off from his hands;

his whole body sweats and shivers;[2] for, how can he kill his own brethren?[3] Would it not be more honourable to beg and survive than to win the war by killing and maiming his own teachers, elders, kith and kin?[4] Having prepared so long for the war, he is now haunted by an ethical dilemma. He is unable to decide whether to take up the arms and fight or retreat and live on alms. Eventually, he takes refuge in Sri Krishna, the omniscient and almighty Lord of the universe, for a verdict.[5]

Sri Krishna exhorts Arjuna to take up arms and fight valorously.[6] It is cowardly to withdraw from war at this stage and thereby suffer perpetual ignominy.[7] Sri Krishna motivates him through several logical arguments. Still, Arjuna is not fully convinced. Finally, Sri Krishna shows His universal form[8] and convinces Arjuna that fighting the war is the only honourable way out of the situation. Arjuna then regains composure and confidence and vigorously participates in the eighteen-day Mahabharata war.

Some thinkers, specifically foreign scholars, have dubbed the Gita as preaching and promoting homicide. What they have overlooked is that it is not the war or killing that is emphasized here but the presentation of a clear concept of karmayoga or the realization of the ultimate truth through the path of selfless work.

We all have certain duties and responsibilities. Side by side, we also have some rights and privileges. These two always go in tandem. To give an example:

A householder has certain duties and responsibilities towards his family, to ensure that all the members of his family live with dignity in the society, his children get adequate education and get settled happily in life with a good job and married life. To this end, he spends all his energy and resources and finally after discharging his duties satisfactorily, he generally lives a life of peaceful retirement supported by his family members.

Suppose another householder does not discharge his responsibilities as above; he squanders away his resources in drinking and other evil indulgences; his children are not given proper education, they are forced to live in disgrace, in such a scenario, he cannot expect them to look after him in his old age. In other words, if he does not discharge his responsibilities properly, he cannot expect any rights or privileges in return. To the extent he is sincere in performing his duties, to that extent, privileges come to him of themselves.

We now extend this example to a teacher who has, say, 100 children under his care. His duty is to see that all the 100 students pass out of the examinations, if possible, with flying colours. He can take some liberty with these 100 children, admonish them and correct them whenever needed. But he cannot command the respect of his students if he does not carry on this job in a responsible way. As long as he discharges his responsibilities towards his students in a proper manner, he enjoys their respect and certain privileges, too.

Expanding this example further, let us take up the case of the head of a nation. He has everything at his command. The privileges he enjoys are almost unlimited, but his duties are also enormous. Any disaster even in a remote corner of his country, be it natural or man-made, has to be attended, without any delay. He should always be prepared for surprises even if he provides good governance. If he simply enjoys the privileges due to the head of a state without duly discharging his responsibilities, he will certainly lose his reputation and job very soon.

From the above examples and discussions, we learn the following principles:

1. Responsibilities and privileges always go hand in hand.

2. The greater the responsibilities one undertakes, the greater the privileges one enjoys.

3. To demand rights and privileges without discharging one's duties and responsibilities would be unethical and suicidal.

4. When a person discharges his responsibilities sincerely, privileges come to him unsought. This is one of the great secrets of karmayoga.

In the context of these four principles, let us take the case of Arjuna in the Kurukshetra war. He was born in a kshatriya family whose *svadharma* is to protect the society from enemies, even by waging wars whenever necessary.[9] Arjuna had been trained by a galaxy of eminent warrior-teachers right from his childhood. His guru made him the greatest archer in the world by not only imparting to him intense training but also by sacrificing the interests of other student-archers like Ekalavya. The whole society had contributed to the emergence of Arjuna as the well known brilliant soldier of the Pandavas.

Now, after receiving so many benefits from the society, if he withdraws just at the critical time of war, it would be nothing but a farce. It will be very similar to the hypothetical case of an Indian soldier who joined the army and served for many years when there was no war. He enjoyed a lucrative salary, got daily consumables at highly subsidized prices at the cost of the general public, and commanded respect from the society by virtue of his position in the armed forces. Suddenly a war broke out with a neighbouring country. This soldier went to the battle-field, but on seeing the enemies, started philosophizing that these enemies were after all his brothers a few years ago just before partition and so it would be wrong to fight and kill his own brethren in the battle. If he thinks in this manner and withdraws at this stage, it would be a betrayal to the nation which had sacrificed so much to keep him and his family comfortable all those years. It would be an eternal disgrace to the soldier. The correct and honourable way would be to face and fight the enemies in the war and win the battle.

This is what Sri Krishna advises Arjuna—'O Arjuna, you have enjoyed so many rights and privileges from the society which has helped to groom you into a great warrior. If at this stage, you desist from fighting, you will incur unpardonable shame.'

We have to note that the emphasis here is not on killing but in discharging one's responsibilities in a disinterested manner.

This is the basis of karma yoga. When we discharge our duties to the society without expecting anything in return,[10] such a type of work gives us maximum benefit and satisfaction and elevating us spiritually.

The Triple Principle: Lessons from Mother Nature

The second stage of work ethic takes us to Mother Nature. Here, Sri Krishna introduces the concept of *yajna* in the Gita and redefines its meaning and scope. In the vedic literature, yajna means a sacrificial fire ritual in which offerings are made to propitiate gods for the attainment of some worldly ends. Sri Krishna speaks of many more types of yajna such as wealth-sacrifice, austerity-sacrifice, yogic sacrifice and knowledge-sacrifice[11] and concludes that unless all our works are done in a spirit of yajna or sacrifice for the good of the society, we will be bound by our own actions.[12] Thus the meaning of yajna, which had hitherto been confined to the relationship between man and God, was transformed to include not only the Creator but also all His creations, be they high or low. Applying this idea, Sri Krishna strongly states that if a person eats food alone without sharing with others, he verily eats sin itself[13] and one who enjoys gifts without giving anything in return is a thief.[14] The implication is that the whole world of things, animals and human beings are interwoven in such a splendid harmony that it will be impossible for any being to survive in isolation without depending upon the rest. We must adopt a policy of mutual give and take.[15]

In this respect, he asks us to imitate Mother Nature which does her work unselfishly, uninterruptedly and without expectation of any reward. A great, mysterious cosmic yajna is going on in Nature without any sort of discontinuity.[16] The earth revolves all the hours of the day and night, and all the days of the year without the slightest respite. The wind has been blowing and will continue to do so for all time to come. Similarly fresh water keeps constantly flowing into the river; vegetables and fruits grow afresh in plants and trees; planets and stars keep moving in their orbits at high speeds without the slightest rest. But for the services rendered by this mysterious Mother Nature, mankind would not be able to survive even for a moment.

The other compelling factor is that Nature always works for others, never for herself. The trees and plants bear vegetables and fruits, not for themselves but for others; similarly the rivers flow for the benefit of others and so on. Yet another point worth noting is that Nature renews herself daily; she never becomes tired, or jaded or old. The flower that blossomed in the morning may wither away by the evening, but the same plant produces equally new and fresh flowers the next morning.

How are we to apply this idea of renewal in our daily lives? Sri Krishna advocates a simple and easy method of prayer and self-surrender. He assures that if we are devoted to Him, sacrifice everything unto Him, considering Him as our highest goal, all our problems, tensions and anxieties will be absorbed in Him.[17] He will refill our spirit with fresh energy and vigour.

To summarise, the following are the lessons that we can learn from Mother Nature:

5. We have to work without respite.

6. We have to work always in the spirit of yajna, without selfish motives.

7. We have to learn to renew ourselves daily, despite tensions and restlessness that are characteristic of today's society.

The Triple Principles on Bondage and Freedom:

In the third and final stage, Sri Krishna speaks about liberation as the goal of life. He is categorical that doing good to the world is only a means and can never be the goal of life. This is because no work is perfect by itself. All works are attended with defects as fire is enveloped by smoke.[18] There is no work which is all good or all bad. In the same way, to conceptualize a perfect world is also a misnomer. Swami Vivekananda likens the world to a dog's tail.[19] As soon as we straighten out a dog's tail, it curls up instantly. Repeated efforts lead only to desperation. Finally wisdom dawns that by attempting to straighten out the dog's tail, which can never be done, we only straighten ourselves. Similarly, by trying to perfect the world through selfless work, we end up by perfecting, not the world, but ourselves. That is why Swami Vivekananda terms this world as a moral gymnasium to which we have come to perfect ourselves.[20] In a gymnasium, the weight blocks are made available for exercising. After a few years of exercising, one is able to build up one's body and muscles substantially, but the weight blocks remain the same as they were years ago. In the same way, after doing much good to the world, we shall one day realize that the world will continue to run with its attendant defects,[21] but we have grown and evolved spiritually.

The world may also be likened to a hospital where, as soon the patients are cured of their illnesses and discharged, new patients with newer diseases occupy the beds; or it is like a laundry where, as soon as the dirty clothes are washed and delivered, new sets of dirty clothes start pouring in.

When we work for money, name, fame or with some other worldly motive, we may get whatever we desire, but they will only bind us more and more to this world. When we do not expect anything from this world and go on doing selfless work, we will be able to get rid of bondages and move towards freedom. To understand this mystery, we need to have a clear grasp of the following three principles:

8. We have to work to remove evils and sufferings and for increasing the good and happiness of the world.

9. As we go on working, we will find that the world will continue to remain a mixture of good and evil, of happiness and sufferings.

10. In our attempt to perfect the world, we will end up perfecting ourselves, which is the goal of human life.

Thus the pragmatic teachings of Sri Krishna help us to look upon all creatures as God's gift to humanity, mutually serving one another. The realisation of this fact helps to forge a strong social commitment, reinforce our belief in ethics as the foundation of our existence, increase our love for the Creator (in whatever way we may address Him) and his Creation, and conduces to our own self-evolution. These teachings have been tested for over thousands of years and every one of Sri Krishna's universal and rational teachings have proved to be eternally relevant, amazingly practical and spiritually rewarding.

References

1. *Srimad Bhagavad Gita*, 1.21-22
2. *ibid.*, 1.28-30
3. *ibid.*, 1.37
4. *ibid.*, 2.5
5. *ibid.*, 2.7
6. *ibid*, 2.37
7. *ibid.*, 2.34-36
8. *ibid*, 11.5 onwards

9. *ibid*, 2.31
10. *ibid*. 2.47
11. *ibid*., 4.28
12. *ibid*., 3.9
13. *ibid*., 3.13
14. *ibid*., 3.12
15. *ibid*., 3.11

16. *ibid*., 3.14-16
17. *ibid*, 9.34
18. *ibid*., 18.48
19. *CW*, 1: 79
20. *ibid*., 1: 80
21. *ibid*., 1: 80

Chapter Twenty

Bhagavad Gita
for
Everyday Living
Some Guidelines

Make Your Destiny

उद्धरेदात्मनात्मानं नात्मानमवसादयेत् ।
आत्मैव ह्यात्मनो बन्धुरात्मैव रिपुरात्मनः ॥

A man should uplift himself by his own self, so let him not weaken this self. For this self is the friend of oneself, and this self is the enemy of oneself.

—*Gita,* 6.5

Man begins to struggle and fight against nature. He makes many mistakes, he suffers. But eventually, he conquers nature and realizes his freedom. When he is free, nature becomes his slave.

—*Swami Vivekananda*

Remember Your Divine Nature

नैनं छिन्दन्ति शस्त्राणि नैनं दहति पावकः ।
न चैनं क्लेदयन्त्यापो न शोषयति मारुतः ।।

This (Self), weapons cut not; This, fire burns not; This, water wets not; and This, wind dries not.

—*Gita,* 2.23

The Background, the Reality, of everyone is that same Eternal, Ever Blessed, Ever Pure, and Ever Perfect One. It is the Atman, the Soul, in the saint and the sinner, in the happy and the miserable, in the beautiful and the ugly, in men and in animals; it is the same throughout. It is Shining One.

—*Swami Vivekananda*

Work but Be Detached

ब्रह्मण्याधाय कर्माणि सङ्गं त्यक्त्वा करोति यः ।
लिप्यते न स पापेन पद्मपत्रमिवाम्भसा ।।

He who does actions forsaking attachment, resigning them to Brahman, is not soiled by evil, like unto a lotus-leaf by water. —*Gita, 5.10*

Just as water cannot wet the lotus leaf, so work cannot bind the unselfish man by giving rise to attachment to results. The selfless and unattached man may live in the very heart of a crowded and sinful city; he will not be touched by sin. —*Swami Vivekananda*

Living a God-centred Life

मन्मना भव मद्भक्तो मद्याजी मां नमस्कुरु ।
मामेवैष्यसि युक्त्वैवमात्मानं मत्परायणः ।।

Fill thy mind with Me, be My devotee, sacrifice unto Me, bow down to Me; thus having made thy heart steadfast in Me, taking Me as the Supreme Goal, thou shalt come to Me. —*Gita*, 9.34

Through the terrors of evil, say— my God, my love! Through the pangs of death, say—my God, my love! Through all the evils under the sun, say—my God, my love! Thou art here, I see Thee. Thou art with me, I feel Thee, I am Thine, take me. I am not of the world's but Thine; leave not then me.
—*Swami Vivekananda*

There is Hope for All

अपि चेदसि पापेभ्यः सर्वेभ्यः पापकृत्तमः ।
सर्वं ज्ञानप्लवेनैव वृजिनं सन्तरिष्यसि ।।

Even if thou be the most sinful among all the sinful, yet by the raft of knowledge alone thou shalt go across all sin.

—*Gita*, 4.36

Let a man go down as low as possible; there must come a time when out of sheer desperation he will take an upward curve and will learn to have faith in himself. But it is better for us that we should know it from the very first. Why should we have all these bitter experiences in order to gain faith in ourselves? We can see that all the difference between man and man is owing to the existence or non-existence of faith in himself. Faith in ourselves will do everything.

—*Swami Vivekananda*

The Power of Steady Mind

शक्नोतीहैव यः सोढुं प्राक्शरीरविमोक्षणात् ।
कामक्रोधोद्भवं वेगं स युक्तः स सुखी नरः ॥

He who can withstand in this world, before the liberation from the body, the impulse arising from lust and anger, he is steadfast (in Yoga), he is a happy man.

—Gita, 5.23

[A man of self-control] controls his own inner forces, and nothing can draw them out against his will. By this continuous reflex of good thoughts, good impressions moving over the surface of the mind, the tendency for doing good becomes strong. . . Such a man is safe for ever; he cannot do any evil.

—*Swami Vivekananda*

The Ideal of Meditation

यथा दीपो निवातस्थो नेङ्गते सोपमा स्मृता ।
योगिनो यतचित्तस्य युञ्जतो योगमात्मनः ।।

'As a lamp in a spot sheltered from the wind does not flicker'—even such has been the simile used for a Yogi of subdued mind, practising concentration in the Self.

—*Gita*, 6.19

Think of that flame as your own soul and inside the flame is another effulgent light, and that is the Soul of your soul, God. Meditate upon that in the heart.

—*Swami Vivekananda*

The Spiritual Basis of Life

आत्मौपम्येन सर्वत्र समं पश्यति योऽर्जुन ।
सुखं वा यदि वा दुःखं स योगी परमो मतः ।।

He who judges of pleasure or pain everywhere, by the same standard as he applies to himself, that Yogi, O Arjuna, is regarded as the highest. —*Gita*, 6.32

If you cannot see God in the human face, how can you see him in the clouds, or in images made of dull, dead matter, or in mere fictitious stories of our brain? . . . When you see man as God, everything, even the tiger, will be welcome. Whatever comes to you is but the Lord, the Eternal, the Blessed One, appearing to us in various forms, as our father, and mother, and friend, and child—they are our own soul playing with us. —*Swami Vivekananda*

The Principle of Moderation

युक्ताहारविहारस्य युक्तचेष्टस्य कर्मसु ।
युक्तस्वप्नावबोधस्य योगो भवति दुःखहा ।।

To him who is temperate in eating and recreation, in his effort for work, and in sleep and wakefulness, Yoga becomes the destroyer of misery. —*Gita, 6.17*

It is the level-headed man, the calm man, of good judgment and cool nerves, of great sympathy and love, who does good work and so does good to himself.

—*Swami Vivekananda*

Devotion Lies in Simplicity

पत्रं पुष्पं फलं तोयं यो मे भक्त्या प्रयच्छति ।
तदहं भक्त्युपहृतमश्नामि प्रयतात्मनः ।।

Whoever with devotion offers Me a leaf, a flower, a fruit, or water, that I accept—the devout gift of the pure-minded. —*Gita, 9.26*

Thou for whom the world of flowers bloom, accept my few common flowers. Thou who feedest the universe, accept my poor offerings of fruits. . . . I do not know how to approach Thee, how to worship Thee, my God, my Cowherd, my child; let my worship be pure, my love for Thee selfless; and if there is any virtue in worship, let it be Thine, grant me only love, love that never asks for anything—never seeks for anything but love.

—*Swami Vivekananda*

Practice of Equanimity

योगस्थः कुरु कर्माणि सङ्गं त्यक्त्वा धनञ्जय ।
सिद्ध्यसिद्ध्योः समो भूत्वा समत्वं योग उच्यते ।।

Being steadfast in Yoga, O Dhananjaya, perform actions, abandoning attachment, remaining unconcerned as regards success and failure. This evenness of mind (in regard to success and failure) is known as Yoga.

—*Gita, 2.48*

Work cannot bind the unselfish man by giving rise to attachment to results. The selfless and unattached man may live in the very heart of a crowded and sinful city; he will not be touched by

The Path to Perfection

वीतरागभयक्रोधा मन्मया मामुपाश्रिताः ।
बहवो ज्ञानतपसा पूता मद्भावमागताः ।।

Freed from attachment, fear, and anger, absorbed in Me, taking refuge in Me, purified by the fire of knowledge, many have attained My Being.

—Gita, IV.10

The road to good is the roughest and steepest in the universe. It is a wonder that so many succeed, no wonder that so many fall. Character has to be established through a thousand stumbles.

—Swami Vivekananda

One Destination, Different Roads

ये यथा मां प्रपद्यन्ते तांस्तथैव भजाम्यहम् ।
मम वर्त्मानुवर्तन्ते मनुष्याः पार्थ सर्वशः ।।

In whatever way men worship Me, in the same way do I fulfil their desires; (it is) My path, O son of Partha, (that) men tread, in all ways. —*Gita*, 4.11

'As the different streams having their sources in different places all mingle their water in the sea, so, O Lord, the different paths which men take through different tendencies, various though they appear, crooked or straight, all lead to Thee.'
—*Swami Vivekananda*
(quoting a verse from Shiva Mahimna Stotra)

A Timeless Assurance

अनन्याश्चिन्तयन्तो मां ये जनाः पर्युपासते ।
तेषां नित्याभियुक्तानां योगक्षेमं वहाम्यहम् ।।

Persons who, meditating on Me as non-separate, worship Me in all beings, to them thus ever zealously engaged, I carry what they lack and preserve what they already have.   —*Gita*, 9.22

Let nothing stand between God and your love for Him. Love Him, love Him, love Him; and let the world say what it will. Day and night think of God and think of nothing else as far as possible. The daily necessary thoughts can all be thought through God. Eat to Him, drink to Him, sleep to Him, see Him in all. Talk of God to others; this is most beneficial.

—*Swami Vivekananda*

God is the Ultimate

सर्वधर्मान्परित्यज्य मामेकं शरणं व्रज ।
अहं त्वा सर्वपापेभ्यो मोक्षयिष्यामि मा शुचः ॥

Relinquishing all Dharmas take refuge in Me alone; I will liberate thee from all sins; grieve not. —*Gita*, 18.66

He who has given up all attachment, all fear, and all anger, he whose whole soul has gone unto the Lord, he who has taken refuge in the Lord, whose heart has become purified, with whatsoever desire he comes to the Lord, He will grant that to him. Therefore worship Him through knowledge, love, or renunciation.

—*Swami Vivekananda*

Chapter Twenty One

Gita's Way to Self-Fulfilment

SWAMI ATMARUPANANDA

The Meaning of Self-Fulfilment

What do we mean by fulfilment, and how do we struggle to achieve it? By boldly examining our search for happiness and unmasking its follies, we become better prepared to receive the Gita's way to self-fulfilment.

There are so many words that we commonly use, thinking that we understand them, without really examining their intent. And part of spiritual practices deal with intent, making our intent conscious and clear. So let us begin by defining our operative term. The word 'fulfilment' refers to the development of the full potentialities of something. If something is fulfilled, it is completed: what was potential has been actualized. *Self*-fulfilment is the development of one's own potentialities; fulfilment of oneself. A synonym of fulfilment would be completion. Synonyms of self-fulfilment would be self-actualization, attainment of perfection. For simplicity's sake we will henceforth use the unqualified term 'fulfilment' for 'self-fulfilment.'

The sense of fulfilment is an elusive thing. Ask most of us, 'Do you feel fulfilled?' and if we are honest we will answer 'no'. . . and, after a pause perhaps, we'll add, 'not yet.' We spend our lives thinking that fulfilment is just around the corner and think thus:

> There is something I want badly, and once I have it I will be happy. There is a problem facing me, and when I solve it life will be smooth. There's a position I want, and once I rise to it I'll have it made.

Sometimes, yes, when life is going our way we do experience periods of satisfaction when all seems right with the world, and we say, 'Life is great! I am so happy!' But such periods are fragile and all too short.

Modern life, starting in the West and now spreading around the world, makes a deceptive promise with cruel results. We are told directly and indirectly through advertising, television, movies, magazines, books, images and songs, that we can be happy, fulfilled, even excited about life. How? By consuming and enjoying, by expressing, by possessing—basically by releasing our life-energy into the world, by engaging with life on its own terms, by grabbing all that life has to offer. It is a deceptive promise because that is not the way life works. The deception is cruel because it leads us to confusion, frustration, and unhappiness: 'I did what I was supposed to do. Why am I not happy?' Now-a-days many people live out their lives in the adolescent belief that, the world is a bowl of cherries, just waiting to be enjoyed, with parental control. In time this may get replaced by 'boss' or 'spouse' or 'the government'.

The Pursuit of Happiness

What are the ramifications of this false premise? First of all, it's especially common in the West to see people trying desperately to look happy, to look excited. It takes time before we can see the sadness behind the smile, the desperation behind the excitement. Not that it is better to go about looking depressed and hopeless. When we are depressed, we can make ourselves feel better by forcing ourselves to smile, to be pleasant. That is therapeutic. But this ebullience covering desperation is a mask which keeps us from dealing with our situation. Even in the midst of difficulties we can find a quiet happiness by changing our attitude and expectations. That is growth. But this show of mirth covering a wail of unhappiness is a tragic loss of integrity. This is not a criticism of those who are suffering, but a criticism of the false belief they have been fed: the belief that they can and should live in perpetual excitement over the adventure of life.

There is a second popular idea that feeds this desperation to be happy. The great scholar of mythology, Joseph Campbell, used to tell people, 'Follow your bliss!'[1] For young people who are afraid of following their dreams, afraid of doing what their better selves love, tied down by ideas of safe, mundane practicality, it is an excellent advice. But by itself, unqualified, it can be an irresponsible advice. If I have a spouse and children but I want to strike out on my own and be independent to 'follow my bliss,' can I find it by abandoning those who depend on me? If I have sick, elderly parents that need my care but I want to squeeze the juice out of life before it's too late by travelling around the world, seeking adventure, should I 'follow my bliss'?

If I do abandon my legitimate responsibilities to others in order to pursue a self-centred goal, I will find eventually that happiness has eluded me, fulfilment has remained hidden.

Thirdly, not only has popular culture promoted this idea that we should be excitedly happy all the time, but elements of New Age thought have promoted another idea—less extreme but also cruel in its result—that if we do the right things and think the right thoughts, life will flow smoothly. Problems, then, are a sign that we are doing something wrong. Illness is a sign that we are not thinking the right thoughts. This teaching also feeds modern desperation.

There may be a higher truth to this New Age doctrine. Yes, if we have surrendered to God and can take whatever happens as the will of God, we gain a higher ease, an acceptance of that which comes our way. We no longer fight our circumstances but work with them. We seem to flow through life as though carried by a warm and loving current—a current that is personal, even considerate—where we don't have to initiate anything. Even though others see us facing great difficulties, we see ourselves as floating in the warm current of the river, participating as things arise, not initiating. But at the lower level where most of us live, this principle does not operate, which makes this New Age teaching cruel because it compounds our problems with a sense of guilt, intensifies our suffering by making us blame ourselves for bringing on illness in some way that we can not even see. Positive thinking is a wonderful tool, but if not grounded in reality, it can itself become a desperate enterprise to repress our emptiness.

These three ideas—that we should be excitedly fulfilled by grabbing life, that we should selfishly follow our bliss, and that problems come because we aren't thinking the right thoughts—each so characteristic in its own way of modern life, fail because they deny the true nature of ordinary life. Life taken on its own terms does not *involve* problem solving, it is not *accompanied* by problem solving, it *is* problem solving. Whenever we think, 'I can't wait to get this problem solved so that I can relax for a change,' another problem is already coming around the corner fully formed.

If we look at very wealthy people who spend their money to buy their way out of problems, we will invariably see that, to the extent that they have bought their way out of the problems which common people face, to that extent very small things become huge problems for them—things that ordinary people would not even notice. Not that all wealthy people use their money to avoid facing the problems of life: some use it well, and some use it very wisely. But those who do try to buy their way out of problems suffer a type of degeneration, a character sickness. This shows that we *need* problems. If we do not have natural problems, we invent problems. And real problems are always better than the imagined problems of the effete.

Is Self Fulfilment Possible?

It depends on what we mean by fulfilment. If we mean 'being high on life' by embracing the world on its own terms, no, that sort of fulfilment is not possible except occasionally in fragile spurts, which really can not be called fulfilment at all because it *is* fragile and occasional, subject to reaction; and it is a 'high' only in comparison to our normal, dull state. Or if by fulfilment we mean following our bliss in a self-centred way, no, we will find in time that bliss has abandoned us, character has not been formed, our mind is uncontrolled, and fulfilment is an empty dream. Or again, if by fulfilment we mean a smooth and joyful life built on doing and thinking right, well, that is not enough to attain true fulfilment, especially as the New Age defines 'right' in this context.

Many of us are attracted to spiritual life because it does promise fulfilment (expressed variously such as Illumination, Enlightenment, Liberation, Union with God, Self-realization or Realization of the Infinite). The problem for us is, the longer we are on the path, the further the Goal seems to recede from us. Not that we move further from the goal, but we begin to realise how vast the goal is, and how meagre our best efforts are, and therefore how difficult a goal it is to reach. Fulfilment thereby once again seems to elude us.

The Hope of Fulfilment

In the Bhagavad Gita, however, Sri Krishna brings fulfilment toward us. He does not tell us: 'Nirvikalpa samadhi or bust.' Rather he says 'Even a little of this dharma carries one beyond the great Fear (death).'[2] But neither does he water fulfilment down to the point where it means nothing more than embracing the world on its own terms in a desperate effort to be happy. He does not promise us that we can enjoy life and be free from problems by following a recipe book of right thoughts and actions. Rather he fully acknowledges the nature of life, but points to that within us which can begin to rise above it.

First Sri Krishna grabs Arjuna and shakes him with the words:

Whence comes this ignoble despair in the face of adversity, contrary to the attainment of heaven and productive of infamy, O Arjuna? Don't give in to this state of neutered weakness. Ill does it befit you! Throw off this small-minded faint-heartedness and stand up, O destroyer of your foes![3]

The Essence of the Gita

Swami Vivekananda said that these two verses express the essence of the *Gita*. How strange! The *Gita* is filled with the most exalted teachings on the nature of the Self, the nature of God and the incarnation, liberation, the vision of God's universal form, surrender of oneself to God, and yet Vivekananda finds here the *Gita's* essence.

I think it is because the rest of the *Gita* stands on this foundation of strength, fearlessness, manliness. To Swami Vivekananda, manliness *is* godliness. When leaving for his wanderings, he told Sri Sarada Devi, 'Mother, if I can become a man in the true sense of the term, then only I shall return; otherwise this will be my last farewell.'[4] Sister Nivedita records the Swami as saying that 'character *is* spirituality,' and it's in this spirit that manliness is godliness.

In most religious traditions we are taught to fear evil, fear temptation, fear hell, fear mistakes, even fear God. But Swami Vivekananda, in his lecture on the *Gita*, said:

> It is a tremendous error to feel helpless. Do not seek help from anyone. We are our own help. If we cannot help ourselves, there is none to help us. 'Thou thyself art thy only friend, thou thyself thy only enemy. There is no other enemy but this self of mine, no other friend but myself.' This is the last and greatest lesson, and Oh, what a time it takes to learn it! . . . That is all I have to say to the world. Be strong! . . . The sign of life is strength and growth. The sign of death is weakness. Whatever is weak, avoid! It is death. If it is strength, go down into hell and get hold of it! There is salvation only for the brave. . . . All weakness, all bondage is imagination. Speak one word to it, it must vanish. Do not weaken! There is no other way out. . . .Stand up and be strong[5]

Yes, 'go down into hell' to get strength! What other great world teacher has ever spoken thus? Only Sri Krishna. None other before Vivekananda.

And so, after giving Arjuna a thunderous shake, Sri Krishna then teaches him about the Self of Man, which is untouched by death, untouched by life, transcendent over all dualities, over all the problems of life. And he tells Arjuna to take his stand there. Then only he teaches Arjuna the secret of work, of yoga, and of devotion.

But are we not back to a far distant goal of Self-realization?

Yes and no. Ultimate fulfilment, indeed, is the rare state of illumination. One expression of that state is the *sthita-prajna*, the person of steady wisdom, whom Sri Krishna describes in the second chapter.[6] Some have said that the state of the *sthita prajna* is not the state of ultimate enlightenment, but the state of one who has awakened the *pratyagatman* or inner, individual self, which is a significant state along the path but not the final state of illumination. But Sri Krishna does not leave us with anything short of illumination. He knows the use and place of everything in life, and so his emphasis is not on denial or rejection. As Swami Vivekananda says:

[Sri Krishna] is the most rounded man I know of, wonderfully developed equally in brain and heart and hand. Every moment [of his] is alive with activity, either as a gentleman, warrior, minister, or something else. . . . He knows the use of everything, and when it is necessary to [assign a place to each], he is there. . . Buddha's activity was on one plane, the plane of teaching. He could not keep his wife and child and become a teacher at the same time. Krishna preached in the midst of the battlefield.[7]

And that is why Sri Krishna begins by insulting Arjuna's sense of manhood. Arjuna, having spoken eloquently of renunciation, of self-sacrifice, of turning the other cheek, is mocked by Sri Krishna: 'Laughing as it were, [Sri Krishna then] spoke to [Arjuna] who had collapsed there between the two armies.'[8] How different from traditional spiritual advice! How delighted most teachers would be on finding a disciple like Arjuna who had seen the vanity of the war, the vanity of victory, of fame, who had seen the superiority of self-sacrifice and renunciation! Yet Sri Krishna saw that Arjuna had come to that 'wisdom' through weakness, through fear which gripped his heart in its cold claws. Arjuna was not conquering life, but giving up defeated.

Therefore Sri Krishna's first advice is, stand up and fight![9] And he doesn't hesitate to appeal to ordinary values, which after all are higher than defeat and depression: he tells Arjuna: 'Killed [in battle] you attain heaven; victorious you'll enjoy the earth!'[10] So fulfilment for Sri Krishna is not one final, ultimate goal, experienced only by a small handful of people in any generation. There is a sliding scale of fulfilment according to our level of personal evolution.

Traditional teachers of most religions emphasize self-denial, self-sacrifice, unselfishness, egolessness, renunciation. One might even question whether the whole concept of self-fulfilment fits into a spiritual path, unless one defines it as 'losing oneself in God.'

What allows these apparent contradictions is the Vedantic doctrine of the Self. Buddhism begins with the denial of the individual self and of the universal Self.[11] Other religions teach self-denial and affirmation of God. Vedanta teaches Self-affirmation. Even the great Ramanuja teaches that true devotion is founded on self-knowledge in the positive sense: 'I can't truly love God unless I know who I am. According to him I must take my stand on the purity and glory of the inner, spiritual—but individual—self.'

Yes, Vedanta also teaches unselfishness, self-sacrifice, transcendence of ego, but it's teaching of 'self-denial' is founded on self-affirmation, and so the term 'self-denial' is really inappropriate—a misnomer—in a Vedantic context. Sri Krishna does not even teach humility as that is understood in the Abrahamic traditions. He teaches same-sightedness (*sama-darshitva*).[12]

This doesn't mean that Sri Krishna teaches egotism or ego-assertion: that has no place in spiritual life. He teaches self-affirmation, where 'self' has to be understood properly. Even the individual self is pure consciousness, only individuated, and it is the door to the infinite Self, whether through knowledge where it is seen as a reflection of one's own highest nature, or through devotion where it is seen as a spark from the fire of God.

And that is why Sri Krishna—the greatest of all Vedantic teachers—begins his teaching with a description of the Self, and asks Arjuna to take his stand there. Stand on the glory of the Self! Stand even on the glory of the self! The great mistake is to think that you are great and others are weak: that is egotism and has nothing to do with standing on the glory of the self. The greater mistake is to think that you are nothing, for that is denial of the self, the very doorway to God.

The Grand Journey

Thus each step on the journey taught by Sri Krishna is a step toward greater and greater self-fulfilment, ending in absolute Self-fulfilment. 'Winning, you attain the earth; losing you attain to heaven.' Take a step higher and stand on the glory of the *pratyagatman*, in the inner self, where the waves of the world can no longer affect you. Yes, we can come to a point, long before liberation, where we feel an increasing freedom from the waves of the world, where we feel an inner quiet and blessedness, a greater fulfilment than we've ever experienced in the world. Take a step higher still and be a *sthita prajna*, steady in wisdom like the ocean which takes in the water of all the rushing rivers of the world and yet remains unmoved.[13]

Or, having known the nature of the self, the nature of the supreme Self, and the nature of God, follow Sri Krishna's advice in the eighteenth chapter: 'Having renounced all supports, take refuge in Me alone'[14] and find absolute, unending, unqualified fulfilment, which is Self-fulfilment.

References

1. See the video-taped series of his interview with Bill Moyers, entitled *Joseph Campbell and the Power of Myth, with Bill Moyers* by Mystic Fire Video, October 2001.
2. *Srimad Bhagavad-Gita,* 2.40; henceforth *Gita*
3. *Gita,* 2.2-3.
4. *Holy Mother Sri Sarada Devi,* Swami Gambhirananda, Channai: Sri Ramakrishna Math, 1969, p.167
5. *The Complete Works of Swami Vivekananda,* Advaita Ashrama, Kolkata, 1: 478-479
6. *Gita,* 2.55-72
7. *Complete Works,* 1: 457.
8. *Gita,* 2.10
9. *Gita,* 2.37
10. *Gita,* 2,37
11. The Mahayana school of Buddhisim, admittedly, brought a modified version of the Self back, but many of the complications in Mahayana philosophy come from the reinstatement of a *de facto* cosmic Self while trying to harmonize it with the doctrine that there is no Self.
12. *Gita,* 5.18
13. *Gita,* 2.70
14. *Gita,* 18.66

Chapter Twenty Two

Gita's View on Ecology and its Maintenance

N V C SWAMY

Gita's Holistic Approach

The Bhagavad Gita is a remarkable scriptural text. Even though it was taught by Sri Krishna to Arjuna on the battlefield of Kurukshetra several millennia ago, it still retains its freshness, because of the universality of its teachings. It is as much relevant today as it was when first enunciated or written down. Millions of people down the ages have benefited by its study and the guidelines suggested by it to lead a purposeful life on this planet.

The Gita is basically a text of Yoga, both theory and practice. Even though it recognizes initially only two branches of Yoga—Jnana and Karma—later it goes on to elaborate the other two branches also, viz., Bhakti and Dhyana. This is because the latter two Yogas can be absorbed into Karma Yoga, since they involve action of some kind. Even the colophon at the end of each chapter of the text recognizes the Gita as *Brahmavidya* [pertaining to Jnana] and *Yogasastra* [pertaining to Karma Yoga].

The Gita is the only book of the scriptural literature of the world that deals with Karma Yoga in a systematic way. So long as we are conscious of our physical bodies, we *have* to perform actions, as otherwise even our survival in the physical body is not possible. Action is, thus, inevitable for all creatures, especially human beings. Species other than human beings have very limited capacity to make choices, whereas the human being is endowed with the capacity to make choices. Human wisdom lies in making proper choices, so that not only one is benefited in the long run, even the rest of the creatures are helped or at least not harmed. Karma Yoga is nothing but making intelligent choices for the greatest benefit to oneself and to humanity.

Karma Yoga can be practised at three levels—personal, societal [or collective] and global. Sri Krishna touches upon all these levels. The focus of our attention in this article is on the last one, viz., Global Karma Yoga, dealing with the responsibility of human beings to the environment.

The Idea of Evolution

To be able to appreciate the current predicament of humanity and the remedy suggested by the Gita, one needs to know how exactly creation has taken place. It is not the intention to discuss here the Vedantic models, but to understand what modern science has to say about it.

Just as Vedanta, modern astrophysics also believes that the manifestation of this universe is a cyclic process. According to the Big Bang theory of astrophysics, this universe came into existence about 16 to 18 billion years ago. Astrophysicists have worked out in detail how the various galaxies evolved out of primordial energy. According to their calculations, the solar system came into existence about 4.5 billion years ago. Very soon the atmosphere of the earth became stable and the earliest life forms appeared on our planet about 1.5 billion years ago.

Evolution then proceeded at its own pace, giving rise to animal species, invertebrates and later to vertebrates. About 250 million years ago, in what is now called the Jurassic era, huge animals and reptiles, now known as the Dinosaurs, made their appearance. They roamed on the surface of the planet for about 180 million years and became extinct around 70 million years ago. The reason for their extinction is now surmised to be a huge meteor that fell on the Yucatan peninsula, raising a huge blanket of dust covering the planet for almost 100 years. This dust blanketed out the sun, thus killing all plant life and herbivorous animals, that work depending on plant life. In turn, carnivorous animals depending on herbivorous animals for their sustenance became extinct.

The next species to appear on our planet were the Apes, the Great Apes and the Humanoids. Around 100,000 years ago, *homo sapiens*, the thinking human being made its appearance. The discovery of fire led to human settlements and an organized way of life. The last Ice Age ended about 12000 years ago, leading to the great Flood, which subsided after about 2000 years leading to the giant river systems. Great civilizations and cultures came into existence on the banks of these rivers.

Science, as we know it today, came into existence around 2700 years ago in ancient Greece. Technology came into prominence about 500 years ago. In this brief period of about three millennia, the world is facing a possible annihilation, thanks to the proliferation of nuclear weapons, air and water pollution and the evolution of deadly diseases like cancer, diabetes, hypertension and AIDS!

The first indication that there was something wrong with the human race was the dropping of the atomic bombs on Hiroshima and Nagasaki. Since that time, humanity has been teetering on the edge of a disaster. After only a brief span of existence of 100,000 years, the human race is facing a real threat of extinction.

When we compare this with the existence of dinosaurs for a period of 180 million years, we start wondering how such huge animals could survive for such a long period of time. If they became extinct, it was for no fault of theirs. The human race, on the other hand, is bent on committing Hara-kiri!

The answer to this poser has been provided by Daniel Quinn in his book *Ishmael*. This is about a dialogue between a human being and a gorilla, called Ishmael. The gorilla is the teacher and the human being the student. The gorilla asks the human being a simple question: 'Before you started tampering with the environment, did you ever bother to consult other life forms, like animals and plants?' The human being has no answer.

The gorilla classifies all species of life forms into two categories—'takers' and 'leavers'. Takers are those who take things whether they need them or not. Leavers are those who take only as much as they need and leave the rest behind. The human beings obviously fall into the first category. They claim to be masters of this planet and even claim to have conquered nature!

Humanity has produced great philosophers, thinkers, and prophets, who have advocated the cause of a simple life with minimum consumption of resources. But, the majority of human beings consist of those, who are discovering fancier and more meaningless means of exploiting the natural resources. They have perfected the art of mass killing of animal species and human beings. Anyone advocating restraint is considered a freak and becomes an object of ridicule.

Humanity is, thus, facing a deep crisis and is desperately looking for solutions. It is an interesting fact that, not finding any suitable remedies in the modern culture, humanity is looking back in time, trying to find solutions in ancient cultures. There is now great interest in ancient remedies like Ayurveda, Yoga, Meditation and Tai chi. One sure source in which some of these solutions can be found is the Bhagavad Gita. We will now examine what the Gita has to say about these problems, especially the one facing the environment.

The Gita's Way to Ecological Balance

The Gita recognizes two kinds of Yoga—Jnana and Karma. In the third verse of the third chapter, Sri Krishna says: 'There are two paths in this world, as I have already described. The path of Knowledge is for the intellectuals and the Path of Action is for the Yogis.' Hence, in the colophon to all chapters, the Gita is described as Brahmavidya (the Knowledge of Brahman) and Yogasastra (the Science of Yoga).

There is a very elaborate description of Karma Yoga in the Gita from the beginning to the end. Selfless action without attachment to the results is the secret of Action. The Gita calls it the attitude of *Yajna*. Elsewhere in the Gita (3:9), Sri Krishna says, 'Action done selflessly, with the intention of serving others, is a liberating force, whereas all other kinds of actions bind us to the world.' It is precisely the lack of this attitude that is responsible for the human race finding itself in a miserable plight. The human being is the only creature that has been given the intelligence to make choices. Time and again, humanity has been found wanting in making wise decisions. The reason for this is the arrogance that the whole creation is meant for the enjoyment of human beings, as if they have no responsibility towards the rest of creation.

Following this verse, Sri Krishna tells us in the following four verses what is expected of us humans. These verses have till now been interpreted in the traditional way, by invoking the duties of human beings towards the gods. But, there is another contemporary view, which is applicable to modern times.

The meaning of these verses (3:10-13) is as follows:

In the beginning of time, the Creator created all creatures along with human beings, and also gave them the gift of Yajna or mutual co-operation. He then told the human beings, 'By this gift of Yajna and its proper use, all of you will prosper. Yajna is like Kamadhenu, the celestial cow, which will fulfil all your needs. Nourish the Devas and they will protect you in turn. Thus, nourishing each other, both of you will prosper. The Devas thus nourished by you will bless you in return. But, he, who having taken from the Devas, gives nothing in return is verily a thief. He, who breaks this chain of mutual cooperation, leads a life of no use either to himself or to the rest of creation.'

The traditional meaning of the word 'Deva' is a celestial being residing in heaven. But, the etymological meaning is the *shining one* that enlightens us. It means a life-giving principle.

The most important factor sustaining human life is Oxygen. No human being or animal can survive without it. We take in oxygen and release in return carbon dioxide, which is used up by plant life. When there is a proper balance between these two, the atmospheric air is pure and clear, conducive to good health. But, when there is excessive consumption of oxygen and equally excessive emission of carbon dioxide, the recycling capacity of the atmosphere is overloaded, leading to accumulation of carbon dioxide, raising the temperature of the atmosphere and causing global warming. Is that not what is happening today? Hence, Sri Krishna admonishes us to lead our lives in such a way that the balance is restored. In this way, we will be nourishing the life-giving atmosphere and will in turn be blessed by it with a healthy life. Our ancients, hence, considered air as Divine and called it Vayu.

All cultures and civilizations had their origins on the banks of rivers, since there was an unlimited supply of water available. But, due to overexploitation of water resources and pollution of existing sources by industrial effluents, pure drinking water has become a luxury. One has to purchase chemically purified water in bottles to survive. Is this not a parody of modern life? Our ancients, again, considered water, a life-sustaining substance, as divine and called it Varuna.

Life in tropical countries becomes endurable by rainfall occurring at the proper time and in proper quantities. According to meteorologists, the pattern of weather has changed so much for the worse, that we have rainless rainy seasons in tropics and snow-less winters in cold countries. All this has happened in living memory. Again, our ancients had recognized the importance of weather and had always prayed to the weather-god for rains at proper times. The name they had given to the weather-god was Indra.

There are many people today who consider the divinization of air, water and rain as rank superstition, without realizing what harm we are causing by not recognizing the truth that lies behind them.

Conclusion

Our planet is the only piece of real estate so far known in the universe. It is also true that the human being is the most intelligent of the species on this planet, since he knows how to choose between options. So, it goes without saying that the future of the planet lies in his hands. Is he aware at all of his great responsibility or has the Good Lord handed over the planet to the wrong species?

The most immediate need today is to spread the awareness about the disaster facing us in the not-so-distant future. This should commence at the school level and continue to the college level. Modern youth is dazzled by the Internet, cellphones, jazzy automobiles, and the likes. They are like condemned people who snatch at any available means of enjoyment, however fleeting it may be. It is high time they are woken up by proper education. It is not that human beings have no remedy for this problem. Only the awareness about the seriousness of the problem is missing. There must be a concerted effort on the part of the media to play the role of educator, rather than frittering away their efforts on cricket, movie stars, etc.

It is indeed remarkable that the Gita had addressed itself to a situation that lay so much in future. Is it likely that such problems were faced in the past also and that

Sri Krishna had suggested this remedy? After all, it is said that history repeats itself. Whatever it may be, this remedy supports the contention of the title of a book by Swami Harshananda [the present President of Ramakrishna Math, Bangalore]—*Ancient Solutions to Modern Problems.*

Chapter Twenty Three

Sri Krishna's Remedy for the Arjuna Syndrome

SWAMI ATMAPRIYANANDA

An Ancient Modern Text

In describing the nature of the Atman, the innermost and immortal spiritual core of every being, the Gita uses the word *purana*[1]. Commenting on this word, Shankaracharya states in his famous *bhashya* [commentary] that it is *pura api nava*—although ancient, it is yet modern[2]. This very phrase applies to the Gita text itself, to be sure.

The Gita is a simple text describing the immortal dialogue between Arjuna, the representative Man (*Nara*) and Krishna, the Supreme Being (*Narayana*), the great Friend of Man (*Narasakha*). This divine dialogue was recorded in the great composition called Bhagavad Gita in seven hundred verses by Veda Vyasa[3], the great grand old sire in the ancient Indian lore symbolizing the essence of all the wisdom embodied in Sanatana Dharma—Veda, Vedanta, Vedanga, Smriti, Purana—describing a complex human situation and seeking solution to this complexity in the simplicity of the realisation of the Divine Inner Essence in all beings, the Atman, the *purana,* the Immortal, Immutable, Unchanging, Eternal Self, the divinity within.

The simple Gita teaching is that sorrow and delusion (*shoka* and *moha*) which are the seeds of unrest called *samsara* (transmigratory existence) cannot be obliterated except through the realisation of the Atman (*atmajnaanaat na anyato nivrittih*).[4] It is eternal because it is ancient and yet modern. It is hence timeless. Such a scripture is truly universal and beyond space-time boundaries. Since it does not belong to any particular country, religion or time period, its appeal too is timeless—to everybody, everywhere and at all times. Being the interplay of the One and the many, it possesses infinite variety in and through the Unity it embodies. The Gita *dhyanam* (verses for meditation on the Gita) therefore calls this scripture Mother, who symbolizes unity in variety in the household, binding great variety in one strong bond of love. This great Mother of all scriptures has been read, studied, chanted, meditated and commented upon, interpreted in innumerable ways by all the *acharyas*. It has been worshipped and lauded over the centuries as no other scripture perhaps has been done, by the scholars and the so-called ignorant, by the saints and the ordinary folk, by the religious people and the worldly ones.

A great Swami once told the author: 'The Gita is like a piece of sugarcane. Everybody can get some juice out of it. Even a child without teeth can feel the taste of it. And a great Acharya with powerful teeth can crush and squeeze plenty of juice out of it.' The beauty and the grandeur of the Gita is that it is both the science of Brahman (*brahma-vidya*) and the technology (called *yoga*) to realize this science. The colophonic phrase marking the end of each chapter of the Gita has four significant components:

(i) that the Gita is the science of Brahman (*brahma-vidya*),

(ii) that the Gita is the technology to realise this science (*yoga-shastra*),

(iii) that the Gita is the dialogue between *nara* and *nara-sakha* (*Narayana*), and

(iv) that the Gita is *yoga* throughout—starting from *vishada-yoga* and ending with *moksha-yoga*—from despondency to liberation. It covers the whole spectrum of human aspirations, endeavours, goals, and enterprise in any situation, in any field, in any direction; the entire human life itself is one continuous state of *yoga*.

Human understanding stands metamorphosed into divine wisdom by the knowledge that life itself is one unbroken continuum of *yoga* and interestingly, the intuitive faculty that opens up the floodgate to this integral new vision of Light and Truth is also *yoga*, which the Gita calls *buddhi-yoga*.[5]

1. It is Yoga Throughout

Every chapter of Gita is called *yoga*, whatever its subject matter. Be it Self-Knowledge (*sankhya*), Knowledge and Special Knowledge (*jnana-vijnana*), Work (*karma*), Devotion (*bhakti*), or even the so-called secular subjects like Threefold qualities of human beings (*guna-traya-*

vibhaga), Qualities of divine and demoniac persons (*daivayaasura-sampad*)— each chapter is considered Yoga.

The Gita starts its teaching with Arjuna's despondency or sorrow in the very first chapter, which is christened *Arjuna-vishada-yoga* (the Yoga of Arjuna's despondency). That is the uniqueness of this immortal text: perhaps nowhere in the spiritual literature of the world would one find 'sorrow-yoga' or 'depression-yoga' discussed in such an elaborate fashion! The deeper significance of putting 'depression-yoga' at the very beginning is to give supreme importance to the *understanding* of human predicament, *human dilemma,* for it is the human being who suffers terrible pain and it is again the human being that reaches divine excellence through dint of *sadhana,* surrender, knowledge and meditation. Thus, the immortal appeal of the Gita to all peoples of all times is because it puts man, *the human being* at the focus rather than God, and teaches how the human being is liberated from the shackles of ignorance and bondage through the paths of *jnana, bhakti, karma,* and *raja yoga.*

Arjuna is *nara*, the representative Man, and the removal of his despondency by Krishna, the Friend of man (*nara-sakha*) is applicable to *all* human situations everywhere and at all times. The secret is to *relate to* Arjuna, to feel through his heart and think through his mind. One could then feel the *presence* of the *nara-sakha,* man's best friend (*suhrid*)[6], and be happily guided by His teachings. Empathetically getting related to the *nara* is achieved through a special faculty that the *nara-sakha* bestows on the *nara*: this faculty is called *buddhi-yoga*[7] and Krishna Himself says that through this faculty, the *nara* reaches Him, intuits Him. This *buddhi-yoga* is the key to unlocking the treasure house of spiritual wisdom Krishna offers through the Gita for the emancipation of man.

2. The Arjuna Syndrome

The malady that was plaguing Arjuna, which we may call the 'Arjuna Syndrome' is a common, universal disease among all humankind. It is breaking out as an epidemic in modern times. This is why the remedy that Krishna prescribes to alleviate and eradicate this universal disease is of supreme importance to the modern man. In the Hindu philosophical and theological parlance, God is described as *bhava-roga vaidya*, the Great Physician Who cures the disease of worldliness which has afflicted man since birth. This 'congenital' disease of all humankind is very much akin to the concept of 'original sin' of the Christian theology. Just like the 'Big Shepherd' as Jesus the Christ is described, the 'Big Physician', Krishna, saves humankind from the unending cycle of birth and death by curing man of *bhava-roga*. Krishna Himself clearly describes His 'Saviour' role in the following verse: *teshamaham samuddhartha mrityu-samsara-sagarat.*[8] Arjuna was overwhelmed (*paraya-vishtah*) with great depression of mind masquerading as compassion.[9] Arjuna himself describes the symptoms of this disease in graphic terms as follows:

My limbs are giving way, my mouth is getting parched, my body is trembling, I am getting (unnatural) horripilations, my (powerful weapon) Gandiva is slipping away from my hand, my skin is also burning, I am unable to stand firm, my mind is reeling (with pain and sorrow).[10]

Krishna, the Great Physician, immediately diagnosed the disease as *kashmala* (loathsome stupidity), *klaibyam* (impotency, unmanliness), and *kshudram hridaya-daurbalyam* (base faint-heartedness)[11], tearing apart the mask of 'compassion' that Arjuna was wearing and exposed the camouflage. These viruses were responsible for the eruption of sorrow and delusion (*shoka* and *moha*) in Arjuna and the cure for these consisted in the direct and immediate (*sakshat, aparokshat*[12]) knowledge of the Immortal Self, the Atman.[13] This was the one and only remedy and the paths to achieve this are the *yogas*. The Arjuna syndrome is seen commonly in all human beings in varying measure, situations and circumstances. The supreme medicine (*paramoushadha*) for its cure is the nectar of the great Gita teaching (*Gitamritam mahat*)[14] prepared through distillation (*dugdham*) by the *bhava-vaidya* Krishna, the Great Physician.

The Syndrome Analyzed—its Origin, Symptoms and Cure

The origin of any disease is one of the most difficult things to detect. On occasions when the origin of any particular type of fever is untraceable, doctors often call it 'fever of unknown origin (FUO)'. *Bhava-roga*, known variously in different religions is the oldest disease known to humankind. *Bhava-roga* was considered an FUO till the saviours, avatars and prophets of various religions traced its origin to *tanha* or desire (Buddhism), *ajnana* or *avidya*, ignorance (Hinduism or in particular, Vedanta), original sin (Christianity), and so on. The divine potion or elixir (*amrita*) that cures this disease has also been described variously—*Jnana* (divine Knowledge), Grace of God issuing from self-surrender and supplication to God (*bhakti, sharanagati, prapatti*), Freedom from desire (*nirvasana*), and so on.

What makes the Gita, the ancient modern text of all time, a unique medicine of *bhava-roga* is that it contains all the ingredients mentioned above, fit to be consumed by peoples of all ages, young or old, male or female, monastic or lay. It is a divine brew, a unique blend, a modicum of different medicines mixed with such technical perfection that even a child could consume it and get cured. The Arjuna syndrome, analyzed and diagnosed by the master physician Sri Krishna, is the starting point of the preparation of this unique brew.

Shankarcharya's description of the Arjuna Syndrome in his *bhashya* on the Gita is simple and remarkable. It is not that Arjuna was unwilling to do his duty as the Army General when he came for war. Arjuna is a picture of courage and self-confidence before the war. In the verses 21 and 22 of the first chapter, he roars like an impatient lion waiting to pounce on its prey:

O Achyuta, please station my chariot between the two armies so that I may, on the eve of this battle, have a view of all those standing ready to fight. I want to see who are all those who need to be fought [and conquered] by me. Let me see all those who have assembled here desiring to favour the evil-minded son of Dhritarashtra in this battle.[15]

Such heroic words! Now, when does Arjuna's mood suddenly change? At what point of time and for what reasons did he become a victim of the Arjuna Syndrome? The Gita verses 28-46 of the first chapter, carefully scanned word for word, give us the clue. Arjuna saw in the huge armies *his own people* (*svajana*)—fathers, grandfathers, uncles, brothers, sons, grandsons, dear companions, fathers-in-law and bosom friends, and was overcome with great pity.[16] The key word here is *svajana*—people who are one's *very own*. Interestingly between verses 28 and 46, Arjuna repeats this word *svajana* four times. Arjuna's lament and depression are rooted in this feeling of *svajanatva*—*own-ness*. Arjuna's ego that strongly felt this attachment engendered by possessiveness—*own-ness* or *svajanatva*—plunged into the abyss of sorrow and delusion (*shoka* and *moha*). Acharya Shankara comments on this pathological behaviour of Arjuna by tracing it to the psychological roots that define the Arjuna Syndrome:

In this way, Arjuna displayed [feelings of] grief and delusion caused by ignorance and confused understanding (*bhranti-pratyaya*) and his attachment for and the sense of separation from dominion, the elders, sons, friends, kinsmen (*svajana*), relatives far and distant— all this arising from the notion that '*I* am theirs and they are *mine'*. It was when discriminative faculty [knowledge] was [thus] overpowered by grief and delusion that Arjuna, who had of himself [that is, naturally, spontaneously] been engaged in battle as warrior's duty (*kshatra dharma*), abstained from fighting and proposed to lead a mendicant's life, which was a duty alien to him (*para-dharma*).

Likewise, all creatures whose intelligence is swayed by evil influences like grief and delusion naturally abandon their proper duties and resort to those which are prohibited. Even if they are engaged in their own duties, their conduct in speech, thought and deed is prompted by a craving for reward and is egoistic. This being so, in their case *samsara* consisting of getting [the experiences of] the desirable and the undesirable births, joy and sorrow, owing to an accumulation of merit and demerit (*dharma* and *adharma*), goes on unceasingly. Grief and delusion are therefore the cause of *samsara*. And seeing that the cessation of grief and delusion is impossible except by Self-Knowledge (*atma-jnana*) preceded by renunciation of all *karma*, Bhagavan Vasudeva (Krishna), wishing to teach that Knowledge for the welfare [and blessing] of the whole world through the instrumentality of Arjuna, began His teaching with the verse (2.11) starting with *ashochyan*, etc.[17]

Thus the Arjuna Syndrome analyzed could be seen to have the following structure: Ignorance—> confused understanding (*bhranti-pratyaya*), the feeling of union and separation—> Feeling of *I* and *mine* (*ahamkara* and *mamakara*)—> sorrow and delusion (*shoka* and *moha*)—> discriminative faculty (knowledge) overpowered—>

abandoning *svadharma* and adopting *para-dharma*—> even in *svadharma* practice, craving for reward and egoism (*phalaabhisandhi* and *ahamkara*)—> accumulation of merit and demerit (*dharma* and *adharma*)—> *samsara* consisting of getting [the experiences of] the desirable and the undesirable births, joy and sorrow[18].

The remedy prescribed by Krishna is Self-Knowledge (*Atma-jnana*), which He teaches at the very beginning as the one sure medicine. In the second chapter, Krishna begins at the highest pitch from verse 11, expounding the very highest wisdom in the form of *ajata-vada* in verses 11 and 12.

This is the greatest relevance of the Bhagavad Gita for the modern world—stress-filled, strife-torn, panic-stricken and conflict-ridden modern world—that human beings, wherever placed, whatever professing, whenever stressed, should look inward into the inner Self (*antaratman*), delve deep within and intuit the Atman, thus deriving all strength, power, knowledge, wisdom, glory and joy from the Atman within which is the source of infinite Strength, infinite Power, infinite Knowledge, infinite Wisdom, infinite Glory and infinite Joy. One devotional practice leading to this Self-Realization is the famous prayer called *viryaprarthana* in the *Vajasaneya Samhita* (19.9):

Tejosi tejo mayi dhehi,
Viryamasi viryam mayi dhehi,
Balamasi balam mayi dhehi,
Ojosi ojo mayi dhehi, manyurasi manyum mayi dhehi,

Sahosi saho mayi dhehi.
Om Shantih, shantih, shantih

Thou art the embodiment of light, fill me with light. Thou art the embodiment of virility, grant virility unto me. Thou art the embodiment of strength, fill me with strength. Thou art the embodiment of Divine Wisdom and Power, grant Wisdom and Power unto me. Thou art the embodiment of indignation [that destroys evil], grant unto me the indignation [to fight against and destroy evil]. Thou art the embodiment of fortitude, fill me with fortitude. Om Peace, Peace, Peace.

References

1. *Bhagavad Gita,* Tr. by Swami Tapasyananda, Sri Ramakrishna Math, Chennai, 2.20
2. Shankara's commentary on the above Shloka
3. Shankara's Introduction to his *Gita Bhashya*
4. Shankara's commentary on verse 2.11
5. *Gita,* 10.10
6. *Gita,* 9.18. See also Gita, 5.29
7. *Gita,* 10.10
8. *Gita,* 12.7
9. *Gita,* 1.28
10. *Gita,* 1.29, 30
11. *Gita,* 2.2, 3
12. *Brihadaranyaka Upanishad,* 3.4.1
13. cf. reference 4 above
14. *Gita dhyanam*
15. *Gita,* 1.21, 22
16. *Gita,* 1.26-28
17. Shankara's commentary on verse 2.11 at the very beginning
18. *ibid.*

Chapter Twenty Four

Management Lessons from the Bhagavad Gita

B MAHADEVAN

Introduction

Modern management practices and theories were developed during the last 150 years, ever since the industrial organisations of the West began to get established. It is a popular belief that globally renowned corporations adopt best practices and manage their organisations very well. Against this backdrop consider the following statistics about how organisations are managed according to a study made in 1997. In his book, *The Living Company*,[1] Geus mentioned that most large and apparently successful corporations are profoundly unhealthy. According to the study, the average life expectancy of Fortune 500 companies was 40-50 years. One-third of companies listed in *Fortune 500* in 1970 vanished by 1983 and 40% of all newly created companies last less than 10 years. Such a high rate of infant mortality of organisations point to primitive stages of management that we are in today.

If we conduct a survey of managers of modern corporations we may infer that managers in these organisations experience stress, struggle for power and control, cynicism and a work environment that stifles rather than releases human imagination, energy and commitment. Many senior executives in companies today will agree to the fact that even after several years of management training, we have hardly made significant progress in addressing some of the vexing issues. These include, among others, dealing with people around us, understanding what motivates oneself, doing one's work in the most efficient manner, making leaders for 'high performance' organisation and creating organisations that can live long. On the other hand, we often notice that there is a disconnect between quality of life at large and work life. We also have serious issues about sustenance of firms and the environment in the long run.

Given this state of affairs, it indeed impels one to look for alternative paradigms for better management practices. The goal of this article is to stimulate thinking in the minds of management researchers and practitioners the enormous potential that ancient Indian literature has in suggesting better alternatives for management. We will explore some aspects of these from one of the sacred spiritual texts of ancient times, viz., *Srimad Bhagavad Gita*—a text for spiritual progress and self realization. Through this article we do not hazard to undermine the primary objective of this holy text nor do we advocate a self-study mode leading to some of the management lessons that one can derive. The sacred texts are to be studied first under the guidance of a competent and spiritually evolved guru. We may later contemplate on multitude of ideas that the texts offer after this initial training. We merely point to the endless list of benefits that the text offers to a management practitioner and illustrate it by culling out some ideas that one may find very useful to apply.

A Compendium of Management Lessons

In simple terms, management is a body of knowledge that enables entities to deal with a multitude of situations involving people, process and the environment, to ensure work is done efficiently to deliver goods and services useful to the society. Good management must result in greater satisfaction for all stake holders. If we carefully study the Gita, we infer that the central issue is all about doing work *(karma yoga)*, in the most efficient manner.

The cardinal principles of कर्मण्येव अधिकारः ['right to work'] and logical explanations leading to the proclamation that योगः कर्मसु कौशलम् ['yoga is skill in action'] laid out in chapter 2 of the Gita and the concept of यज्ञः ['sacrifice'] laid out in chapter 3 of the Gita amply demonstrate that the fundamental requirements of good management are contained in the Gita.

Gita offers a framework for stimulating high levels of motivation. Otherwise how can one explain the magic transformation that Arjuna has gone through from a state of fear, mental agony and hair raising experience (सीदन्ति मम गात्राणि, रोमहर्षश्च जायते) to one of waging a war against a battery of most credible and competent leaders in the society and eventually winning the war. A careful study of Gita from this perspective will lead us to important principles that managers must inherit to create rightful and long living organizations. Such a study will help us discover certain aspects of high performing organizations and may provide vital clues for alternative paradigms of management.

Alternative Paradigms from Gita

Notion of time

One of the pressing problems that modern organizations face arise out of their notion of time. Modern organizations suffer from extreme levels of 'short termism.' Software companies in India provide what is known as quarter-on-quarter guidance. In simple terms what it means is that they inform the market players and their stakeholders what can be expected of them in the next quarter. Invariably they project a positive outcome quarter after quarter and in order to meet these guidelines they engage in a variety of activities that create stress, and a short term oriented approach to managing business. This invariably brings negative results in the long run. For instance, to cut costs and show impressive results, it is customary in several organizations to slash training budgets and expenditure on Research and Development (R & D). Clearly, this will make the organisation less equipped for the future. Unfortunately, a series of short terms never makes a long term for any organization. While some have understood this aspect they have not been able to change the way they work and take decisions that are consistent with this requirement.

In the Bhagavad Gita, Sri Krishna's first lesson to Arjuna is to train his mind to the notion of time that is essentially long term (Chapter 2, Slokas 11-13). A good understanding of this helps managers to feel less pressurized of performance targets in the short run and instead develop some conviction to engage in activities and decisions that seek to create a balance between short term and long term. Change management becomes easier as they develop comfort in the fact that people come and go and good principles and ideas must remain and drive choices in organisations. They will also begin to realise (as it happened to Arjuna) that whenever they face complicated and apparently insurmountable problems, one way to broad-base the problem and search for acceptable solutions is to revisit the notion of time.

Performance Metrics and Assessment

The biggest constraint for modern management is the mindset towards performance metrics and assessment. Modern management practices approach this issue in the context of a world of duality. It works at two stages. In the first stage, the dual perspectives are first established. For example, all actions and outcomes are first classified using a framework of duality; good Vs bad, desirable Vs undesirable, performer Vs non-performer, belongs to my camp Vs opposite camp, positive Vs negative and so on. Based on these, expectations are set that pertain only to the positive aspects of this world of duality. At the second stage, the managers begin to develop a false notion that only good things are going to happen. In modern management practice, it is a bad thing to expect negative outcomes in this scheme of duality. Consequently, they develop no skills to expect negative outcomes, to understand why these happen and evolve no methods to face these. This is clearly unrealistic. In the absence of these, managers develop needless tension, experience stress in their work place, deal with their sub-ordinates in non-managerial and at times unprofessional ways and even carry these negative emotions and stress back home and spoil their family life as well.

One of the greatest contributions of the Bhagavad Gita is to develop a good understanding of the risks of living in this contrived world of duality and equipping the managers to rise above the plane of duality. Shri Krishna had devoted much time on this critical aspect of managing the world of duality. In chapter 2 verse 14 he urges Arjuna to learn to tolerate the ups and downs that characterizes the world of duality (तांस्तितिक्षस्व भारत). Later in chapter 2 verse 48 he proclaims that developing a sense of equanimity begets a composed and a complete personality (समत्वं योग उच्यते), which is a quintessential attribute for a leader/manager. In several chapters he revisits the notion of sense of equanimity and reminds Arjuna of the virtues of it[2]. Slokas 24 and 25 in chapter 14 provide in a nutshell all the important attributes pertaining to the world of duality that a leader/manager must possess to be successful in his/her work place. If managers can develop a sense of equanimity as indicated in the Gita, the quality of leadership will dramatically improve and so will the quality of management.

Work and Efficiency

Perhaps the most profound insight that the Bhagavad Gita offers to managers in modern corporations is the definition of work and efficiency. The definition of work presents itself as a paradoxical and often an unacceptable idea to an uninformed and casual reader of the Gita. It is important to note here that many verses in Chapter 2 and the following chapters of the Gita build[2] on this central idea and therefore it requires a good understanding in its totality. It requires deep contemplation and guidance of a guru to understand the concept. There are four aspects to the definition of work that Shri Krishna articulates:

(a) The doer has the right to work (**कर्मण्येव अधिकारः**)

(b) The doer has no control on outcomes/fruits of action (**मा फलेषु कदाचन**)

(c) The doer has no control on the root causes of the fruits of action (**मा कर्मफलहेतुर्भूः**)

(d) There is no choice to revel in inaction (**मा ते सङ्गोऽस्त्वकर्मणि**)

Explaining the fourth component of this definition is easier. On seeing the first three components, one may come to the conclusion that one may rather choose not to engage in work. Krishna has ruled out this option. In chapter 3 he also explains why the so called state of inaction does not exist in reality.

Managers will revolt at the idea of doing work but having no desire and/or control on outcomes. However, we do not realize that during our life time there have been several occasions when we indeed practiced this virtue. Is it not common for us that when we do good work, we tend to say 'I was lost in the work'? What do we mean by getting lost in the work? It merely means we ceased to look for outcomes and fruits of action during those moments of time. Simply extending this logic, we can easily conclude that मा फलेषु कदाचन concept simply enables us to get lost in the work for ever and enjoy doing it.

There are other important reasons for managers to actively consider practicing this idea. Some of them are as follows:

Too much of result orientation breeds a sense of fear and discomfort as several of us are wary of failures. Moreover, a desire to have control on fruits of action will invariably force us to focus on ends instead of means. Because of this, process orientation will give way for result orientation. Getting results somehow will dominate individual's behaviour. As we see nowadays, such behavioural patterns have the potential not only to destroy individuals but also institutions. Results and outcomes are a matter of future and work is a matter of present. Therefore with excessive result orientation one tends to escape the dynamics of 'present' and go after 'future'.

The Take Away

Based on these illustrations from the Gita, mangers can take away some simple yet powerful lessons.

Developing a good sense of neutrality is an important pre-requisite for discharging one's work very effectively. This may appear like a simple idea. However it requires deep contemplation of this idea and a conviction of its usefulness. Only out of such a conviction can one generate new behavioural patterns consistent with this idea. The current dominant paradigm 'I must enjoy fruits of action—else no work' will generate enormous amount of wasteful effort.

Embracing the overarching principle of karma yoga will have to be the alternative paradigm for improving the quality of management in organizations. If managers can take these two important lessons from the Gita, we can not only build an alternative paradigm of management but also succeed reasonably in the practice of management. That can be the greatest tribute we can offer to the sacred text of Bhagavad Gita. May Lord Krishna bestow his divine blessings on us to achieve this goal.

References

1. Geus, A. (1997), *The Living Company*, Harvard Business School Press
2. cf., *Gita,* 5.18-19, 6.7-9, 29, 32, 12.4, 13, 13.10, 39, 14.24-25

৪০ঞ্জ

Chapter Twenty Five

Living the Gita Way

PRAVRAJIKA BRAHMAPRANA

The Rajarishi Ideal

A retired Indian devotee, who was a manager in a computer technology company, once told me an interesting story. Years ago he had attended a conference on personnel management at which one of the top management consultants in America was invited to speak. The devotee was so impressed with his talk, that he later approached the speaker: 'How did you become such a renowned specialist in your field?'

'I have read and studied the Gita,' was his surprising response. He then added, 'All psychological training necessary for developing a strong leader is there.'

'What do you mean?' the devotee asked.

'The Gita teaches how to accept failure,' the consultant explained, 'develop patience, detachment, forgiveness, and love—traits essential for a strong leader.' The devotee listened, flabbergasted. Here was an American businessman revealing to him—an Indian devotee—the unprecedented and practical relevance of one of the most widely read scriptures in Hinduism—the Bhagavad Gita.

The consultant continued. 'After all,' he said, 'a successful manager must learn to cultivate the *rajarishi* attitude of royal wisdom that we find in the Gita—in other words, that of the kingly seer who owns everything, but not for his own personal benefit. That is the secret of leadership—selfless service.'

For our devotee such advice coming from the lips of a corporate consultant suddenly lifted the Gita off his library shelf and into his suit pocket. The Gita was no longer simply a scripture to worship with flowers and then forget. It had become an essential guidebook for daily life—and, in his case, corporate life.

If we want to become a seer in the workplace— whether blue collar or white collar, monastic or lay devotee—we have to harvest from the Bhagavad Gita Sri Krishna's kernels of practical wisdom. If one method does not germinate, another will, depending on our own temperament and preference.

A rajarishi like King Janka became free while living by doing his duty without anxiety. As a king, he had nothing to gain in the world and nothing to lose. But through his actions he showed his subjects how duty done in a disinterested spirit is holy. In this way he set an example, not only for his own subjects, but for spiritual seekers in ages to come.[1]

For those drawn to the path of Yoga, Sri Krishna stresses the method of action governed by the power of one's higher will. On this path, aspirants are challenged to gather all forces of the mind in order to re-channel their actions along the path to union with Brahman.[2]

But, if this method seems beyond our capacity, Sri Krishna encourages us to perform actions as worship of God, and thus bypass their karmic effects altogether. When we work as worship, we sanctify our actions and become free from the law of karma in a world otherwise imprisoned in its own activity.[3]

However, if we aspire to jnana yoga, the path of knowledge, then Sri Krishna exhorts us to *affirm* and *know* that we are not the doer. Vedanta teaches that it is simply the sense of ego that deludes us into thinking that we act. But when we assume the standpoint of jnana, we remain poised in the knowledge that it is only our prakriti that acts as our senses attach themselves to objects, and thus gunas attach themselves to other gunas. In this way, when we become the witness of our actions, we stand free from all effects of action.[4]

As we work and perfect any one of these methods— that of the rajarshi, the yogi, the bhakta, or the jnani—patience, detachment, forgiveness, and love naturally follow in its wake.

In the Bhagavad Gita, Sri Krishna's words have special power because they are not attributed to his individual personality, but rather to his transcendental aspect—the supreme Soul of all souls, whose Universal Form is described in the eleventh chapter of the Gita. Therefore, Gita teachings have a universal ring because Sri Krishna's words were uttered from the same transcendental plane of consciousness as that of other incarnations of God, such as Rama, Buddha, Christ, or Ramakrishna—namely, the Universal Self.

The Right Way of Studying Gita

The power of the Bhagavad Gita is also anchored in its antiquity. Its verses have been chanted and sung by royalty and commoners throughout the ages, and its message has crossed rivers, oceans, mountains, and national boundaries. The wisdom of the Gita applies to people of all temperaments, whether active or meditative, intellectual or devotional. Therefore, its teachings have sunk into the collective unconscious of a world civilization—not just that of a particular religious tradition, people, race, or nation. Along with its universality and power, the Gita is considered one of the three main scriptures of the Hindus—the Hindu Bible, as it were, which encapsulates the essence of the Upanishads. So in order to go straight to the source of Hinduism, we can simply turn to the Gita.

However, it is best not to be tricked by the simplicity of this spiritual classic. In fact, we might well ask: 'Is there a secret to studying the Bhagavad Gita?' Swami Turiyananda, disciple of Sri Ramakrishna, answered,

> Take one verse at a time, meditate on its meaning, and live the verse for a week at a time before going on to the next verse. In this way, the entire Gita is to be studied.[5]

This particular method was brought home to me when I used to make my annual pilgrimage to the Vedanta Society of Portland during Swami Aseshananda's lifetime. Every day devotees would gather to perform outdoor karma yoga on the Centre's premises and the swami, who was a disciple of Sarada Devi, would join them, watering the garden and sweeping the paths. But at those times Swami Aseshananda wore an almost formidable expression. I asked various devotees what the swami was thinking about when he was doing his gardening chores, but nobody knew. And nobody dared to ask. So one day, I queried: 'Maharaj, how do you occupy your mind when you are gardening?'

His answer rang a bell in my heart. 'I take a verse from the Gita,' he smiled, 'and meditate upon its meaning. That is how Swami Turiyananda used to instruct all of us to study the Gita.' The mental picture of this venerable old swami pushing his broom and watering the plants with the utmost concentration always generates the memory of this privy counsel—how to actively study the Gita so that it works its way into our conscious and subconscious mind and then into our nerves, muscle, flesh, and bones. No matter what we do, how we do it, where we are, or what time of the day it is, we can cultivate a habit of rigorously contemplating the meaning of a select Gita verse so that it becomes one with our system.

The Bhagavad Gita is a treasure chest for anyone who wishes to cultivate self-development. It teaches us how to work and worship, how to meditate, and how to die. It also teaches us how to eat and sleep, how to behave, and how to relax. 'Yoga is not for the man who overeats, or for him who fasts excessively. It is not for him who sleeps too much, or for the keeper of exaggerated vigils'(6.16). Gita further cautions:

Let a man be moderate in his eating and his recreation, moderately active, moderate in sleep and in wakefulness. He will find that yoga takes away all his unhappiness.[6]

By meditating on these verses, we can assimilate a middle path to stabilise and sustain our spiritual life, otherwise truncated or aborted by the physical and mental havoc of prideful excess. Sri Krishna guides us with the promise that if we can control an outer show of enthusiasm and carefully cultivate an inner routine of spiritual practice, we will ultimately attain supreme peace and joy.

Learning to Make Uncomfortable Choices

Aside from basic guidelines, the Bhagavad Gita also instructs us how to make uncomfortable choices. I still marvel at the timeless relevance of Sri Krishna's ancient words of wisdom to Arjuna, who trembled with fear as he faced his own kinsmen on the field of battle. 'What is this weakness?' Sri Krishna admonished, 'It is beneath you. . . Shake off this cowardice, Arjuna. Stand up.'[7] Perhaps it was this divine command that inspired a couple to boldly deal with their daughter's addiction. She had been arrested for a traffic violation while under the influence of alcohol—just one of many wayward incidents in her youth. But this time when the daughter called her parents to release her from jail, they refused. At first their decision seemed cruel, until I discovered that it was this act of 'tough love' that turned their daughter's life around. 'Dedicate all your actions to me,' Sri Krishna prompted Arjuna. 'Then go forward and fight.'[8] In this case, by doing what was outwardly heartless, yet righteous, the concerned parents forced their daughter to face the consequences of her own dangerous and self-destructive behaviour. Her night in jail jolted the daughter awake and prompted her to join Alcoholics Anonymous and gain control over her life.

The Bhagavad Gita is as bold in its teachings as it is relentless in pointing out subtle dangers and pitfalls. If we fear temptation, the Gita shows us how to reach for just the right arrow in our quiver. 'Thinking about sense-objects will attach you to sense objects,' Sri Krishna warns.

Grow attached, and you become addicted;
Thwart your addiction, it turns to anger;
Be angry, and you confuse your mind; you forget the lesson of experience;
Forget experience, you lose discrimination;
Lose discrimination, and you miss life's only purpose.[9]

Empowered, once we see how attachments can lead the mind downward, step by step like a runaway tennis ball, this singsong, rhythmic verse almost invites us to memorize it for safekeeping. Thus stored in our mental quiver, it becomes an ever-ready arrow in our bow the moment an object of enjoyment looms on our horizon.

Or if it is death we fear most, Sri Krishna takes us right into its jaws. Select verses from the second chapter of the Gita are often chanted at the deathbed of a loved one, such as:

Know this Atman, Unborn, undying,
Never ceasing, Never beginning,

Deathless, birthless, Unchanging forever.
How can It die, the death of the body?[10]

Throughout the second chapter, Sri Krishna's teachings on life and death, our real and apparent nature, are like fodder to chew and ruminate. As we meditate on death, we build our lives to prepare for death. In chapter seven, *The Way to Eternal Brahman*, Sri Krishna instructs: First, '...close all the doors of the senses.'

.... Hold the mind firmly within the shrine of the heart, and fix the life-force between the eyebrows. Then let him take refuge in steady concentration, uttering the sacred symbol OM and meditating upon me. Such a man reaches the highest goal.

Sri Krishna then divulges the secret of success:

When a yogi has meditated upon me unceasingly for many years, with an undistracted mind, I am easy of access to him, because he is always absorbed in me.[11]

Spiritual success is not a hit or miss affair. It comes to those who live the Gita way throughout life.

Some of the most well-worn passages that aspirants have memorized and practiced are those that follow Arjuna's famous question in the second chapter:

Krishna, how can one identify a man who is firmly established and absorbed in Brahman? In what manner does an illumined soul speak? How does he sit? How does he walk?[12]

The eighteen verses that follow, describing the inner and outer life of a seer of Knowledge, when memorized and contemplated, become like intimate friends that we can take to heart, imitate, and follow. Living one verse at a time, we actually feel as though we are living in the company of a seer. And by acting as though we are *already* illumined, we take a giant step forward on our own spiritual journey. In the Gita, this is called 'raising the self by the Self.'[13]

In so many ways, we can live the Gita way. When we do, we will feel a spiritual current growing within, our problems will gradually dissolve, and our spiritual life will become a blessing to ourselves and others.

References

1. *Bhagavad Gita*, 3.20-21
2. *ibid.*, 3.7
3. *ibid.*, 3.9
4. *ibid.*, 3.27-28
5. Pravrajika Anandaprana's Unpublished *Reminiscences of Swami Prabhavananda* (Vedanta Society Archives, 29)
6. Swami Prabhavananda and Christopher Isherwood,

trans., *The Song of God: Bhagavad Gita* (Hollywood: Vedanta Press, 1969), 6.17
7. *ibid.*, 2.3
8. *ibid.*, 3.30
9. *ibid.*, 2.62-63
10. *ibid.*, 2.20
11. *ibid.*, 8.12-14
12. *ibid.*, 2.54
13. *ibid.*, 6.5

૭૦૦૮૭

Chapter Twenty Six

Work As Worship
Guidelines from the Bhagavad Gita
SWAMI YUKTATMANANDA

Work is inevitable in life, be it physical, mental, or intellectual. We can never give up work, says the Bhagavad Gita, since even the bare maintenance of the body is impossible without work.[1] Work occupies most of our day, and we often long for relief from it. We look forward to the time when we won't need to work and can do what we like to do. But, paradoxically, when we get a break from work, we don't know how to make use of the time. Again, the Gita cautions us that if out of conceit we resolve not to work, the resolve will be in vain, since our nature will compel us to work.[2] So work we must, but the challenge is how not to be frustrated by work, but find fulfilment in it.

Though we feel trapped by work, our own mind is responsible for our feeling bound or free. In Sri Ramakrishna's words,

Bondage is of the mind, and freedom is also of the mind. A man is free if he constantly thinks: 'I am a free soul. How can I be bound, whether I live in the world or in the forest? I am a child of God, the King of Kings. Who can bind me?'[3]

So the motive behind work, and how we do it are more important than the nature of the work itself.

What Impels us to Work?

'The Infinite is bliss; there is no bliss in anything finite,' declares the *Chandogya Upanishad*.[4] The Infinite refers to our true, divine nature. Vedanta teaches us that we are not just body-minds, but are essentially the divine Self. This divine Self is called the Atman. This eternal Self is the source of infinite Knowledge and infinite Bliss. But Self-knowledge remains latent in most of us: we are unaware that we ourselves are the source of eternal Bliss. Ignorance makes us identify with our body and mind, and we imagine that we are limited beings. The world occupies our whole being, and we desire happiness and fulfilment from finite things. Actions prompted by desire only further our ignorance. It is a self-perpetuating chain of ignorance-desire- action. As long as we are ensnared by this chain, our work will bring us only frustration and bondage.

The Gita teaches us how to break this chain and realize the Atman—our true nature. It shows us how to work without desire, and how to convert work into a tool for attaining freedom from the bondage of the body, mind, and senses.

What Causes Desires?

Desires arise from samskaras, or impressions. Every action and thought leaves an impression on our mind. This impression deepens with every repetition of the action or thought. Each one of us is a huge bundle of good and bad impressions accumulated over many lives. Swami Vivekananda defines character as the sum total of these impressions.[5] These impressions account for what we are at any moment, how we work, and how we react to situations. We can escape from the influence of bad impressions by increasing our stock of good impressions with good thoughts and actions. Good character is preferable to bad character, but just being good is not the ideal. If someone is bad in spite of himself because of the power of bad impressions, then someone else is good in spite of himself because of the power of good impressions. Both good and bad are chains that bind us; we need to be free from both. Says Swami Vivekananda:

> Good is near Truth, but is not yet Truth. After learning not to be disturbed by evil, we have to learn not to be made happy by good. We must find that we are beyond both evil and good. . . . Evil is the iron chain, good is the gold one; both are chains. Be free, and know once for all that there is no chain for you. Lay hold of the golden chain to loosen the hold of the iron one, then throw both away.[6]

The Gita way is to work without gaining good or bad impressions.

'To Work, Alone, You Have the Right. . .'

We shall consider the oft-quoted teaching from the Gita:

> To work, alone, you have the right, not to its fruit. Never let the fruit of work be your motive for work, but don't be attached to inaction either.[7]

Then again there is the saying, 'Even a fool doesn't embark on an enterprise without a purpose.' But there is no contradiction between the two. Every work leads to a definite result. The Gita teaches us not to be attached to the result or be anxious about it *while doing the work*. Hankering after the result, or worrying about achieving it, will only dissipate our mental energy; it will certainly not help us to do the work better. The Gita teaches us how to work calmly, free from restlessness and anxiety. Swami Vivekananda describes the effect of calmness:

> The calmer we are, the better for us, and the more the amount of work at hand we can do. When we let loose our feelings, we waste so much energy, shatter our nerves, disturb our minds, and accomplish very little work. The energy which ought to have gone out as work is spent as mere feeling, which counts for nothing. It is only when the mind is very calm and collected that the whole of its energy is spent in doing good work.[8]

We need to be careful never to let the end justify the means. Questionable means will leave a bad impression on the mind, which will be difficult to erase. Swami Vivekananda puts this in the right perspective:

> Proper attention to the finishing, strengthening, of the means is what we need. With the means all right, the end must come....*Once the ideal is chosen and the means determined, we may almost let go the ideal, because we are sure it will be there, when the means are perfected*. When the cause is there, there is no more difficulty about the effect, the effect is bound to come. If we take care of the cause,

the effect will take care of itself. The realization of the
ideal is the effect. The means are the cause: attention to
the means, therefore, is the great secret of life.[9] [*Emphasis
added*]

Work as Worship

The Gita shows us how to be unaffected by the
good and evil effects of work:

Whatever you do, whatever you eat, whatever you offer
in sacrifice, whatever you give away, and whatever you
practise in the form of austerities, do it as an offering to
Me. Thus shall you be free from the bondage of actions,
which bear good or evil results. With your mind firmly
set on the yoga of renunciation, you shall become free
and come to Me.[10]

Offering actions and their results to God strengthens
our will and awakens our sense of discrimination: we
scrutinize our work carefully and see if it is worthy of
being offered to God. Work done with a such a mindset
gradually turns into worship, and such worship leads us
to perfection, promises the Lord in the Gita:

From whom have originated all beings, and by whom
the whole universe is pervaded—by worshipping Him
by his own duty man attains perfection.[11]

We learn more about doing work as worship from
Swami Vivekananda:

When you are doing any work, do not think of anything
beyond. Do it as worship, as the highest worship, and
devote your whole life to it for the time being.[12]

When we do not think of anything beyond the work at hand, and devote our whole life to it for the time being, we become calm, more focussed, and less selfish. Besides improving the quality of work, a worshipful attitude lessens our egotistic impulses towards work, increases our devotion to God, and leads us to perfection.

The Journey from *tamas* to *sattva*

In the last part of verse 2.47 of the Gita, Sri Krishna sounds a word of caution against inactivity: 'Don't be attached to inaction either.' Sattva, rajas, and tamas constitute Prakriti, or nature, and inhere in our body and mind in varying proportions. Tamas manifests as inertia, sleep, laziness, and carelessness; rajas as passionate activity; and sattva as equanimity and calmness in the midst of activity. Often the dullness of tamas gets mistaken for the calmness of sattva. This misperception will make us all the more ignorant of our divine nature. Work done as spiritual discipline involves the journey from tamas to sattva, which necessarily has to pass through rajas. There is no straight jump from tamas to sattva. Intense activity helps us get rid of inertia and carelessness. Established in rajas, we face the next challenge: how are we to ascend to sattva?

Calmness in the Midst of Activity

The qualities of a sattvic worker described in the Gita (18.26) can serve as guidelines in our journey from rajas to sattva.

1. Freedom from self-conceit and attachment to the fruits of action: Since God is the Prime Mover of all activities,[13] it is unwise to appropriate to ourself the results of our actions. A sattvic worker mentally offers his actions and their outcome to God. Says Swami Vivekananda:

> Do you ask anything from your children in return for what you have given them? It is your duty to work for them, and there the matter ends. In whatever you do for a particular person, a city, or a state, assume the same attitude towards it as you have towards your children—expect nothing in return. If you can invariably take the position of a giver, in which everything given by you is a free offering to the world, without any thought of return, then will your work bring you no attachment. Attachment comes only where we expect a return.[14]

2. Fortitude, and enthusiasm for work: Fortitude, or *dhriti,* is an attribute of buddhi, the seat of discrimination, decision-making, and will-power. A sattvic worker is not discouraged by obstacles in the path of work, but steadfastly pursues the chosen means to the end. Though he is detached from the outcome of an action, he is no less enthusiastic about his work. With his mind under control, adverse circumstances do not dampen his enthusiasm for work.

3. Even-mindedness in success and failure: Our natural tendency is to seek pleasure and avoid misery, celebrate good and be depressed by pain. Besides helping us retain sound judgement, even-mindedness improves the quality of our work. This even-mindedness, which Sri Krishna defines as yoga,[15] is the effect of offering the fruits of actions to God.

The work ethic of the Bhagavad Gita teaches us to do work as worship, free from egotism and attachment to the results of work, and be even-minded in success and failure. Such a worshipful attitude transforms work into yoga, detaches our will from desires, uncovers our true Self, and leads us to eternal peace and supreme Bliss.

References

1. *Bhagavad Gita*, 3.5, 8.

2. *ibid.*, 18.59.

3. M., *The Gospel of Sri Ramakrishna,* trans. Swami Nikhilananda, Sri Ramakrishna Math, Chennai, 1985, p. 138.

4. *Chandogya Upanishad*, 7.23.1.

5. *The Complete Works of Swami Vivekananda*, 9 vols. (Calcutta: Advaita Ashrama, 1-8, 1989; 9, 1997), vol. 2: 255.

6. *CW*, 7: 4-5.

7. *Gita*, 2.47.

8. *CW*, 2: 293.

9. *ibid.*, 2.1.

10. *Gita*, 9.27-8.

11. *ibid.*, 18.46.

12. *CW*, 1.71.

13. *Gita*, 15.4.

14. *CW*, 1.59.

15. *Gita*, 2.48.

৪০৬৪

Chapter Twenty Seven

Teachers as Mentors— Lessons from Gita

M SIVARAMKRISHNA

The Teacher Ideal

Almost every month, I interact with a group of teachers (mostly higher secondary level) drawn from several states. These sessions focus on values in education and life-skills for personality development. To know their attitude to teaching, I ask questions like:

a) Do you like—if not love—your profession?

b) Do you like the subject you teach?

c) How do you deal with the so-called weak students?

d) Do you focus on areas 'outside' the syllabus, such as personality development and values?

By and large, they are positive to the teaching of life-skills. But one question crops up always: 'how do we teach them?' One cannot generalise, but some hints can be drawn on how the Gita can help the teachers in this matter.

To begin with, the teacher should be a *mentor*—'an experienced person who *advises* and *helps* somebody with less experience, over a period of time' (*Oxford Advanced Learners' Dictionary*). S/he should be a role-model who sets high but achievable standards for work and behaviour of students without being authoritarian, shedding the 'I know more than you do' fixation. And, above all, be open to learn, remaining a student, like an *avadhuta*—the ever-eager-to-learn-ascetic mentioned in the *Bhagavatam*—and alert to every experience. In this perspective, who could be an ideal example than Sri Krishna who was the model of friend, philosopher and guide to Arjuna?

Arjuna-Krishna dialogue, as enshrined in the Gita, is the best way to understand it. But how does the Gita help us? Sri Ramakrishna said: 'eliminate "the head and tail", that is, emphasise the essentials.'[1] This process has to reckon with the existing situations. Sri Ramakrishna, the Great Master himself, described it: 'The situation is very difficult. There is so much confusion in the world' (*Gospel*, p.246). The contexts of violence and war are now both global and local. There are also cultural convulsions of a speed and range that are nearly uncontrollable. The teacher-student relations are purely functional, all *learning oriented to earning*. In such a context, can a teacher hope to reach each student, with the pragmatics of the Gita?

Teacher – Student Dialogue

Sri Krishna's core teaching can *contain* the chaos and offer alongside, as its subversion, a map for the creative unfoldment of the students. The structure of the

Gita itself is that map: the song is a *dialogue* which dramatizes the basic concerns of a confused ward. It is also an *intimate*, informal dialogue, where the seeker can lay bare every doubt of his. In offering strategies of fighting (phobias and traumas), it also *shows* how all strategies are rooted in oneself. The most enduring help is in one's mind—one's activated, holistic consciousness (the code word being *yoga*). For the teacher, the Gita unfolds the possibility of a dialogue, drawing insights from both sides, knowing the grey areas, and tapping strength and wisdom from the perennial springs of one's infinite potential.

'Whatever a great man does,' says Sri Krishna, 'the same is done by others as well. He sets up a standard and it is followed by the world.' (Gita, 3.21.)[2] This is the crux of awareness that a teacher ought to achieve in his/her own setting and background. They show tremendous energy in following a model when their *emotions* are drawn to.

Let us take fear and faith as the basic contours of the teacher and students in the context of the Gita. What are the fears of the student (at various levels with different degrees of intensity)? An effective corollary here would be the teachers' introspection about his/her *own* experience as a student of such fears. Did s/he succeed in overcoming them and how? Do they work for his/her students now? As J. Krishnamurthi says: 'Parents and teachers who recognize the psychological processes which build up fear and sorrow should be able to help the young to observe and understand their own conflicts and fears.'[3]

Some Fears of Students

Students may fear the teacher himself or herself; of parents who may have expectations which arise from privileging some professions as concretions of a successful life—defined in terms of plenty of money and pleasure-filled matrimony. There are, of course, fears from fellow students, some of them held up as models for mostly counterproductive comparison.

Can the teachers help the student? Yes, if the experience of fear and overcoming it are both shown as natural. Arjuna—a great hero in all respects, succumbing to cowardice when courage is needed—shows the indissoluble link between strength and weakness. Arjuna's nerve failed for a positive reason: affection for kinsmen. But in this context it was misplaced. Elsewhere fear is positive: fear of not performing one's *dharma*, fear of deviation from ethical norms—so long as they don't breed guilt. And the crisis itself is a context to actualise the already available creative action. Interestingly Gita or the Song of the Lord emerges in the context of the distressing sorrow of his beloved disciple who contemplates running away from the realities of life. Indeed, difficulties are a fertile ground for developing strength and maturity. One may also recall here how *The Gospel of Sri Ramakrishna* originated in the agony (*vishada*) of the scholarly-teacher Mahendranath Gupta, the chronicler of the *Gospel*, who was so troubled by events in his life that he had even contemplated suicide. Sri Ramakrishna, the modern Gitacharya, rescued him through his gentle chidings and counseling. The message of the Gita, thus, continues in a new form.

It is interesting that Sri Krishna *smilingly* exhorts: 'Give up this cowardice' (II.3). The non-verbal gesture of a smile is powerful. This is not a derisive kind of smile. It is one of mutual trust suggesting that Krishna can be relied upon. It requires surrender from the seeker and a good deal of love from the teacher. Can there be a more sorrowful life than that of Sri Krishna? And yet is there a more lovable incarnation and an exemplary teacher, ever smiling at tears, facing every crisis with courage and conviction? And his worldly wisdom is superb. This wisdom can be seen as resting on *four* integral life-skills:

❖ *Interconnectivity and interdependence;*

❖ *Equality that is horizontal and functional variations which are vertical;*

❖ *Comparisons and contrasts as natural tools for excellence and not for elimination;*

❖ *Finally, blending all these with, balance as the key for the journey into joy.*

In terms of psychological patterns of behaviour they correspond, by and large, to the four pillars of the Gita:

❖ Desirelessness *(nishkama),*

❖ Detachment *(anasaktata),*

❖ Steadfast wisdom *(sthithaprajna)* and

❖ Total surrender*(prapatti)*.

But the important question is: how do we achieve the strength, where do we seek, the energy to actualise them? How do we do that, especially in moments of acute crisis?

The Gita is remarkable in suggesting a way out, without recourse to a presiding deity in heaven: 'Raise yourself by yourself, don't let yourself down, for you alone are your own friend and you alone are your enemy.' *(ibid*, VI. 5) This is one of the most effective and *natural* of all strategies the Gita identifies. Absorbed by the mentor, it can easily communicate itself to the youngster. It can also be paraphrased: 'Your self' can direct 'your mind.' We cannot blame fate; we cannot rebel against a vengeful God. The seeds of all destinies, all rebellions are innate. No wonder, Sri Krishna affirms: 'He who has conquered himself is a friend of himself; but he who has not conquered himself is hostile to himself as a foe' *(ibid*, 6.6). 'Mind is all,' declares Sri Ramakrishna.

What is the nature of the mind? It is 'mighty enemy,' says Sri Krishna, 'comes in the guise of desire who is hard to overcome.' *(ibid,* III. 43) Behind desire is an uncontrolled mind. Arjuna, who, in one context, could focus his mind only on the reflected eye of a target he has to shoot, in another, voices his fickle nature and expresses, thereby, a *universal* phenomenon: '. . . the mind is restless, Krishna, it is violent, powerful and obstinate. To control it is as difficult, it seems to me, as to control the air.' *(ibid*, VI. 34).

Mind is desire-oriented and desires have a wide range. A choice ought to be made. For the majority it is certainly a high-salaried job. In a consumer-based economy, this is a compelling choice. The economist Tim Harford points out, that 'rational people... will bear in mind not just the *costs* and *benefits* of their choices' but the overall '*constraints* upon them.' Above all, they will 'consider the future consequences'[4] which arise from unresolved stress and tension inevitably leading to health hazards. What is earned now may, in all likelihood, be spent on recovering the health lost in earning later. Can the teacher effectively offer a counter weight for this?

The Gita also gives to the teacher an insight into natural, *horizontal equality* and *job-wise, hierarchically vertical* functioning. Each has its role unique to itself (*svadharma* and *svabhava* equation). All students get the same lesson but performance-wise, they are hierarchical. Implicit here is the tendency to compare and virtually destroy the individual talent of a child. Can we, in spite of our teaching, refrain from tampering with the faith of the child in his/her innate creativity, refusing to slot him or her into a coveted but highly unsuitable niche? Can the innate quality of detachment and joy be maintained by the right understanding of desire?

'Hierarchy' or functional privileging is suggested in the chapter eleven wherein Sri Krishna shows his cosmic form. He singles out Arjuna as the one, among Pandavas, with whom he identifies himself (*ibid*, 10.37). This is an extraordinary assertion of the basic and potential identity between the teacher and his disciple. Hence, two important insights are here available for us. Unless there is genuine empathy between the teacher and the student, there is hardly any teaching. A 'good' teacher will progressively make himself *dispensable*. No fence is needed when the plant grows up.

'Steadfast wisdom' (*sthithaprajna*), for our context, is the nurturing in our students, what Professor Gayatri Chakravorthy Spivak, in her original analysis of the Gita describes as, 'how to act *knowingly* but without desire.'[6] If one can paraphrase this, it could mean knowing that we are *free* to the extent we can conceive, plan and execute an action. All the three are motivated by *our* expectations regarding the result. *Result is implicit in the action* and action is perfected by knowledge of factors which impel it. A student can be a little bit relaxed, even inattentive, in a classroom lecture. But at the time of taking a crucial, competitive test, during that period, does s/he *think* of the result? After the test also, the result may or may not be identical with what s/he expects. Therefore, *acting* for a desired result, but *knowing* that what one desires may often be denied is sound psychology. Desire and detachment are thus interlinked.

Conclusion

Surrender in this sense would mean *natural joyous acceptance of what is*. Surrender in psychological terms is neither pessimistic nor optimistic but *realistic*. In short, it is freedom from fantasies about desired results often undesirable. This is a combination of *skill in action* and *samesightedness towards its results* which ties in with the realities of life. In this sense it is 'tagi', Sri Ramakrishna's reversed recovery of the essence of the Gita. Tyaga is taming all excesses. That requires courage and as Andre Comte-Spoonville says, 'All the virtues are interdependent and they all depend on courage.'[7]

Krishna's clarion call is just that.

References

1. Swami Nikhilananda, tr; *The Gospel of Sri Ramakrishna*, Ramakrishna – Vivekananda Center, New York. 1992; p.685. Further references are given in the essay itself.

2. D.S. Sarma, (tr), *The Bhagavad Gita* The Chennai Law Journal Office, Chennai. 1952. Further references are given in the essay itself. I found this translation very readable.

3. J. Krishnamurti, *Education and The Significance of Life*: Harper & Brothers, New York, 1953; p.11.

4. Tim Harford, *The Logic of Life : Uncovering the New Economics of Everything* (emphasis added) Little, Brown; New York; 2008; p. 8.

5. Sri Ram, *Journey into Joy*; Letters for Spiritual Seekers. Sterling Publishers Private Ltd; Delhi, 2008, p.174.

6. Gayatri Chakravorty Spivak, *A Critique of Postcolonial Reason*; Seagull; Calcutta: 1999, p. 51.

7. Andre Comte-Spoonville, *A Short Treatise on the Great Virtues: The Uses of Philosophy in Everyday Life*: William Heinemann, London; 2002, p. 59.

৩০০৪

Chapter Twenty Eight

Countering Stress and Lack of Motivation
Gita's Advice to the Modern Youth
SWAMI BODHAMAYANANDA

Gita's Ageless Relevance

There is a wrong notion among the youth that the scriptures such as the Bhagavad Gita are meant for old and retired people and for gaining a little 'peace of mind'. And some feel that it is not possible to apply the profound teachings in today's context and are difficult to comprehend. By a sincere and serious study of the Gita, however, such misnomers and false perceptions can surely be erased from the mind. The youth should keep in mind that the Gita is a scripture of the mankind. Arjuna, the recipient of Sri Krishna's teachings, represents the modern man. Like the modern man, Arjuna is confused by the chaotic situations of life and the fear of failure. Sri Krishna teaches Arjuna to face the battle of life.

Solving the Problems

Gita addresses the modern youth's problems squarely and plainly—the issues such as how to achieve success in life, controlling one's passions, learning to be an effective leader, decision-making and so on. While

270

many modern schools of thought deal with these problems at material, external and peripheral levels, the Bhagavad Gita goes to the root of the problem—setting right our world-view and the resultant thinking. Once our thoughts change, there is a visible change in the quality of our actions, as also our response to their result. Gita's teachings help us to change from within.

There are numerous ways in which these teachings can be applied in the context of modern youth. Let us, however, focus on two very vital areas—overcoming stress and lack of motivation or focus.

1. Overcoming Stress

Stress is the reaction to a demanding situation and it can occur at two levels—physical and psychological.

❖ Physical stress is caused by physical causes such as accidents, burns, infections and so on. It is a reaction of the body to face the strain and trauma caused by diverse factors.

❖ Psychological stress, on the other hand, is a reaction to mental situations such as fear, anxiety, tension, anger, emotional conflicts and so on. These situations may be of just a short period but may affect a person for long time leaving deep impressions on his subconscious mind.

Restlessness is a common problem of mind. A youth, who has to prove his ability and rise up to the expectations of society, peers and others, undergoes a taxing time and it results in accumulation of stress. With many things to do, he lives a fast life and then there is no time for him to take stock of things. The modern youth may be thinking and working faster than what his counterparts did earlier twenty years ago, but, then, at what cost? Psychological breakdown and negative thinking. Added to this is the scourge of violence and restlessness.

Gita provides valuable guidelines to overcome stress and restlessness. The battle-field of Kurukshetra, the scene in which Gita was delivered, underlines a point with regard to its relevance in overcoming stress. Just consider this. Even after the war drums have been sounded, the conchs and the trumpets blown, Arjuna is not able to convince himself of the utility of the war and the purpose of killing his own cousins, teachers and others in the impending war. He is horrified and becomes mentally nervous when he thinks about the disastrous consequences of war. Arjuna, having lost his inner steadiness, trembling with fear and confused, is unable to even lift his bow and arrow and sinks into depression.

This situation has aptly been named as *vishada* [depression] of Arjuna. The strong and mighty stature of Arjuna can be found in many modern youth's life as well. At the time when they are supposed to carry out their responsibilities, a little failure or a small obstacle here and there, makes them feel weak and totally helpless. Some of them even think of running away from life itself. But what does Sri Krishna advise Arjuna in this context? He admonishes Arjuna and is pained at his behaviour. He nudges Arjuna thus:

Whence, O Arjuna, has this weakness, neither entertained by honourable men, nor conducive to (the attainment of) heaven, and leading to ill-fame, come on you at this crisis? Yield not to unmanliness, O Partha, it is not worthy of you; shake off this mean faint-heartedness, arise, O scorcher of foes.[1]

Every youth should daily repeat the essence of these two verses. And their essence is—face life; do not run away from it. Running away from the challenges of life does not solve them. It only weakens the mind and makes it more incapable to face them in future. One should think over it deeply and try to focus on one's strength instead of weakness. One can quietly sit in one's room or in any silent place and meditate on the meaning of these verses. He should allow the message to soak into his subconscious mind, which is the storehouse of all our inner motives—positive and negative. This practice, if done regularly, will take away a good deal of stress and weakness of mind. In fact, stress itself is a kind of tremendous energy, which, when not channelled, can cause considerable damage to a person's life.

Further, this idea should be brought into our daily life. We should keep this attitude of facing life, and not avoiding it, always burning in our mind.

2. Overcoming Lack of Motivation

How to remain motivated, despite all hurdles, is a major issue in life. We need a constant drive and enthusiasm. This means we have to handle our negative thoughts and anxiety about the future. Everyone faces doubt and depression in life sometime or the other. What determines success is our ability to overcome these and keep moving forward.

The key to self-motivation is to understand our thoughts and how to handle them. By learning how to nurture positive thoughts, we learn the art of remaining focused. This means being proactive and not reactive.

When Krishna chides Arjuna for his unbecoming behaviour, Arjuna's response is quite educative. He understands how he has been misguided by wrong thoughts and pleads:

I ask you—tell me that which is definitely good for me. I am your disciple; teach me who have taken refuge in You.[2]

In fact, this is where the real teachings of the Bhagavad Gita commence—when Arjuna is ready to learn. He is willing to perform his duties as a kshatriya.

The second chapter of the Gita is rightly called as the *Yoga of Knowledge*. Here Sri Krishna teaches Arjuna about the Atman or the Indwelling Self which is deathless, birthless, pure and the ever changeless. This means temporary issues of life should not take away our motivation and interest. We should think of the eternal and inexhaustible source of strength present in each one of us. Recalling this eternal nature of every human being, Swami Vivekananda said:

If the fisherman thinks that he is the Spirit, he will be a better fisherman; if the student thinks he is the Spirit, he will be a better student. If the lawyer thinks that he is the Spirit, he will be a better lawyer.[3]

The Gita further says that we should learn to 'work with dexterity' and 'to take refuge in *Buddhi* or the higher intellect'. Many youth work only through raw emotions. They do not know how to use their power of discrimination. To work with dexterity means not becoming attached to the fruits of action but enjoying the joy of working without any self-defeating thoughts. As a curio display put it: No matter how bad a situation is, you can make it worse by resorting to negative thoughts.

Man is great and superior to animals only because of his faculty of discrimination. Whenever a man falls or suffers, it is due to loss of this power of discrimination. Sri Krishna advices that one should not be swept away by problems and obstacles which are after all temporary and passing in nature. Through proper self-control, one can invoke one's hidden potential which is the source of all success and consolation. One should always strengthen oneself. Says Swami Vivekananda, 'Every idea that strengthens you must be taken up and every thought that weakens you must be rejected.'[4]

Again, Sri Krishna's message to the modern youth is that one should develop oneself *by* oneself. Let him not wait for external help but derive strength from his inner core. He says,

Man must lift himself by himself; and having lifted himself, let him not allow himself to be dragged down.

For this, self alone is your friend, and indeed, this self alone is your enemy.[5]

Conclusion

Gita contains enough insight to help a young, struggling person to develop into a wise and responsible personality. What is needed is sincerity and faith. He would be willing to change, willing to undergo the training required to make him a better person. He must not focus on what he does not have but what he *has*. Let him count his blessings and as Sri Krishna says:

Therefore, at all times constantly remember Me and fight. With mind and intellect dedicated to Me, you shall, without a doubt, attain to Me alone.[6]

And that 'Me', the God Himself, is present in us all. Where is the cause for stress and hopelessness? Let every youth try to renew his life by thinking Gita's message of faith and inherent strength.

ॐ

Chapter Twenty Nine

Bhagavad Gita—Song of Culture

K SUBRAHMANYAM

The Meaning of Culture

The Bhagavad Gita is a celestial song, a divine song of true human culture. When a person is pure and inwardly polished and is placed lovingly at the disposal of the needy, he is said to be truly cultured. Sri Krishna, himself a personality of great culture has sung this song of eternal culture to elevate mankind to the pinnacle of culture.

Oils and metals are available in the bowels of earth. But they are to be drilled, processed and purified before they are made usable. So also, man to be of use has to undergo the process of purification. The rawness, then, gives rise to refinement at every level. It is through the cultural processing that we evolve to blossom as a fragrant flower. This is how the Bhagavad Gita can be viewed, as both the means and goal of human evolution. In other words, man becomes a better human through the study of the Gita.

Rishis are researchers and seers. They have been able to see beyond and unravel the Truth hidden to the un-evolved perceptions. Only a purified vision is able to discover the Vedic wisdom. That wisdom, the fruit of aeons of cultural evolution, is preserved and placed before mankind in the sacred Upanishads. The collective consciousness, thus accumulated in the Upanishadic lore, is sweetly and systematically simplified for our use as the song of culture in the form of Bhagavad Gita.

This song of culture has many a soft petal. They are: 1. Physical Culture 2. Work Culture 3. Emotional Culture 4. Intellectual Culture 5. Self or Spiritual culture.

Physical Culture

Body is an essential vehicle to transport us to higher levels of evolution. It is also a temple housing the all-pervading soul or God. Therefore, it is to be kept clean and pure. It is but the entire cosmos in microcosm. The five elements—earth, water, fire, air and space—are very much available both in the macrocosm (universe) and in the individual body of every human being (microcosm). Their disciplined functioning is but dharma.

Also, the individual body has to work in tune with the cosmic body. All beings have a responsibility to practise dharma, so that all can live in peace. Yoga it is, when there is harmony at all levels and Bhagavad Gita emphasises Yoga throughout. At the physical level, a disciplined life along with adherence to a principle is a sign of culture. A cultured person does not disturb nature. Methodical life of routine is the mark of a cultured person.

Dharma is a self-imposed discipline for a harmonious coexistence of all. People established or settled (Asana) in life with discipline (Yama) and principle

(Niyama) are of culture. They lead a regulated life (Pranayama) of self-confidence, self-reliance and self-dedication. It is proper pranayama, when we breathe out more and breathe in less. It is a cultured life of pranayama and yoga, when we take less from society and contribute more for its well-being. Yama, Niyama, Asana and Pranayama of Raja Yoga are but the essential aspects of physical culture leading to individual and social health.

Yama denotes discipline—discipline of space, discipline of time and discipline of procedure. If we are capable of allotting a place to every object and cultivate the habit of keeping things in their respective places, we will be free from tensions and anxieties. We need not have to search for the misplaced articles. Time and energy are thus not only saved, but they will be very much in surplus to be utilised for higher and nobler pursuits. When every item in the house is neat and tidy, house will be a heaven, a veritable temple. Similarly, civic sense and its observance in society will make our lives pleasant and harmonious.

The second dimension of discipline pertains to time. Set apart a time for every action and strictly abide by the time schedule! There will, then, be no scope for worry. Not only do we plan our day's routine, but we can streamline our lives as well. 'Play while you play and work while you work' is the time-tested proverb. Let not the 'office' make the home sour. Let not the houses distract our attention in the work place. Brahmacharya (celibacy and tutelage), Grihastha (marital life and money making manhood), Vanaprastha (retirement and self-analysis) and Sannyasa (life of detachment and absolute self-dedication) are the time-schedule of planned lives to unfold the divinity.

The third and final aspect of discipline is 'procedure'. There is an established methodology for every worthwhile human activity. Even animals have a set track for their lives. Human beings cannot afford to revert to lead a life of indiscriminate indulgence. As a human being one has to exercise restraint over basal instincts and try to overcome as much as is within one's capacity.

The efforts of Sri Krishna in the Gita are entirely to highlight the need for discipline—from the physical to the spiritual. Unless the body with all its senses is kept under strict control, nothing can be achieved. Patanjali, in the footprints of the Lord, lays stress on yama and niyama, asana and pranayama as the primary physical requirements for any noble pursuit. The most basic discipline prescribed to everybody consists of regulated diet and sleep. In the chapter titled *Shraddha Traya Vibhaga Yoga*, Sri Krishna describes the nature of food needed for higher pursuits. In his infinite generosity and boundless compassion, the Lord directly and indirectly presents to all, the essentials of discipline. Inertia is to be shed. Diffidence is to be dropped. Impulses are to be checked. Instincts are to be controlled. Intellect is to be channelled properly. Intuitive eye is to be nourished and one is thus gradually to be established in perfection through steady discipline.

Work Culture

The entire universe is ever engaged in action. It is constantly working. All the five elements are ever on the move. There is change everywhere. Unavoidable is work to anybody. *Jagat* it is, since it is 'ever in a state of flux'. Sri Krishna in the Gita highlights the cosmic activity taking place incessantly when he says, 'no one can sit idle even for a moment'. When action or work is ceaselessly happening, there is bound to be a reaction or the fruit of work.

Action is a combination of good and evil. Every activity is only relatively good or bad depending upon the attitude of the doer and the awardees. Killing, for example, is an activity. Good it is, when it is on the battlefield. Same is but an evil and a crime in social life. Similar are the qualities of reactions equally relative and they are but a combination of good and evil. The inference, therefore is, everybody is caught in actions and reactions which are both good and evil. If they are good, they are golden shackles; if they are bad, they are but barbed wires of iron. Bondage is unavoidable, since work is inevitable. Arjuna, then, as a representative of mankind, requests Krishna, the eternal master, to show the way out.

Sri Krishna, suggests to Arjuna the best method which is nothing but 'work culture.' Work or action performed for gratification of senses is but the crude form of work. Effort to eat and sleep, works to enjoy the pleasures of the body are but beastly expressions of uncultivated activity. The worst form of work is to use energy only to enjoy the pleasures of life without striving for them. Those that feed on others' labour resort to all sorts of corrupt means to make their lives indulgent. They mercilessly exploit the meek and the innocent. Every thought, word and deed of theirs is self-centred. Self-assertion and aggression are characteristic of their make-up. They are like Ravana of the Ramayana and Duryodhana of the Mahabharata.

A little more evolved work culture is seen in cooperative activity. Selfishness, to a great extent, is reduced but not eliminated. People come together and work together for mutual benefit and comfort. They share both the effort and fruits. Higher than this is the work culture of total self-dedication. People of evolved work culture are free from all shades of selfishness. They strive for the welfare of all. Swami Vivekananda says, 'Him I call a Mahatma whose heart bleeds for the poor.'

The lowest form of work is to grab from others, loot others and to suck their very blood. The highest and purest form of work culture is to give, serve and save all, all the time and at every level. It is like a tree giving the fruit of its labour to society. No tree eats its own fruit. It strives to produce the fruit and gives it up for the use of others. Sri Krishna speaks of this highest form of culture when he says, 'To work alone you have the right not to the fruits thereof.'

As the crude oil is to be rid of all the impurities to make it refined, work is to be freed from the impurity of selfishness to make it refined and cultured.

Emotional Culture

Love is a basic feeling present in every heart. Whom we love, when we love, and what for we love, how we love and the intensity of love may vary from person to person. Love, as such, is never absent in any human heart. It is love that guides, governs and motivates one's thoughts, words and deeds. To guide this emotion from the lowest form to the most refined expression and expansion is emotional culture.

When the clear and colourless ray of light passes through a prism, it gets reflected and refracted, resulting in the seven colours: VIBGYOR. If the prism is removed, colours disappear. Similarly, when the pure love, the trait of divinity, passes through the prism of a person's egoism, it acquires qualities such as lust, greed, anger, conceit, possessiveness, envy and infatuation. If egoism is slain, pure love shines resplendent. It is emotional culture to restore sublimity to love. The raindrop is free from impurities. If it falls in the sea, it becomes salty. If it falls in the ditch, it becomes dirty; if it falls in the Ganges, it becomes Gangajal. To become the pure distilled water, it has to pass through a process. It is this purification process that restores the original sublime purity to the raindrops. Similarly, the contortions of love on account of its contact with egoism are to be removed.

In emotional culture, the entire pursuit is to purify love, by directing it towards infinite love of divinity. The means and the end in emotional culture are but Bhakti. Sri Krishna speaks at length of it in Bhakti Yoga. When the flood of emotion is spontaneous, incessant, sublime and all-embracing, it is called devotion or Bhakti. When a person is established in this flood of Bhakti, no action will be antagonistic to anybody. Everything and everybody then will be acceptable. Nay, all will be lovable. Both heat and cold will be comfortable. Insults and eulogy will all be equally welcome. Enmity and antagonism can never arise in the heart filled with pure love.

Every action is prompted by love in a devotee. Even the apparent surgical deeds are prompted by love. Devotion is a culture making one vibrant, fragrant, sweet and sublime. Love *is* God, when it is rid of egoism and selfishness.

Intellectual Culture

As love is a gift from God, reason too is a blessing from the almighty. As much as love is intrinsic in all, so is rationalism hidden in everyone. It is ever thirsting to know more and more about everything and everybody. At long last, tired of seeking knowledge from outside, it turns within to know more about the hidden knowledge. It is then real self-study—*svadhyaya*. That is *svadharma* as well.

Intellect is the seat of logic, analysis, reasoning, inference, discrimination and decision-making. When it is crude and undeveloped, it is mere superstition, believing all without questioning. It yields easily to silly sentiments as well. A little logical thinking would dispel all false deductions. Religion, when it is not accompanied by right thinking will lead to all sorts of superstition. An evolved intellect will observe a judicious combination of reason and religion.

At the inert level of matter, cosmic intelligence is available as inertia. The same is pervasive as impulse in the vegetable kingdom —impulsively the leaves go up in search of sunlight and the roots go towards the water resource. At the level of subhuman species such as animals and birds, it is perceptible as instinct. Procreative urge and fear are but instincts. At the human level, it manifests as intellect available in every brain. It is left to mankind to foster it to perfection wherein it shines as superhuman intuition. The evolution from a crude state of body bound instincts to an enlightened intuition is intellectual culture.

Intellect is initially deployed as a tool to acquire knowledge and to discriminate the wrong from the right, the favourable from the unfavourable, the impermanent from the permanent, etc. Finally, it attains the seat of a judge passing judgements wise or otherwise depending upon its evolved state of culture. At the highest state of unfoldment of intellect, its threefold activity of knower, known and the process of knowing will be shed. There will then remain only knowledge without any duality, as a river losing its identity when it merges with the sea. There remains nothing but the vast sea, the infinite ocean of knowledge and absolute consciousnesses.

Sri Krishna through the path of knowledge—Jnana Yoga—takes us to a state of consciousness absolute. God then will be seen everywhere. Nay, one realises God within and without. As the ornaments have the same gold metal in them all, as the same earthen soil is available in all the pots, as the same water is present in all the waves, an evolved person of intellectual culture will be able to see the same truth and divinity inherent in all, the same God shining in all.

Self Culture

No saviour has saved any society or individual so far. One has to save oneself. One has to purify oneself. At the most, there may be a conducive atmosphere provided for one's unfoldment or evolution. The bud blossoms on its own. Gardener may water the plant, remove the weeds, facilitate its growth. Never does he touch the bud, nor can he force its blossoming. Similarly, the small self has to grow and evolve further to be the cosmic Self. It is a journey of the small individual self into the large infinite Self. When the impurities of the small self are removed, it is facilitated to unfold its infinite inner Self.

In other words, one has to strive for self-purification through self-culture and evolve to be the cosmic Self.

The small self is selfish and body bound, self-centred and earthbound, ego-centric and materialistic. The large Self is unselfish, loving, universal and infinite. It is sublime and spiritual. Materialism and spirituality have three components in each of them. The first two are the same in them. Only the third one is different.

The first component: Each soul is potentially divine; everyone has the spark of divinity within; every person is born with a talent; each is endowed with a gift.

The second component: The hidden soul, latent spark, the intrinsic talent or the gift should be identified and brought out through a purification process or training.

The third component: The perfected talent or gift has to be given a direction. If the evolved talent is encashed for bodily comforts and sense-indulgence, it is materialism. If the same is utilised for unfoldment of the self through service to humanity, it is spirituality.

Swami Vivekananda, therefore, beautifully explains in a single expression the entire process of purification and self-culture when he says *atmano mokshartham jagat hitayacha,* ['For the liberation of oneself and for the good for the others']—echoing Sri Krishna's exhortation to Arjuna.

Conclusion

A person of materialism seeks to indulge in the pleasures of the body. All abilities, talents and gifts will be ushered in only to experience in full the sense pleasures such as eating and mating. Slowly, pleasures will give way to emotional enjoyments such as love and hate. Further, in the process, we find the intellectual happiness growing to be very vibrant. Sense-pleasures may, then, be either eclipsed or totally eliminated. It is peace, peace and peace that will be sought after. Neither pleasures nor enjoyments nor even happiness then will appear to be worthy of pursuit. Peace blossoms, finally, as bliss and that is the state of fulfilment, the finest flower of self-culture. He or she is a yogi who is ever peaceful, ever blissful, at all times, at all levels. Sri Krishna asks Arjuna the representative man to be a Yogi—a useful person, a peaceful individual, a blissful soul, a man of self-culture.

Chapter Thirty

'What is in a Name?'

Bhagavad Gita is a dialogue between Sri Krishna and Arjuna. At several places in the Gita, Sri Krishna addresses Arjuna by various names as also Arjuna addresses Sri Krishna by different names. All these names are supposed to be contextually relevant and have a significance of their own. These names at times are repeated also. Following is list of various epithets—without repetition—with which both have

*been called in the Gita. The meaning of every name has also
been given.*

Sri Krishna

अच्युत—	One eternally established in his supreme glory.
अक्षर—	The indestructible one.
अव्यय—	One for whom there is no decay.
अनन्त—	The eternal.
अनंतरूप—	One with innumerable forms.
आदिदेव—	The primordial being. The divinity who is the source of all devas.
अरिसूदन—	Destroyer of enemies.
ईश्वर—	One who has unlimited lordliness or power over all things.
कमलपत्राक्ष—	The lotus eyed one.
काल—	Time. One who measures and sets a limit to everything.
किरीटिन्—	One with a diadem.
केशव—	One who is himself the three— *kah* (Brahma), *ah* (Vishnu) and *isa* (Siva).
केशिनिषूदन—	One who destroyed the asura Kesi.
कृष्ण—	*Kri* denotes existence, *na* denotes bliss. He is Satchidananda.
गदिन्—	One who has the mace known as Kaumodaki which stands for the category of Buddhi.
गोविंद—	The Lord of the earth, of cows, and of words.
चक्रिन्—	One who sports the discuss known as Sudarshana which stands for mind. Or one who turns the wheel of Samsara.

चतुर्भुज—One with four arms as Vasudeva is always represented.

जनार्दन— One who inflicts suffering on evil men. Or He to whom all devotees pray for worldly success and liberation.

जगत्पते— The Lord of the Universe.

जगन्निवास—One in whom the universe dwells.

त्वम्— Thou.

देवदेव— The Lord of gods.

देव— The resplendent or shining One.

देववर— The supreme one among the devas.

देवेश— One who is the Lord of all Devas.

धर्मगोप्ता— The one revealed through Dharma.

परमेश्वर— The supreme one who holds sway over all beings.

परब्रह्म— The supreme Brahman.

परंधाम— The ultimate abode of all beings.

पवित्र— The auspicious one.

परम-पुरुष— The supreme Purusha or Spirit.

पुराण पुरुष— The primordial Purusha.

पुरुषोत्तम— The greatest among all Purushas—spirits. Or one greater than all individual spirits.

प्रभो— The Lord. One who surpasses all.

भगवान् — Lordliness, prowess, fame, beauty, knowledge, non attachment—the combination of all these six attributes is *Bhaga*. One who possesses these is Bhagavan. The origin, dissolution, the bondage and salvation of creatures, knowledge, ignorance—one who knows all these is Bhagavan.

भवान्— Thou.

भूतमहेश्वर— The supreme Lord, who is the great Being presenting himself in the form of all beings.

भूतानाम् ईश्वर— The supreme Lord of all beings.

माधव— Consort of ma or Mahalakshmi. Or one who is Lord of ma or knowledge.

मधुसूदन— The destroyer of the demon Madhu.

महाबाहो— One with mighty arms.

महात्मन्— High-souled one.

यादव— One of Yadava clan.

योगिन्— One adept in Yoga.

योगेश्वर— The Lord revealed through and the Master of all yogas.

लोकमहेश्वर—The Lord of all lokas or abodes.

वार्ष्णेय— One who has incarnated in the Vrishni race.

वासुदेव— The Paramatman in whom all beings live and one who lives in all beings.

विभो— One who becomes many from Hiranyagarbha downwards.

विश्वरूप— The one manifested as the universe.

विश्वेश्वर— The Lord of the universe.

विश्वनिधान—The support of the universe.

विष्णो— Lord Vishnu, the all-pervading One.

विश्वमूर्ते— The one manifested as the universe.

वेदान्तकृत्— One who revealed the path of Vedanta.

वेदैःवेद्य— One to be known through the Vedas.

वेदविद्— One who knows all the Vedas.

वृष्णीनां— One of the Vrishni race.

शाश्वत— The Eternal.

सर्वम्— The all.

सर्वलोकमहेश्वर— The Lord of all lokas or abodes
सनातन पुरुष— The eternal Lord.
सहस्रबाहो— One with innumerable arms.
सर्व— The all.
हरि— One who attracts devotees to Himself.
हृषीकेश— The master and controller of the senses (*hrisika*-s).

Arjuna

अर्जुन— One who is pure in action.
अनघ— The sinless one.
कपिध्वजः— One with the monkey (Hanuman) as the crest of his banner.
किरीटी— One with a diadem.
कौन्तेय— Son of Kunti.
कुरुसत्तम— Best of Kurus.
कुरुश्रेष्ठ— Best of Kurus.
कुरुप्रवीर— Best of Kurus.
कुरुनंदन— Descendant of Kuru.
गुडाकेश— One who is master of sleep and is ever alert and energetic.
तात— Child.
धनंजय— Arjuna is so called because by his conquest of the kingdoms in the four quarters he acquired wealth.
धनुर्धर— One sporting the bow.
देहभृतांवर— Best among embodied jivas.
पाण्डव— Son of Pandu.
पार्थ— Son of Pritha (Kunti).
परंतप— Scorcher of foes.

पुरुषव्याघ्र—	Best (tiger) among men.
पुरुषर्षभ—	Best (bull) among men.
भारत—	Descendent of Bharata.
भरतर्षभ—	Best (bull) of Bharatas.
महाबाहो—	Mighty armed one.
सव्यसाचिन्—	One who can discharge an arrow even with one's left hand.
भरतसत्तम—	Best among those endowed with knowledge and discrimination.

Chapter Thirty One

Values in the Bhagavad Gita

SWAMI VIRESHANANDA

In his younger days, an eminent monk met Sri Ramana Maharishi, the great sage who lived in Tiruvannamalai in Tamilnadu. Recalling his only meeting with the sage, he said: 'I could not comprehend whether Sri Ramana was a realised soul or not, but one thing I observed about him: I saw excellence in every little action that he did—be it dressing vegetables or cleaning a place and so on. This perfection in daily life, in small acts of life, reveal a person's inner being. In Ramana's case, the state of inner perfection was evident and hence I consider him to be a man of realisation.'

What are Values?

By values are meant the practice of those principles and patterns which bring perfection in life. Values make life perfect and truly valuable. But, then, there is one thing we must consider here. Perfection in Sri Ramana's actions was a *fact* whereas for most others it is only a *value* yet to be achieved. Hence, there is a distinction between a *value* and a *fact*. When we see something directly or learn of it indirectly then it is called a *fact*. This knowledge produces a sense of wanting or avoiding and thus are born values. Values are thus, those virtues which we think as desirable and worthy of inculcation (from the view point of personal and collective good). In other words, before we seek to cultivate values, we perceive them as possible facts or potential values and after we become established in them, they become actual facts for us. They also become natural to us.

Bhagavad Gita—A Repository of Values

The importance of Bhagavad Gita is best known by the remarks of Warren Hastings, the first Governor General of India, in his introduction to the first-ever English translation of *Bhagavad Gita* by Charles Wilkins published in 1784. He wrote:

Works as the *Gita* would live long after the British dominion in India has ceased to exist.

What is the secret of this tremendous appeal of the Gita? It lies in the fact that it deals with practical problems of life. It teaches how a man can perform his duties in the society and at the same time, lead a moral as well as religious life. The Bhagavad Gita begins with an ethical problem (Arjuna's dilemma in fighting a righteous war), and in the process of solving this problem, it works out a noble and wholesome philosophy of life.

Whatever be our profession and station in life, we should be enthusiastic in all our endeavours, keep a calm and tranquil mind in the midst of all troubles and practice moral and ethical values. Apart from this, we should also have a clear-cut goal in our life and should be aware of the inexhaustible strength and capabilities within us. Our life goal should be very   lofty and unselfish to the core. Only then can our life be termed *worthwhile*.

The Gita teaches us how to transform our life into a meaningful one and at the same time, be helpful to the society at large. In this sense, the Gita is a lasting source of inspiration for everyone and for all times to come. It is all the more relevant today than ever before. Let us enumerate some abiding values that Gita mentions.

1. Courage to Face Life

The Gita is a manual for learning to face the challenges we encounter in daily life. Arjuna's dilemma, which we find in the beginning of the Gita, reflects our own misgivings and lack of self-esteem. Sri Krishna traces the root of this problem to the lack of awareness of our own personality and infinite capabilities and potential that we are endowed with. The very first words of Sri Krishna echo this idea:

O Arjuna! Yield not to unmanliness! It befits thee not. Abandoning this petty faint-heartedness, rise up, O dreaded hero![1]

Swami Vivekananda says in the same vein,

'Stand up and fight! Not one step back—that is the idea. Fight it out, whatever comes; let the stars move from the spheres! Let the whole world stand against us! . . . You gain nothing by becoming cowards. . . you are infinite, deathless, birthless. Because you are infinite spirit, it does not befit you to be a slave. Arise! Awake! Stand up and fight![2]

2. Efficiency in Work

Sri Krishna says that with a calm and steady mind, we can work more efficiently. He says, 'Perform your duties without selfishness. Doing actions without self-interest for the benefit of everyone is what is called sacrifice (*Yajna*).'

Whenever we are engaged in an action, our mind is distracted. Hence, is it not better to give up work? 'No', says Sri Krishna, 'You should do your duty. But be aware of what you are doing. Don't be egotistic or think too much about the results of your actions. Concentrate on how efficiently, neatly, lovingly you can perform your duties. Work done in a spirit of detachment in this way is equal to the worship of God. Through this, you can get knowledge that will ultimately lead you to enlightenment.'

3. Knowledge is Power

Knowledge is what a person should seek in life. The Sanskrit term for a student is *vidyarthin*—a seeker of knowledge. Sri Krishna says, 'Verily there exists nothing in this world purifying like knowledge. In good time, having reached perfection in Yoga, one realises that oneself in one's own heart' (4.38). For acquisition of knowledge, the foremost requirement, says the Gita, is *Shraddha*. *Shraddha*, of course, has a much wider significance than its English equivalent 'faith.' Swami Tapasyananda has elegantly brought this out thus:

> The three qualities absolutely necessary for progress in spiritual life (*as a matter of fact, in any endeavour*) are mentioned here (in the verse quoted above). These are: 1. *Shraddha* or faith, 2. Ardent practice, 3. Control of the senses. . . *Shraddha* or Faith is not a superstitious acceptance of unknown and unverifiable entities and claims of individuals. . . Faith is as much a unique quality of the human mind as Reason. . . Anything that has become a matter of faith in a man, unlike what is mere belief, works as an operative force, enthusing him to put the content of his faith to practice, and to struggle towards the realization of the ideal it presents. Ardour and sincerity are of the very stuff of faith. . . Faith is firm and active acceptance unlike belief or a conventional conformity which has no power to move a person to action.[5]

Sri Krishna says, 'Knowledge burns up all your weaknesses and makes you aware of your inner strength and potential. This is what is called enlightenment.' We should perform every action as an act of sacrifice. Among them, *jnana yajna*—pursuit of true knowledge or contemplation, which leads to learning, is the best one because as Sri Krishna stresses, 'Verily there is nothing so purifying as knowledge in this world.'[3] The very next verse specifies qualification for a seeker of knowledge:

> A man of deep faith (*shraddha*) obtains divine knowledge if he is full of zeal and devotion for knowledge and has achieved mastery over his senses.[4]

4. The Practice of Concentration

All great achievements come through contemplation and steadiness of mind. A meditative man is not disturbed by physical or mental activities. This mental condition gives never-ending and pure joy that cannot be found in external objects. Through meditation, one gets supreme peace and contentment. The practice of concentration is the *core* of meditation enabling us to perform our duties like reading, playing, cleaning, serving, and so on with greater effectiveness and awareness. Through this, all these works cease be a burden to us for they become easier and highly enjoyable.

Sri Krishna gives a striking example to illustrate the unperturbed and tranquil state of mind that one should cultivate in the time of meditation: 'The flame of a lamp sheltered from wind does not flicker. This is the comparison used to describe a Yogi's mind that is well under control and united with the Atman.'[6]

5. Overcoming Lust and Anger

Why does a man do wrong? Sri Krishna pinpoints that it is lust (sexual desire) and anger which prompt man to commit wrongs. He tells Arjuna to consider them as enemies in one's life journey.[7]

Sri Krishna elucidates the terrible impact, lust and anger make on one's pursuit of knowledge: 'As fire enveloped by smoke, the knowledge is overcast by lust.

It is the eternal enemy for an aspirant of knowledge.' He also identifies the locus of this dreadful passion, so that we can be ever alert to counter its awful effects: 'The *senses*, the *mind* and the *intellect* are said to be its seat. With these it veils knowledge.' Hence Krishna calls upon us to control the senses right from the beginning. [8]

In today's world, in the midst of declining standards of moral and spiritual values, one is likely to forget this and get influenced by baser and animal instincts in man. Hence it would profit everyone to heed to the counsel of Krishna and try hard to lead a pure, wholesome life.

6. Living a Pure Life

Arjuna raises a question of practical significance in the sixth chapter of the Bhagavad Gita. He says,

O Krishna! Verily, the mind is fickle, turbulent, powerful and unyielding. To control it, I think, is as difficult as controlling the wind itself.

To this Krishna replies:

Arjuna! Undoubtedly the mind is fickle and difficult to be checked. Yet, it can be brought under control by steady practice and dispassion.[9]

Steady practice (*abhyasa*) and cultivation of disinterestedness towards unimportant things (*vairagya*), according to Sri Krishna, are the two essential practical tools to gain control over the senses and in turn to attain higher standards of concentration and character. In the very next verse, Krishna cautions that 'Yoga (can also mean, success in one's endeavour in this context) is difficult for attainment by men of uncontrolled mind. But for those who have their minds under control, it is possible to attain, if they strive with proper means."[10]

7. The Signs of a True Devotee

'Devotion to God is the easiest path to divinity and the most natural to follow,' says Sri Krishna. He continues, 'Practice whole-hearted devotion to Me. Do all work as an offering to me and to please Me.' He then explains qualities we should cultivate in order to develop true devotion to God:

❖ Friendship towards all

❖ Freedom from pride

❖ Cheerfulness and calmness in all circumstances

❖ Perseverance in whatever we undertake

❖ Self-surrender to God

❖ Not troubling others in body, mind and speech

❖ Being unperturbed by irritation caused by others

❖ Always maintaining purity in thoughts and actions

❖ Not being troubled when someone abuses us or becoming over-ecstatic when one praises us

❖ Looking upon the whole world as our own home [11]

Conclusion

Gita is a repository of values. In essence, what it tells is this: We should have faith in ourselves, towards instructions given by our elders and also towards God. There is a saying, 'Man is what his faith is.' The quality of all our actions depends upon the faith we have in performing them. Work done without vanity and motivated by the good of others is the best kind of work. Whatever is done with desire, vanity and for self-glorification is inferior and whatever is done carelessly with evil motive and thoughtlessness is useless.[12]

We should not neglect our duties. We should always perform our duties with all dedication and without craving for results. We should lovingly offer all our duties and their results to God. True Knowledge leads to understanding of unity in diversity. It frees us from our ego-sense and brings about control over our body and mind. Following these teachings may be daunting in the beginning but it ends in great happiness.

Thus we get in the Gita a complete value system leading to perfection in life—where intense action combined with concentration, coupled with knowledge and love towards God is made practicable.

References

1. *Bhagavad Gita*, 2.3
2. CW, 1: 461
3. *Bhagavad Gita*, 4.38
4. *ibid*, 4.39

5. *Srimad Bhagavad Gita,* The
   Scripture of the Mankind,
   Tr with Notes by Swami
   Tapasyananda, p.144
6. *Bhagavad Gita,* 6.19
7. *ibid,* 3.37

8. *ibid,* 3.38-40
9. *ibid,* 6.34,35
10. *ibid,* 6.36
11. *ibid,* cf. Chapt. 12
12. *ibid,* Chapt. 14

∞౧

Chapter Thirty Two

Gita's Ideal of
Emotional Stability

SWAMI SARVAPRIYANANDA

Let us set on a journey to learn the art of emotional stability. We shall visit an ancient battlefield and acquire wisdom from God Himself—wisdom which is the source of eternal freedom and permanent serenity.

The Crisis

The Bhagavad Gita commences with a crisis—emotional crisis. Arjuna, the warrior prince, is confronted with the awful necessity of killing his own friends, teachers and relatives. Like any decent human being, he shies away from violence. Grief overwhelms him. When we listen to Arjuna speak of his suffering, we can straightaway identify the symptoms of acute emotional distress. He says:

Seeing these kinsmen, O Krishna, arrayed with a view to fighting, my limbs fail, and my mouth is parched up. My body quivers, and there is horripilation; the Gāndiva [Arjuna's bow] slips from my hands, and my skin burns. I am not able to stand, my mind is reeling, as it were, and I see, O Keshava, adverse omens.[1]

Faced with this moral dilemma, unable to choose an appropriate course of action, Arjuna is frozen into

305

inaction. He appeals to his friend-cum-charioteer, Sri Krishna, thus:

> With my natural traits [i.e. courage and decisiveness] overcome by [a sense of] helplessness and sin, and my mind perplexed regarding my duty, I ask You—tell me that which is definitely good for me. I am Your disciple; teach me who have taken refuge in You.[2]

Then ensues the greatest dialogue of all of human literature. It is the dialogue between suffering man and a loving God, in the most dramatic setting—the battlefield of Kurukshetra.

The Response

How does Sri Krishna respond to Arjuna's plea? Does he remind Arjuna of his duty as a Kshatriya? Does he appeal to his pride? Does he recommend meditation? Philosophy? He does all of this and more, but, above all, Sri Krishna's response is spiritual.

Our emotional responses to any situation depend ultimately on our reality-perception. As long as we believe that we are limited creatures, subject to birth and death, sorrow and suffering, with infinite desires and finite means, we are bound to be tossed around by passions, by emotional turbulence. Sri Krishna's first teaching, hence, is, 'Do not give in to weakness—sentimentality'. For this weakness is rooted in an erroneous perception of the reality of our self.[3]

What do we truly consider ourselves to be? Body? Mind? Body-mind? But this is entirely wrong. We are not bodies, nor even minds. We are not born with the body nor do we die with the body. Arjuna learns that he is spirit, that he has taken many bodies in the dim past and can do so into the far future if he so wishes. He learns of the Atman, which is pure consciousness, immortal and ever pure. Sri Krishna corrects Arjuna's reality-orientation by showing him that man is neither body nor mind, but the atman—pure consciousness, existence and bliss (Sat-Chit-Ananda). And this Atman is not only his inner reality, but is also the reality of the entire universe. *Atman is Brahman*. This eternal wisdom is the central philosophy of the Gita. Arjuna is urged to attain this wisdom and thereby be transformed into a *sthitaprajna*—a man of stable wisdom which includes emotional stability.

Sthitaprajna—The Man of Stable Wisdom

With goal of attaining the highest Advaitic wisdom shining before him, Arjuna is naturally eager to know the characteristics of a man who has already attained this goal. Arjuna asked:

What is the definition, O Keshava (Sri Krishna), of a man of stable wisdom, absorbed in contemplation? How does a man of steady wisdom talk, how does he sit, and how does he walk?[4]

Sri Krishna's answer to this question not only delineates the characteristics of the person who has attained stable wisdom, but also gives clear pointers for practice for those who have yet to attain this lofty goal.

What is natural and effortless to the perfected is attained by the aspirant through strenuous effort. In other words, characteristics of the perfected are practices for seeker; those who want to attain emotional serenity would do well to study and emulate the man of stable wisdom.

> When a man gives up all desires of the mind, O Pārtha, and himself delights in his Self, then he is said to be a 'a man of stable wisdom'.
> He who is unperturbed in misery and free from desires amidst pleasures, who is devoid of all attachment, fear and anger—that sage is said to be of stable wisdom.
> He, who is free from affection everywhere, and who getting whatsoever, good or evil, neither welcomes nor hates them, has stable wisdom.[5]

The serenity and even-mindedness of the *sthitaprajna* is born of the realization of his own infinitude. He delights in the infinity of the atman and, as Sridhara Swami, a well-known commentator on Gita, remarks, *kshudravishaya abhilashan tyajati* . . . 'the desires for paltry sense-objects are easily given up'.[6] Events which would make most men miserable, leave him unshaken, for he sees the same infinite atman shining through. In other words, he sees that events, fortunate or unfortunate, have no intrinsic reality apart from the atman.

However, the journey is far from over. The seeker soon realizes that intellectual knowledge is one thing and the ability to *live* that knowledge, to 'walk the talk' as the saying goes, is quite another. When assailed by temptation or buffeted by misfortune, he finds himself unable to translate this intellectual conviction into emotional stability. As Erich Fromm said, 'Insight separated from practice remains ineffective'. Intellectual knowledge is weak, the passions and ingrained habits are enormously powerful. This is the great paradox, the great tragedy, of human life that insight is often divorced from practice. Duryodhana, the eldest of Kaurava brothers, complained in Mahabharata,

> I know what is good (*dharma*), and I know what is evil (*adharma*), but (the problem is) I possess neither the desire to do good nor the restraint to stop doing evil!

Why are we unable to practice what we know to be good? Why are we unable to restrain ourselves from doing what we know to be evil?

The Elephant and the Rider

The psychologist Professor Jonathan Haidt has studied this perennial human problem from both ancient and modern perspectives. He uses an ancient metaphor, that of rider and elephant, to describe the human condition.[7] The intellectual self, which grasps philosophy and morality, is like the rider and the rest of the body-mind system is the elephant. The rider has limited control over the elephant and can tell it to walk or stop, turn left and right. But, the elephant is mighty and has a will (or tendencies) of its own. If it really wants to do something, like snatching a bunch of bananas from a vendor, there is very little the rider can do. Similarly, the intellectual self is seldom able to direct the powerful physical system.

Let alone the body, the mind itself is mostly beyond conscious control. Most mental (and sensory) processes are automatic. We are always in the midst of a stream of consciousness, which flows by its own rules of association, often without the control or even awareness of the intellectual self. Self-aware action is rare, but automatic, habitual, instinctive action is the norm. The automatic system is the product and slave of nature. It is ruled by the genetic imperative—by pleasure or pain, by flight or fight. Its aims are security, food and reproduction. This automatic system is the elephant and not very responsive to high philosophy. The intellectual self is the rider placed on the elephant's back to help the elephant make better choices. The rider can guide the elephant towards long-term goals (called *purusharthas* in Hindu philosophy), but the rider cannot order the elephant against its will.

Haidt's use of the elephant-rider imagery reminds the Vedantist immediately of the chariot model of the *Kathopanishad*. The body is the chariot, the senses the horses, the road is the field of experience, the intellect is the driver while the self is the passenger. Only a skilful driver and well-trained horses will enable the passenger to reach the goal (*purushartha*). The unregenerate body-mind system sabotages spiritual life, just as a foolish driver and untrained unruly horses drags the chariot with its hapless passenger to doom.

The elephant-rider problem was well known to Indian philosophers. Sri Krishna warns Arjuna:

The turbulent senses, O son of Kunti, forcibly lead astray the mind of even the struggling wise person.[8]

Just as the unruly elephant can derail the rider, the intellectual self can be easily overcome by demands of the sensory system. This process, where the rider is overpowered by the elephant, is dramatically narrated by Sri Krishna:

For a person thinking of the sense-objects, there grows an attachment for them; from attachment arises desire, from desire results anger.

From anger results delusion, from delusion results confusion of memory, from confusion of memory results destruction of intelligence, and *from destruction of intelligence he perishes.*[9]

Taming the elephant is a must for stability in wisdom. Sridhara Swami comments—*indriyasamyamam vina tu sthitaprajnata na sambhavati....* 'Since without the control of the senses it is not possible to attain stability in wisdom, therefore, during the period of spiritual practice (Sādhanā), one should struggle hard for this end.'

After revealing the wisdom born of one's true nature to Arjuna, Sri Krishna teaches him the secret of stabilizing this wisdom by controlling the senses. This is a secret to be learned from the tortoise.

The Way of the Tortoise

Revealing this secret, says Sri Krishna:

And when he completely withdraws his senses from the sense-objects, *even as a tortoise its limbs (then) his wisdom is steady*.[10]

The tortoise has a unique defensive technique. When threatened, it immediately withdraws all its limbs (four feet, its head and tail—six in all) into its shell, thus protecting itself from external harm. The seeker too must be similarly able to withdraw his senses from sense-objects to preserve emotional stability in the face of temptation and provocation.

Controlling all these (senses), the self-controlled one should sit meditating on Me. Verily, his wisdom is steady, whose senses are *under control*.[11]

Taming the elephant is what transforms the scholar into the saint, the scattered mind into a self-poised mind.

Clearing a Wrong Notion

Emotional stability might be misunderstood as cold-blooded emotionlessness. There is a long and unfortunate history of motivated misreading of the message of the Gita, mostly by Western interpreters. In a recent work, David E. Cooper comments[12]

'... many western readers are chilled by those paintings, in more gaudily illustrated editions of the Gita, which portray the serene and smiling Arjuna scything his way through the enemy as if through a field of corn.'

Now this is a gross misreading of Sri Krishna's message—on at least two counts. First, (and this is an oft-repeated calumny against the Gita), let us remember that the Gita does not support violence at all. Since the dialogue is in the context of a war, some superficial commentators are quick to link the Gita with war, whereas it only teaches karma yoga (the way of attaining God through selfless work). Possibly, the collective guilt and psychic burden of centuries of militarism culminating in the two world wars weighs heavily on these commentators and is projected into their reading of the Gita. The history is a witness to peaceful disposition of Hindus, even though their scripture be set in the battlefield.

Second, the ideal of *Sthitaprajna*—the person of steady wisdom—does not mean emotionlessness but the sublimation of emotions. Emotional stability is not emotionlesness but keeping oneself emotionally stable in the midst of numerous challenges of life.

The Ultimate Goal

Hearing, thinking and meditating on the eternal wisdom in this manner, and protecting the wisdom gained through control of the senses, the seeker attains *aparoksha-anubhuti*—the direct experience of non-duality—and finds that the entire universe, including his apparent (body-mind) self has no existence apart from Brahman, Existence Absolute (Sat)–Consciousness Absolute (Chit)–Bliss Absolute (Ananda). The empirical dichotomy of the elephant and rider disappears, no more is there danger of a fall, he is truly and permanently free, even while living (*jivanmukta*). And that is the final state of emotional stability.

References

1. *The Bhagavad Gita* (Tr.) Swami Swarupananda I. 28-30 (all further references are to the same work).
2. *ibid*, II. 7
3. Shankaracharya's Commentary on the Bhagavad Gita (Gita Press)
4. *Gita*, II. 54
5. *ibid*, II. 55, 56, 57
6. Sridhara Swami's Gloss on the Bhagavad Gita (Tr.) Swami Satyapriyananda (unpublished manuscript)
7. Haidt, Jonathan Haidt *The Happiness Hypothesis* Arrow Books 2006.
8. *Gita*, II.60
9. *ibid*, II. 62-63
10. *ibid*, II.58
11. *ibid*, II.61
12. Cooper, David E. *World Philosophies* 2003

ೞಅ

Chapter Thirty Three

Gita for Housewives

SUMITA ROY

I

The perennial nature of the *Bhagavad Gita* has been stressed by many savants time and again. Its relevance is illimitable, cutting across all boundaries in an inclusivistic sweep. From the time of its composition to the present, the *Gita* has been analyzed and commented upon in an endless variety of ways. Multiple levels of engagement with the text continue even today. An issue of the *Journal of South Asian Literature* (Summer, Fall 1988) published from Michigan State University, is exclusively devoted to the *Gita* on the occasion of the bi-centennial of its first translation into English. In one of the essays in this seminal volume, the author Milton Eder puts forward the view that,

> In the Bhagavad Gita Krishna speaks not only to Arjuna to resolve his dilemma, he also speaks to a multifarious audience with a multitude of dilemmas, and his instruction serves them too.[1]

Obviously, women—especially housewives—cannot be excluded from this wide group.

Closer home there is the Gita Swadhyaya Samithi which brought out a volume entitled *Bhagavad Gita and*

Modern Problems comprising of papers presented at the International Seminar on Gita held at Thiruvananthapuram in December 2000. In yet another interesting volume titled *The Gita in World Literature,* which traces the global influence of the text, the editor C.D. Verma suggests:

> The Gita resolves the existential dilemma of worldly beings . . . combines the two orders of reality, the transcendental and the empirical . . . [and is a] journey from crisis to liberation.[2]

The *Gita* therefore is a kaleidoscope in which the individual can find any pattern which she/he needs/desires, as long as that pattern emerges from the basic tenets which the text enshrines. Some criticism may have been levelled against the text because of its gender bias arising out of its predominantly patriarchal stance. But this has to be viewed and analysed cautiously from the social dynamics of the period when the text was composed.

In a verse (IX.32), which says that *even* women can attain to the highest spiritual goal, there is enough fodder for strong objection from radical feminists. But in the twenty-first century, the fundamentalist notions of early feminism have been toned down ushering in a post-feminist era. More and more attempts are now being made to establish 'the alliance between faith and feminism'[3] because in the initial stages of the women's movement in the West, 'Many consider[ed] feminism to be a secular movement with a bias against organised religion.'[4]

Elaborating the link between faith and feminism, Helen LaKelly Hunt suggests,

As a political movement, feminism seeks to transform society by challenging and changing social institutions. Religion, on the other hand, seeks first to transform individuals through a personal relationship with God, which then results in a desire to work for the transformation of society. Religion and feminism share many common ideals.[5]

What this search for common ideals between the religious/spiritual and social dimensions implies is that the two are complementary and one without the other is dysfunctional. The imbalances which were brought about in the life of individuals, families and society as a whole in the name of gender equality is now a murky chapter in history. True empowerment of women is believed to lie in strengthening their spirit and helping them forge an individual identity, not in taking on roles that are usually considered male bastions, or gaining entry into economic or public power structures. From this point of view, the *Gita* can be taken as a roadmap and a blueprint of empowerment because 'the Gita tries to ignite . . . [a] divine spark in all of us.'[6]

Relevance of Gita for Housewives

How relevant is the *Gita* for women whose spheres of influence are the home and family? We will try answering this with an illustration.

The electronic media, which at this moment seems an arbiter of taste and formulator of opinions, more powerful than any other single factor one can think of, gives us the clue. Just one instance of how the *Gita* has found its way into this arena should be sufficient to reiterate that this immortal poem is as relevant today as it was at the time it was composed and housewives can certainly use it as a tool for social and spiritual evolution.

A Bangla TV serial called 'Kurukshetra' on a channel called *Aakash Bangla* has in its theme song one of the most significant slokas of the *Gita* (XI.33):

Tasmat tvam uttistha yaso labhasva
    jitva shatrun bhumksva rajyam samriddham
may'aiv'aite nihatah purvam eva
    nimittamatram bhava savyasachin

Therefore arise! Win renown! And destroying your enemies, enjoy the prosperous kingdom. For these warriors have already been slain by Me. Be you but an instrument thereof, O thou master-bowman, Arjuna.[7]

The story depicts three women revolting against evil in the form of unfair domination, conflict and familial crisis in a joint family where they are the daughters-in-law. It is truly remarkable how the so-called unexceptional and ordinary housewives take on the ills in the lives of women and battle with them against almost impossible odds.

Of the three women, the youngest is the protagonist with a deeply symbolic name, *Ananya*. Explaining the significance of this 'highly suggestive term' in his notes on chapter IX of the *Gita*, Swami Tapasyananda writes:

> In a pure Advaitic sense it can mean—those who do not think of Him as different from their real Self. In a purely devotional sense it can mean—those who love Him, looking upon Him, the Supreme Being, as their 'own', and not as a strange power to be propitiated for favours . . .. *Anya* means a 'stranger', and *Ananya*, its opposite, is therefore 'one's own'. It indicates intimacy and unselfish love.[8]

How the protagonist comes from a state of doubt to deep conviction and devotion as she battles with social and familial ills is creatively retold through this serial narrative—of Arjuna's Kurushetra experience.

The women—and the housewives in particular—can take up this rewarding task of putting into practice Gita's teachings with a two-fold purpose: the first is to evaluate the present situation (made up of all that they consider as the crises), and the second is to resolve the crises/conflicts in order to aspire for an elevation, a moving ahead (or higher) from where they are at present. The *Gita* provides the parameters both for evaluation and elevation in almost all the slokas, but one can use a few illustrations (and leave the rest for individual readers to interpret and utilize).

The beginning can be made with a self-analysis: women are famed to be changeable like the weather and emotionally charged, often excessively so. And discussions about what action they do, they ought to do or should not do can fill volumes. Many internal and external crises arise from these temperamental traits and existential dilemmas. Stress, lack of confidence, unnecessary aggressiveness or unpleasantness, crisis of values, material leanings, peer pressure to prove oneself at all costs and running after meaningless goals are all part of our daily experience. The two important correctives we can look for are attitudinal and behavioural—with an example or two for each from the indelible melody of the song of the divine teacher.

The *Gita* tells homemakers how to measure and correct ourselves in many places, but one of the most poignant is the 56th sloka of chapter II:

Dukhesvanudvigna manah, sukhesu vigata-sprihah
Vita-raga-bhayakrodhah sthita-dhir muniruchyate

Whose mind is not agitated in adversity, who is free from desire, and who is devoid of attachments, fear and anger—such a person is called a sage of steady wisdom.[9]

To analyse and evaluate our inner being is the first step to reading, contemporizing and learning from these words. How does the mind respond to adversity? Do we not immediately desire relief from it? Or curse its unfairness in leaving others and afflicting us? Is it possible for us to welcome adversity with the same warmth and cordiality as we do prosperity? How do desires affect us? And how do we behave in contexts of fear, anger, attachment?

Once we begin this process of self-analysis, we are already on the way to reaching the goal—which is becoming a 'sage', a person who is not 'agitated', who is not overtly disturbed by sorrow/suffering and overwhelmed by joys/pleasures. Every instance in the day of a housewife becomes a measure of how far she is progressing on this path of inward balance, moderation and stability. The gains are not only individual—imagine a family and a society where the mother, wife and homemaker is always calm, unperturbed, not hankering for pleasures and not making superhuman efforts to escape from sorrow, and is unmoved by excessive desires, fear or anger. If we can achieve this internal equilibrium, most of the 'enemies' on the battlefield of life are automatically slain.

Work for Holistic Health

A significant pointer in the *Gita* is about action—work which we do and the behavior pattern that is inherent in us. Do we work only with selfish motives? Do we devote some of our time each day, each week, each month or each year in working for others? Do we perform all our duties? Do we consider our duties as unpleasant tasks and shirk them? Do we carry out our actions with some expectation?

One of the most oft-quoted slokas from the text is the following (2.47)

Karmany ev'adhikaraste ma phalesu kadachana
ma karma-phala-hetur bhur mate sango'stvakarmani

To work alone you have competence, and not to claim their fruits. Let not the longing for fruits be the motive force of your action. At the same time let not this attitude confirm you in indolent inaction.[10]

The Holy Mother, Sri Sarada Devi is a dynamic model of this illustration. Always engaged in the so-called mundane housework, uncomplaining, considering work as the greatest worship, not expecting anything from those who she served selflessly for almost the entire length of her mortal existence, she is a worthy interpreter of the kind of work the *Gita* specifies.

The Holy Mother's words echo the ideas inherent in the *Gita*. Obviously, when she says[11], 'Always be engaged in some work or other. It is conducive to the health of both the body and the mind,' it is an injunction worth implementing. According to her,

One must do some work. Through work alone can one remove the bondage of work, not by avoiding work. Total detachment comes later on. One should not be without work even for a moment.[12]

Therefore, working with commitment and a sense of detachment is the best means to train the mind. It helps forge the mind-body link to bestow happiness and holistic health on the housewife who is the maker of homes in all families the world over.

References

1. Eder, Milton, 'A Review of Recent *Bhagavadgita* Studies', *Journal of South Asian Literature*, Volume 23, No.2, Summer, Fall 1998, MI: Michigan State University, pp.20-46.

2. Verma, C.D. ed. *The Gita in World Literature*. New Delhi: Sterling Publishers,1990, p.x.
3. Hunt, Helen LaKelly, *Faith and Feminism: A Holy Alliance*, New York: Atria Books, 1970, p.xxii.
4. *ibid.*
5. *ibid.*, p.12
6. *Bhagavad Gita and Modern Problems:* Papers Presented at the International Seminar on Gita, Thiruvananthapuram: Gita Swadhyaya Samithi, 2000, p.52.
7. Tapasyananada, Swami. *Srimad Bhagavad Gita*: The Scripture of Mankind. Sri Ramakrishna Math, Chennai, 1984, p.300.
8. *ibid.*, p. 258
9. *ibid.*, p. 65
10. *ibid.*, p. 61
11. *The Gospel of the Holy Mother*, Sri Ramakrishna Math, Chennai, 1986, p.7.
12. *ibid.*, p. 14-15

Chapter Thirty Four

Bhagavad Gita and the Ideal of Service

SWAMI VEDAPURUSHANANDA

Introduction

'I have made a new path and opened it to all,'[1] proclaimed Swami Vivekananda to one of his brother disciples. That new path is the path of service—serving God in all beings. However, the blueprint of this path was long given out by Sri Krishna in his immortal poem, Bhagavad Gita. Selfless work and the reconciliation of the different paths of *dharma* are the two special characteristics of the Gita.[2] Swamiji's service ideal incorporates both these ideas and issues forth in action as the manifestation of the divinity.

We shall see how this great book, a veritable mine of multi-faceted, universal, eternal, inclusive and above all practical teachings, has in its bosom the ideals of the path of service.

What is Service?

Service, as understood by the commoner, is to alleviate the physical distress of the needy by providing food, clothes and shelter. Saving or sustaining life by medical treatment and conducting relief is service.

Spreading knowledge, both academic and moral that helps man to face the problems of life and overcome them is service. Finally, guiding a man to manifest his innate divinity—a fact central to Vedanta and Swamiji's teachings—by counselling, initiation and religious publications is also service. In short, every good action done selflessly is service.

Philosophy of Service

To the exalted vision of the Upanishadic seers all that exists is Brahman. They saw the divine every-where—in natural forces, animals, plants, and above all in humans. Echoing their words, Sri Krishna says in the Gita that Brahman exists in creatures pervading them all.[3] And to the worshippers of personal God he says, that the Lord resides in the region of the heart of all creatures.[4] The server, the served, the means of service and the result to be attained are all Brahman, says Krishna in a profound verse in the language of sacrifice.[5]

The immense potential of these teachings in transforming the way in which we see the world and deal with it remained untapped till the advent of Sri Ramakrishna. The simple question of this unlettered person, 'If God can be worshipped through an image, why not also through a living man?'[6] has changed forever our conception of religion. And the teaching, 'Not compassion for others, but rather the service of man, recognising him to be a veritable manifestation of

God'[7]—is the modern gospel and the basis of all service activities.

This perception of the divine in all beings turns the secular into sacred, matter into spirit, work into worship and ultimately transforms man into God. This lies at the core of the ideal of service and its practice. Service, however, has several facets.

Facets of Service:

Action becomes transformed into service when accompanied by a set of four mental qualities. These are the four pillars of service.

1. Renunciation (*tyaga*)

Sri Ramakrishna says that renunciation is the keynote of the Gita.[8] There can be no service without sacrifice. These two are our national ideals. In the context of service renunciation implies giving up of the results of work and willingness to forego one's likes and dislikes, pleasures and preferences, time and money, and even life and liberation, if needed. Sri Krishna defines tyaga as the giving up of attachment to all work and to their results.[9]

An easy way to practice this renunciation is self-surrender. Krishna says:

O son of Kunti, whatever you do, whatever you eat, whatever you offer as a sacrifice, whatever you give and whatever austerities you undertake, all that you offer to Me.[10]

2. Selflessness

Selfishness is sin and unselfishness is virtue. Selfishness binds while unselfishness liberates. Every action becomes service when this self-centred ego is given up. Gita strongly condemns selfishness. It says that a person who enjoys things without sharing them with others is a thief and incurs only sin for his actions. It urges men to hold their life as a sacrifice and promises that they will spiritually evolve by such actions and attain supreme Brahman. Let them share whatever they have got with others. This is the way to purify the mind of selfishness.[11]

In this context, Gita's concept of *yajna* meaning sacrifice, merits special consideration. Krishna lifts *yajna* from its ritualistic moorings and gives it a broad ethical and humanistic turn. He points out that God intended all the inhabitants of this world live and work in mutual harmony, to help and not exploit one another. Krishna shows that human beings and nature are closely interrelated. The failure to appreciate this mutual interdependence had led to the extinction of many species, environmental degradation resulting in global warming, etc.

3. Unity

Gita says that Brahman, though undivided, appears to be divided in all beings and the correct vision is to see a unitary, indestructible, undivided Entity in all the diversified things of the world.[12] A realized soul with such a vision sees his self existing in everything and everything in his self. Due to this unifying outlook, he identifies himself with all beings and is happy in their happiness and suffers at their miseries and is actively engaged in doing good to all beings.[13]

Swami Vivekananda forcefully reiterated this ideal of oneness in modern times. He said:

> The one central ideal of Vedanta is this oneness. . . .
> There is but one life, one world, one existence. Everything
> is that one, the difference is in degree and not in kind.[14]

4. Sameness

A person venturing to serve has to transcend all differences based on race, language, religion, sex, caste, etc. He should try to see the same divine essence in humans, animals and plants. Even a small act of service connects one with others at a deeper level. In fact service ideal is a powerful tool to obliterate all divisions in our society. What happens to a person who succeeds in attaining this sameness of vision? Gita says:

> Here itself is rebirth conquered by them whose minds
> are established on sameness. Since Brahman is the same
> in all and free from defects, therefore they are established
> in Brahman.[15]

One may despair that these four qualities are beyond the reach of ordinary mortals like us to acquire in one life. But the silver lining is that we do possess these qualities and manifest them in our daily life, but only within a limited circle of our family and friends. What is required is to deepen them and expand them to include one's society, nation and ultimately the whole world. This expansion is the fruit of the service ideal of Swamiji.

Service Ideals—Sri Krishna's Assurance: *Cultivate Faith*

Some of us may wonder, we see Brahman neither in ourselves nor in others. So is it not self-deception to say that we serve God in Man? Will any good come out of it?

Swami Brahmananda replies:

One must have faith that the one Brahman is in man, woman, in all creatures; and with that faith one should learn to serve Shiva in the form of Jiva. As you practice this, suddenly one day the veil will be lifted and you will see that it is He who has become everything.[16]

Gita also puts a lot of emphasis on faith and says that 'a person is made up of faith as the dominant factor. He is verily what his faith is.' and 'The man who has faith attains knowledge.'[17]

Work and Worship should go Together

Our elders say that to prevent oneself from straying away from the ideal i.e. God Realization and to serve in true spirit, it is necessary that service activities are combined with spiritual practices like japa and meditation. Krishna also advises in the same vein. He says,

Renouncing all actions to Me, with mind centred on the Self, getting rid of hope and selfishness, fight on, free from mental tension'. . . . 'think of Me at all times and fight.[18]

Lord Protects the Good

What will happen to one who serves selflessly? Who will take care of those who are dependent on him?

To this legitimate question, Krishna replies:

O Partha, there is certainly no ruin for him here or hereafter. For the doer of good, never comes to grief, My son. Those persons who becoming non-different from Me and meditative, worship me everywhere, for them who are ever attached to Me, I arrange for securing what they lack and preserving what they have.[19]

Service and Svadharma

Should I—a student or a professional or a housewife or a retired person—give up my vocation and take to service for my spiritual growth?

No, tells Gita. It isn't necessary to change one's station or avocation in life. Rather it advises to worship the all-pervading Supreme Reality in and through one's duties.[20] Everyone should do some selfless service as it presents itself before him or her. That itself will lead to spiritual perfection as testified in the lives of Dharma Vyadha and the housewife in the Mahabharata.

The Silent Minority Serves the World

Sankaracharya in his introduction to his commentary on the Gita says that spiritual ideas spread when they are understood and practised by men and women of more than ordinary good qualities. Incarnations and spiritual leaders set in motion a wave of sublime ideas by their lives and teachings, which slowly spreads and leavens the society. We see right in front of us how the service ideal preached by the holy trinity has slowly penetrated and changed the thought-patterns of the world. Now it is being increasingly accepted and practised by thousands of people silently in their lives. They may be in minority. But they are the 'salt of this earth'. And society survives intact because of them. Therefore if we believe in the service ideal, if our heart commands us to help others in need, we should go forward and take the plough. We will find help and guidance coming to us from unknown quarters.

Universality of Service Ideal

Gita places before humanity the concept of universal welfare as opposed to regional or national welfare. It's 'One World' now—one in sorrow and happiness; one in war and peace. It can no longer be split into isolated fragments. The well-being of the individual lies in the universal. So Gita's concepts of universal welfare (*loka samgraha*), Yajna as service to all, helping one another (*parasparam bhavayantah*), the right way of giving (*sattvic dana*) and the world pictured as interconnected cosmic cycle—all have immense universal and practical relevance.

Conclusion

In spite of impressive achievements in science and technology, in spite of overall economic development, the world today is faced with many serious challenges. The problems of social inequity, fundamentalism, environmental degradation, etc., cannot be tackled by material forces alone. The power of religion, broadened and purified, has to be brought into play. The ideal of service should permeate all levels of the society, if it has to survive. Seeds of love, equality, mutual respect and cooperation have to be sown in the hearts of people. The change has to begin at the level of individual. The spiritual development of human beings should proceed side by side with the social progress. As we pursue our noble intent, the teachings of Bhagavad Gita and the holy trinity will guide and serve as our unfailing sources of inspiration and support.

References

1. Swami Chetanananda, *God Lived with them*, Advaita Ashrama, p.369
2. *CW*, 4:107
3. *Bhagavad Gita*, 13.13. (Similar shlokas are 10.8,42; 7.6,7; 15.7; 13.17,30; 9.4,5 and 8.22)
4. *ibid.*, 18.61 (Similar shlokas are 10.20, 13.2)
5. *ibid.*, 4.24.

6. *The Gospel of Sri Ramakrishna*, Sri Ramakrishna Math, Chennai, p.688

7. *The Life of Swami Vivekananda* by his Eastern and Western Disciples, vol.1, p.139.

8. *The Gospel of Sri Ramakrishna*, p.917

9. *Bhagavad Gita*, 18.2,9

10. *ibid.*, 9.27. (See also 5.10; 3.30;12.6)

11. *ibid.*, 3.9-16

12. *ibid.*, 13.16; 18.20.

13. *ibid.*, 6.29,32; 5.25,12.4.

14. *CW*, 2:297

15. *Gita*, 5.19

16. *Eternal Companion*, p.136

17. *Gita*, 17.3 and 4.39

18. *ibid.*, 3.30 and 8.7

19. *ibid.*, 6.40; 9.22. see also 9.31.

20. *ibid.*, 18.46,47.

ৰাণ্ড

Chapter Thirty Five

What They Say

Some Eminent Persons on the Bhagavad Gita

❖ The Gita is the universal mother. She turns away nobody. Her door is wide open to anyone who knocks. A true votary of the Gita does not know what disappointment is. He ever dwells in perennial joy and peace that passeth understanding. But that peace and joy come not to the sceptic or to him who is proud of his intellect or learning. It is reserved only for the humble in spirit who brings to her worship a fullness of faith and an undivided singleness of mind. There never was a man who worshipped her in that spirit and went back disappointed. . . I find a solace in the Bhagavad Gita that I miss even in the Sermon on the Mount. When disappointment stares me in the face and all alone I see not one ray of light, I go back to the Bhagavad Gita. I find a verse here and a verse there, and I immediately begin to smile in the midst of overwhelming tragedies—and my life has been full of external tragedies—and if they have left no visible or indelible scar on me, I owe it all to the teaching of Bhagavad Gita. . . Today the Gita is not only my

Bible or my Koran, it is more than that—it is my
mother. . . . When I am in difficulty or distress I seek
refuge in her bosom.

—**Mahatma Gandhi**

❖   The Srimad Bhagavad Gita is one of the most brilliant
and pure gems of our ancient sacred books. It would
be difficult to find a simpler work in Sanskrit
literature or even in all the literature of the world
than the Gita, which explains to us in an
unambiguous and succinct manner the deep, and
sacred principles of the sacred science of the Self,
after imparting to us the knowledge of the human
body and the cosmos, and on the authority of those
principles acquaints every human being with the
most perfect and complete condition of the Self.

—**Bal Gangadhar Tilak** (1856-1920), *social reformer
and Indian Independence fighter*

❖   The Gita is the greatest gospel of spiritual works
ever yet given to the race. . . . our chief national
heritage, our hope for the future.

—**Sri Aurobindo** (1872–1950), *Indian nationalist,
scholar and mystic*

❖   I believe that in all the living languages of the world,
there is no book so full of true knowledge, and yet
so handy as the Bhagavad Gita. . . . It brings to men

the highest knowledge, the purest love and the most luminous action. It teaches self-control, the three-fold austerity, non-violence, truth, compassion, obedience to the call of duty for the sake of duty, and putting up a fight against unrighteousness (adharma). . . . To my knowledge, there is no book in the whole range of the world's literature so high above all as the Bhagavad Gita, which is a treasure-house of Dharma not only for Hindus but for all mankind.

—**Madan Mohan Malaviya,**
Indian nationalist and the founder of Banaras Hindu University

❖ When I read the Bhagavad-Gita and reflect about how God created this universe everything else seems so superfluous. . . .
—**Albert Einstein,** *Scientist and Nobel Laureate*

❖ The Bhagavad-Gita has a profound influence on the spirit of mankind by its devotion to God which is manifested by actions.
—**Dr. Albert Schweitzer**(1875 – 1965), *an Alsatian musician,*
philosopher, and physician. Awarded Nobel Peace Prize in 1953

❖ I owed a magnificent day to the Bhagavad-Gita. It was as if an empire spoke to us, nothing small or unworthy, but large, serene, consistent, the voice of an old intelligence which in another age and climate had pondered and thus disposed of the same questions which exercise us.

—**Ralph Waldo Emerson**(1803-1882), *an American essayist, philosopher, and leader of the Transcendentalist movement*

❖ In the morning I bathe my intellect in the stupendous and cosmogonal philosophy of the Bhagavat Geeta, since whose composition years of the gods have elapsed, and in comparison with which our modern world and its literature seem puny and trivial; and I doubt if that philosophy is not to be referred to a previous state of existence, so remote is its sublimity from our conceptions. . . . One sentence of the Gita is worth the State of Massachusetts many times over.

—**Henry David Thoreau** (1817-1862) *American author, naturalist and transcendentalist*

❖ Among the priceless teachings that may be found in the great Indian epic *Mahabharata*, there is none so rare and priceless as the Gita.

—**Annie Besant** (1847-1933), *a prominent Theosophist, and a notable political leader during India's freedom struggle*

❖ [Gita is] the most beautiful, perhaps the only true philosophical song existing in any known tongue . . . perhaps the deepest and loftiest thing the world has to show. I read the Indian poem for the first time when I was in my country estate in Silesia and, while doing so, I felt a sense of overwhelming gratitude to God for having let me live to be acquainted with this work. It must be the most profound and sublime thing to be found in the world.

—**Wilhelm von Humboldt** (1767-1835), *Prussian Minister of Education*

❖ The Bhagavad Gita is one of the noblest scriptures of India, one of the deepest scriptures of the world. . . . a symbolic scripture, with many meanings, containing many truths. . . . [that] forms the living heart of the Eastern wisdom.

—**Charles Johnston**, *an English civil servant in Bengal, in his a translation of Gita in 1908*

❖ I hesitate not to pronounce the Gita a performance of great originality, of sublimity of conception, reasoning and diction almost unequalled; and a single exception, amongst all the known religions of mankind.

—**Lord Warren Hastings** (1754-1826), *The first Governor General of British India*

❖ [Gita is] the most beautiful philosophical song existing in any known tongue.

—**Robert Oppenheimer** (1904-1967), *The developer of the atomic bomb*

❖ [Bhagavad Gita is] a compendium of the whole Vedic doctrine to be found in the earlier Vedas, Brahmanas and Upanishads, and being therefore the basis of all later developments: it can be regarded as the focus of all Indian religion.

—**Dr. Ananda K Coomaraswamy** (1877-1947), *Historian and an early interpreter of Indian culture to the West*

❖ The Bhagavad Gita and Upanishads contain such godlike fullness of wisdom on all things that I feel the authors must have looked with calm remembrance back through a thousand passionate lives, full of feverish strife for and with shadows, where they could have written with such certainty of things which the soul feels to he sure.

—**John Elignton,** *Well-known author*

❖ [Gita is] a work of imperishable significance [which] gives us not only profound insights that are valid for all times and for all religious life, but it contains as well the classical presentation of one of the most significant phases of Indo-German religious history. . . Here Spirit is at work that belongs to our Spirit. We are not called to solve the meaning of life but to find out the deed demanded of us and to work and so, by action, to master the riddle of life.

—**Jacob Wilhelm Hauer** (1881-1961), *German writer*

❖ The Gita is one of the clearest and most comprehensive summaries of the Perennial Philosophy ever to have been done. Hence its enduring value, not only for Indians, but for all mankind. . . . The Bhagavad Gita is perhaps the most systematic spiritual statement of the Perennial Philosophy.

—**Aldous Huxley** (1894-1963)
Eminent English writer and noted philosopher

❖ I believe the Gita to be one of the major religious documents of the world. If its teachings did not seem to me to agree with those of the other gospels and scriptures, then my own system of values would be thrown into confusion, and I should feel completely bewildered. The Gita is not simply a sermon, but a philosophical treatise.

—**Christopher W. B. Isherwood** (1904-1986),
American translator, biographer, novelist, and playwright

❖ This famous and marvellous Sanskrit poem occurs as an episode of the Mahabharata, in the sixth [section]—or 'Bhishma-Parva' of the great Hindu epic. It enjoys immense popularity and authority in India, where it is reckoned as one of the 'Five Jewels'—*pancharatnani*—of Devanagari literature. In plain but noble language it unfolds a philosophical system which remains to this day the prevailing Brahmanic belief blending as it does the doctrine of Kapila, Patanjali, and the Vedas.

—**Sir Edwin Arnold** (1832-1904), *poet and scholar and Author of The Song Celestial, one of the earliest translations of the Gita*

❖ The Bhagavad Gita is known as the Lord's Song— or the Song Celestial—and it represents one of the highest flights of the conditioned spirit to its unconditioned Source ever achieved.

—**L. Adams Beck** (?-1931), Author of *The Story of Oriental Philosophy*

Chapter Thirty Six

Splendour of the Bhagavad Gita
Some Important Sayings on the Gita

Meditation on the Bhagavad Gita

ॐ पार्थाय प्रतिबोधितां भगवता नारायणेन स्वयं
व्यासेन ग्रथितां पुराणमुनिना मध्ये महाभारतम् ।
अद्वैतामृतवर्षिणीं भगवतीमष्टादशाध्यायिनी-
मम्ब त्वामनुसन्दधामि भगवद्गीते भवद्वेषिणीम् ।।

ॐ Om भगवता by the Lord नारायणेन (the one Refuge of all beings) Narayana स्वयं Himself पार्थाय प्रतिबोधितां with which Partha was enlightened पुराणमुनिना by (through the lips of) the ancient sage व्यासेन Vyasa महाभारतम् मध्ये in the Mahabharata ग्रथितां incorporated भगवतीम् the blessed Mother अद्वैतामृतवर्षिणीं showering the nectar of Advaita (the philosophy of non-duality) अष्टादशाध्यायिनीम् in the form of eighteen chapters भवद्वेषिणीम् destroyer of rebirth अम्ब loving Mother भगवद्गीते (the Lord's song) Bhagavad-Gita त्वाम् Thee अनुसन्दधामि I meditate upon.

Om! O Bhagavad Gita—with which Partha was en-lightened by the Lord Narayana Himself and which was incorporated in the Mahabharata by the ancient sage Vyasa—the blessed Mother, the Destroyer of rebirth, showering down the nectar of Advaita, and consisting of eighteen chapters—upon Thee O Bhagavad Gita! O loving Mother! I meditate.

सर्वोपनिषदो गावो दोग्धा गोपालनन्दनः ।
पार्थो वत्सः सुधीर्भोक्ता दुग्धं गीतामृतं महत् ।।

सर्वोपनिषदः All the Upanishads **गावः** the cows **गोपालनन्दनः** Son of the cowherd (Krishna) **दोग्धा** the milker **पार्थः** Partha (Arjuna) **वत्सः** the calf **सुधीः** (men) of purified intellect **भोक्ता** the drinkers **महत्** the supreme **अमृतं** nectar **गीता** Gita **दुग्धं** the milk.

All the Upanishads are the cows, the Son of the cowherd is the milker, Partha is the calf, men of purified intellect are the drinkers and the supreme nectar Gita is the milk.

[On being asked whether God accepts food that is offered to Him by devotees, the Holy Mother replied:]

'Why? Have you not read in the Gita that God receives the fruits, flowers, water, and other things that are offered to Him with devotion?'

—*The Gospel of the Holy Mother,* p.331

Quotes by Swami Vivekananda

Than the Gita no better commentary on the Vedas has been written or can be written. The essence of the Shrutis, or of the Upanishads, is hard to be understood, seeing that there are so many commentators, each one trying to interpret in his own way. Then the Lord Himself comes, He who is the inspirer of the Shrutis, to show us the meaning of them, as the preacher of the Gita, and today India wants nothing better, the world wants nothing better than that method of interpretation. It is a wonder that subsequent interpreters of the scriptures, even commenting upon the Gita, many times could not catch the meaning, many times could not catch the drift. . . But you find in the Gita there is no attempt at torturing any one of them. They are all right, says the Lord; for slowly and gradually the human soul rises up and up, step after step, from the gross to the fine, from the fine to the finer, until it reaches the Absolute, the goal. That is what is in the Gita. Even the Karma Kanda is taken up, and it is shown that although it cannot give salvation direct, but only indirectly, yet that is also valid; images are valid indirectly; ceremonies, forms, everything is valid only with one condition, purity of the heart. For worship is valid and leads to the goal if the heart is pure and the heart is sincere; and all these various modes of worship are necessary, else why should they be there? Religions and sects are not the work of hypocrites and wicked people who invented all these to get a little money, as some of our modern men want to think. . . They are all here to satisfy the hankering and thirst of different classes of human minds, and you need

not preach against them. The day when that necessity will cease, they will vanish along with the cessation of that necessity; and so long as that necessity remains, they must be there in spite of your preaching, in spite of your criticism. . . These forms, and all the various steps in religion will remain, and we understand from the Lord Shri Krishna why they should.
—*CW*, 3: 261-62

Shri Krishna says in the Gita (VII.16), 'Four classes of people worship Me: the distressed, the seeker of material things, the inquirer, and the knower of truth.' People who are in distress approach God for relief. If they are ill, they worship Him to be healed;if they lose their wealth, they pray to Him to get it back. There are other people who ask Him for all kinds of things, because they are full of desires—name, fame, wealth, position and so on. They will say, "O Virgin Mary, I will make an offering to you if I get what I want. If you are successful in granting my prayer, I will worship God and give you a part of everything." Men not so material as that, but still with no faith in God, feel inclined to know about Him. They study philosophies, read scriptures, listen to lectures, and so on. They are the inquirers. The last class are those who worship God and know Him. All these four classes of people are good, not bad. All of them worship Him.
— *CW*, 8:120

The good cook concentrates his whole self on the food-material he handles; he loses all other consciousness for the time being. But they are only able to do perfectly a single work in this way, to which they are habituated. The Gita teaches that all works should be done thus. He who is one with the Lord through Yoga performs all his works by becoming immersed in concentration, and does not seek any personal benefit. Such a performance of work brings only good to the world, no evil can come out of it.
. .

The result of every work is mixed with good and evil. There is no good work that has not a touch of evil in it. Like smoke round the fire, some evil always clings to work. We should engage in such works as bring the largest amount of good and the smallest measure of evil. Arjuna killed Bhishma and Drona; if this had not been done Duryodhana could not have been conquered, the force of evil would have triumphed over the force of good, and thus a great calamity would have fallen on the country. The government of the country would have been usurped by a body of proud unrighteous kings, to the great misfortune of the people. Similarly, Shri Krishna killed Kamsa, Jarasandha, and others who were tyrants, but not a single one of his deeds was done for himself. Every one of them was for the good of others. We are reading the Gita by candle-light, but number of insects are being burnt to death. Thus it is seen that some evil clings to work. Those who work without any consciousness of their lower ego are not affected with evil, for they work for the good of the world. To work without motive, to work unattached, brings the highest bliss and freedom. This secret of Karma-yoga is taught by the Lord Shri Krishna in the Gita.

—*CW*, 5:249

This is the central idea of the *Gita*—to be calm and steadfast in all circumstances, with one's body, mind, and soul centred at His hallowed feet!

—*CW*, 7: 273

The teachings of Krishna as taught by the Gita are the grandest the world has ever known. He who wrote that wonderful poem was one of those rare souls whose lives sent a wave of regeneration through the world. The human race will never again see such a brain as his who wrote the Gita.

—*CW*, 7: 22

If one reads this one Sloka—

क्लैब्यं मा स्म गमः पार्थ नैतत्त्वय्युपपद्यते ।
क्षुद्रं हृदयदौर्बल्यं त्यक्त्वोत्तिष्ठ परन्तप ।।

—One gets all the merits of reading the entire Gita; for in this one Sloka lies embedded the whole Message of the Gita.

—*CW*, 4: 110

Study the Gita every day. By such study the mind can be cleansed of all unnecessary thoughts and anxieties. This I know from personal experience.

—*Swami Brahmananda*

Make Gita your constant companion. Be always of good cheer. Never allow sorrow or dejection to take possession of your soul which is ever free and blissful.

—*Swami Ramakrishnananda*

Attachment produces confusion and that, in turn, often leads to weakness, deflecting a person from the path of duty and truth. Prior to the battle, Arjuna stood for truth, not selfishness. He wanted to have a peaceful settlement by having only five villages. How much he tried to avoid the clash! Only when he realized that avoiding the battle would encourage injustice, impropriety and evil, did he get ready to fight for the cause of truth. To eliminate oppression is the duty of a person who belongs to the class of warriors.

Wherever you see injustice and oppression, you must oppose it. Everyone in the world is interconnected. If you are hurt, I too am hurt. Suppose you see me being oppressed by somebody and you keep silent. You say to yourself, 'That's OK. *I* haven't been oppressed. Why should I bother about what happens to someone else?' You are clearly in a deluded state. You should realize that along with me you also have been oppressed. The nobility of your mind has been attacked. Blinded by selfishness, you have today refrained from opposing injustice. When you are oppressed tomorrow, you will not have the strength to retaliate. In this way a person gradually marches along the road to degradation and slavery. . . Blinded by beauty and the lure of wealth, we often lose sight of the goal. If we are practising spiritual disciplines *(sadhana)*, we may be able to recover the forgotten goal. But without it, everything comes to naught.

—Swami Saradananda

A man finds fulfilment in his life if he can somehow offer everything to God, regard him as his own, and direct all his thoughts and actions towards him. As the Master said this, so did Krishna repeatedly tell Arjuna in the Gita:

Whatever you do, whatever you eat, whatever you offer in sacrifice, whatever you give away, and whatever you practise in the form of austerities, O son of Kunti—do it as an offering to me. Thus shall you be free from the bondage of actions which bear good or evil results. With your mind firmly set on the yoga of renunciation, you shall become free and come to me.

—Swami Turiyananda

In the Gita, Sri Krishna emphasizes svadharma, one's own dharma. The word "dharma" is really untranslatable.

"Religion," "duty," "righteousness," and the other English equivalents give only a partial meaning. Dharma is derived from the root *dhri,* meaning to hold or sustain. The word signifies the attitude behind a man's action or duty that sustains him in his present stage of evolution and also helps him to realize his ultimate destiny. The dharma of a man is determined by his past experiences and tendencies. The beginningless Soul assumes different forms in different births for the gaining of experience. The works performed in every birth leave impressions, which are stored up in the subconscious mind and are not destroyed with the death of the body. When the Soul assumes a new body, these impressions begin to operate. Thus they form his svabhàva, or character; they determine his dharma—his duty, his religion, his sense of right and wrong. Education and environment only help a man to manifest what he has inherited from his own past. ... So a man's dharma is the basis of his thought and action; he cannot get rid of it any more than a dreaming person can get rid of his dream. To try to act against one's dharma is to do violence to one's nature. The duty determined by a man's dharma is his natural duty. That is the only real thing for him; all other duties are alien to his nature, imposed from outside and therefore sources of confusion. Krishna asks Arjuna to cling to his kshatriya dharma though it does not seem perfect from other standpoints. 'Better is one's own dharma, though imperfectly performed, than the dharma of another well performed.

—Swami Nikhilananda

In the Bhagavad Gita, Arjuna raised the problem of the difficulty of controlling the mind. He said: *tasyaham nigraham manye vayoriva suduskaram*—'I find it as difficult to hold the mind as to hold air within one's fist.' Sri Krishna answered: *asamsayam mahabaho mano durnigraham calam, abhyasena tu kaunteya vairagyena ca grihyate.*—'Yes, O mighty-armed one, mind is no doubt very powerful and hard to control, but through *abhyasa* and *vairagyam* this mind can be brought under control.'

In other words Sri Krishna propounded two methods: *abhyasa*—that is to say, repeated practice, doing the same thing over and over—and *vairagya,* renunciation. Repeated practice I have dwelt upon: again and again try to bring the consciousness of the ideal spiritual state to the mind. *Vairagya,* or renunciation, is also necessary. If you have come to the conclusion that something you are doing is not in consonance with your ideal, then give it up. Don't at that time say, 'Oh, I shouldn't give it up. What would my friends say!' Will your friends take you to salvation? And what kind of friends are they if they cannot appreciate these things? I am a cynic, no doubt, but my definition of a friend is one who is a playmate. I want to enjoy certain things; I cannot enjoy them alone, so I want a few others to enjoy them with me. Those fellow enjoyers you call friends. No, they are not friends; they are conveniences. If you didn't want to do certain things along with them, you would shun them. So let friends say whatever they like; you should not make too much of it. And if they are real friends, you may be doing them good by changing your habits. The way things generally happen is that when you take to spiritual life, your friends at first ridicule you, hate you, shun you; but as you make progress, they become proud of you; they feel a vicarious enjoyment. Then if you fail to live up to your own spiritual ideal, they become your bitterest enemies—which is only natural, because they were enjoying this wonderful thing through you, and you have deprived them of it. But if you persevere in spiritual life, you can really help them.

—**Swami Ashokananda**

Have you grown spiritually? Have you realized something of the divine spark that is within you? Have you gone beyond the body-mind complex and its pulls and pressures, and become calm and steady within yourself? All these are profound questions that some people in modern western civilization are asking. What has happened to the human being? He or she has been a good worker. But he or she has become a broken person after years of productive efficiency. Work has done no good to the worker, except his or her salary and whatever creature comforts could come out of that salary. What about the inner life of the worker? Is he or she rich within, peaceful and fulfilled? In this way, Sri Krishna defines the yoga taught in the Gita as a double efficiency: productive work efficiency, and inward personal or character efficiency. These must go side by side. Don't separate these two. By the same work, if one can achieve two great things, how much greater will be our profit thereby?

—**Swami Ranganathananda**

A Poetic Liberty

Says Sri Krishna in the Gita (9.27):

यत्करोषि यदश्नासि यज्जुहोषि ददासि यत् ।
यत्तपस्यसि कौन्तेय तत्कुरुष्व मदर्पणम् ॥

'Therefore, Arjuna, whatever you do in the world, whatever you eat, sacrifice, give up, or give away even your suffering—offer it all to Me. Dedicate everything to Me.'

Here is a poetic change done in order to make the above idea more easily understandable and practical.

यत्करोमि यदश्नामि यज्जुहोमि ददामि यत् ।
यत्तपस्यामि भगवन् तत्करोमि त्वदर्पणम् ॥

'Whatever I do, whatever I eat, whatever I offer in sacrifice, whatever I give away, whatever austerity I practice, O Lord, I offer it all to you.'

Sources and Contributors

Chapter One
❖ **Swami Atmashraddhananda** is a monk of the Ramakrishna Order. This article appeared as the Editorial of December 2008 issue of *The Vedanta Kesari*. This volume has been edited by him.

Chapter Two
❖ Complied from the *Gospel of Sri Ramakrishna*, Translated from original Bengali by Swami Nikhilananda, Sri Ramakrishna Math, Chennai.

Chapter Three
❖ Excerpts from the lectures delivered in San Francisco, on May 28-29 1900. cf. *The Complete Works of Swami Vivekananda* (hereafter *Complete Works*), Advaita Ashrama, 5, Dehi Entally Road, Kolkata, 1: 459-480.

Chapter Four
❖ Based on lectures delivered in California, on April 1, 1900 and San Francisco, on May 26, 1900; cf. *Complete Works*, 1: 437-445, 456-458.

Chapter Five
❖ **Swami Ranganathanandaji** (1908-2005) was the 13th President of the Ramakrishna Order. He was a prolific

writer and a speaker of international acclaim. The following are excerpts from his three volume book, *Universal Message of the Bhagavad Gita—An Exposition of the Gita in the Light of Modern Thought and Modern Needs*, published from Advaita Ashrama, Kolkata. 1: 13-20.

Chapter Six
- **Swami Smaranananda** is Vice President of Ramakrishna Math and Ramakrishna Mission.

Chapter Seven
- **Swami Sridharananda**, a senior monk of the Ramakrishna Order, is the Head of Vedanta Centre of Sydney, Australia.

Chapter Eight
- **Swami Prabuddhananda**, a senior monk of the Ramakrishna Order, is the Head of the Vedanta Society of Northern California, San Francisco, U.S.A.

Chapter Nine
- **Swami Harshananda**, a senior monk of the Ramakrishna Order, is the Head of Ramakrishna Math, Basavanagudi, Bangalore. He is a versatile speaker and a prolific writer having several publications in English, Kannada, and Sanskrit to his credit. His monumental work *A Concise Encyclopaedia of Hinduism* was published in 2008.

Chapter Ten

◆ **Swami Gautamananda**, a senior trustee of the Ramakrishna Math and a member of the Governing Body of the Ramakrishna Mission, is the Head of Sri Ramakrishna Math, Chennai.

Chapter Eleven

◆ **Swami Bhaskarananda** is the Head of Vedanta Society of Western Washington, Seattle, USA. He is the editor of *Global Vedanta*, a quarterly published from there and has several books to his credit.

Chapter Twelve

◆ **Swami Adiswarananda** (1925-2007) was the Head of Ramakrishna-Vivekananda Center, New York. A deep thinker and prolific writer, he authored many insightful books on Vedanta and its contemporary significance. This article is an excerpt from his book Meditation and Its Practices, Advaita Ashrama, Kolkata, Pp. 357-360.

Chapter Thirteen

◆ **C S Ramakrishnan**, a former editor of *The Vedanta Kesari*, was a long-standing and close devotee from Chennai.

Chapter Fourteen

◆ **Swami Dayatmananda**, a senior monk of the Ramakrishna Order, is the Head of Ramakrishna Vedanta Centre, Buckinghamshire, United Kingdom.

Chapter Fifteen

◆ **Swami Atmaramananda**, a former editor of *Prabuddha Bharata*, is a Trustee of the Ramakrishna Math and a member of the Governing Body of the Ramakrishna Mission. He is presently the Secretary of Ramakrishna Mission Vidyalaya, Coimbatore.

Chapter Sixteen

◆ **Swami Nityasthananda** is a former editor of *Viveka Prabha*, Ramakrishna Order's Kannada monthly, and is presently the President of Sri Ramakrishna Ashrama, Mysore, Karnataka. He has many books in Kannada to his credit.

Chapter Seventeen

◆ **The Spot Where the Gita was Delivered.** By a special reporter of the Vedanta Kesari Office.

Chapter Eighteen

◆ **Dr. Prema Nandakumar** is a devotee from Srirangam. She has several publications to her credit, and regularly reviews books for *The Vedanta Kesari* and other journals.

Chapter Nineteen

◆ **Swami Abhiramananda** is the Manager of Sri Ramakrishna Math, Chennai. His thoughtfully written articles appear in *The Vedanta Kesari* occasionally.

Chapter Twenty

◆ **Guidelines from the Gita.** Complied from the Vedanta Kesari office.

Chapter Twenty One
◆ **Swami Atmarupananda**, a monk of the Ramakrishna Order, lives at the Ramakrishna Monastery in Trabuco Canyon, California, USA. He travels to Mexico and around the United States giving talks and retreats on Vedanta.

Chapter Twenty Two
◆ **Dr. N.V.C. Swamy**, a former Director of the Indian Institute of Technology, Chennai, is currently the Dean of Academic Courses at the Swami Vivekananda Yoga Anusandhana Samsthana, a Deemed University in Bangalore.

Chapter Twenty Three
◆ **Swami Atmapriyananda**, a monk of the Ramakrishna Order, is the Vice-chancellor of Ramakrishna Mission Vivekananda University (Deemed), with its headquarters at Ramakrishna Mission Sarada Pitha, Belur Math.

Chapter Twenty Four
◆ **B Mahadevan** is EADS – SMI Professor of Sourcing & Supply Management, Dean (Administration), Indian Institute of Management, Bangalore.

Chapter Twenty Five
◆ **Pravrajika Brahmaprana** is a nun at the Vedanta Society of Southern California, Hollywood. In addition to writing articles for various publications in America

and abroad, she has also edited *With the Swamis in America and India*, by Swami Atulananda, the *Vivekacudamani of Sri Sankaracarya*, translated by Swami Turiyananda, and volume 9 of *The Complete Works of Swami Vivekananda*.

Chapter Twenty Six

◆ A former editor of *Prabuddha Bharata*, **Swami Yuktatmananda** is the Head of Ramakrishna-Vivekananda Center, New York.

Chapter Twenty Seven

◆ **M. Sivaramkrishna** is the former Head of the Department of English, Osmania University, Hyderabad, and has several books to his credit.

Chapter Twenty Eight

◆ **Swami Bodhamayananda** is a monk of the Ramakrishna Order, at Ramakrishna Mission Ashrama, T. Nagar, Chennai. He has been actively engaged in conducting workshops, lectures and seminars on Personality Development for the youth.

Chapter Twenty Nine

◆ **Dr. K. Subrahmanyam** is retired Principal of National Defence Academy, Khadakwasla, Pune, and Vivekananda College (Gurukula), Madurai. In his doctoral work, he specialised on Swami Vivekananda, and also has several books to his credit.

Chapter Thirty
◆ 'What is in a Name?'. Compiled by the volunteers of the Vedanta Kesari office.

Chapter Thirty One
◆ **Swami Vireshananda**, a monk of the Ramakrishna Order, is the present editor of *Viveka Prabha*, the Kannada monthly of the Ramakrishna Order, published from Sri Ramakrishna Ashrama, Mysore, Karnataka.

Chapter Thirty Two
◆ **Swami Sarvapriyananda**, a monk of the Ramakrishna Order, teaches at the Monastic Probationers' Training Centre at the Belur Math, Howarh, West Bengal.

Chapter Thirty Three
◆ **Prof. Sumita Roy** teaches at the Department of English in Osmania University, Hyderabad.

Chapter Thirty Four
◆ **Swami Vedapurushananda** is a monk of the Ramakrishna Order at the Ramakrishna Mission Vidyapith, Purulia, West Bengal.

Chapter Thirty Five
◆ Compiled from various sources.

৩০০৪